IN VIEW OF THE MOUNTAINS

by
Jennifer Patten

Printed by Commercial Printers & Signs
208 Main St - Fort Morgan, CO 80701
(970) 867-9709

Patten, Jennifer
In View of the Mountains: A History of Fort Morgan,
Colorado

Copyright © 2011 by Jennifer Mishra

ISBN-13: 978-0-615-49703-7
ISBN-10: 0-615-49703-9

Library of Congress Control Number: 2011911037

First Edition
First Printing

agedpage@gmail.com

Front Cover: Indian Encampment on the Platte River (1868)
by Thomas Worthington Whittredge

To my husband Michael,
whose love makes everything possible.
And to my father who shared my wonder and inspired me
to finish.

Preface

From my youth I brought with me only a vague impression of the history of the small town in which I was raised. Fort Morgan, Colorado, built on the site of a short-lived military fort in the heart of the great American desert; a fort that had never been attacked, never seen a battle. On little more than a whim I went in search of the fort's operational dates, expecting this information would come readily to hand and that would end my curiosity - the fort once again fading into the midst of vague memory. To my surprise, I instead found a door opening to the history of the west. The history of Fort Morgan included connections with early explorers, nearly a dozen Native American tribes, the Colorado gold rush, the Indian Wars, and the rise of the mid-west as the agricultural center of the United States.

But I also found that Fort Morgan was a resting point, just as it remains today; a place to refresh the weary traveler worn from days on the road, a place to stop and prepare for the journey ahead. It is a place to pass through – on the way to a destination, but rarely a destination itself. In some ways, the land surrounding Fort Morgan has changed little over the centuries and in other ways, the land has transformed dramatically.

The history of Fort Morgan will never rival that of Denver or glisten with the same gold dust of the mountain mining towns, but this little town on the plains was central to the story of the Romantic west; it's story connecting with the major events of the age. Everyone has a history and every place is central to a story. What follows is the story from the land - of the land - on which Fort Morgan would rise.

Jennifer Mishra née Patten
March 21, 2010

Table of Contents

Acknowledgements

I wish to thank the librarians at the University of Houston, Southern Illinois University – Edwardsville, and the Houston Public Library. I would also like to thank the Houston Metropolitan Research Center, Newberry Library, the Missouri Historical Society, the Colorado Historical Society, and the Bloedorn Research Center at the Fort Morgan Museum.

I would also like to thank my family and Paul who provided a sounding board; allowing me to shape my ideas.

Brief Timeline of Fort Morgan

1739	Mallet Brothers travel from St. Louis to Santa Fe along the South Platte River Trail.
1819-20	Major Stephen H. Long Expedition
1824-25	General William Ashley Expedition
1835	Dodge leads company of Dragoons to Rockies
1842	Fremont's First Expedition
1842	Rufus B. Sage tours the Rocky Mountains
1843	Fremont's Second Expedition
1856	Bryan Expedition
1857	Cheyenne Expedition
1858	Gold discovered at Cherry Creek
1859	Colorado Gold Rush begins
1859	Leavenworth & Pike's Peak Express Co. establish mail route along South Platte River to Denver
1860	Central Overland & Pike's Peak Express Company takes over mail and stage route Cut-off established between Junction and Denver
1861	Colorado territory formed
1863	Telegraph line opened from Julesburg to Denver via Junction

1864	Battle at Fremont's Orchard begins Indian wars in area
	1st troops sent to the Junction
	Sand Creek Massacre
1865	Indian raids from Julesburg to Junction
	Fort Wardwell established
1866	Fort Wardwell renamed Fort Morgan
1868	Fort Morgan abandoned May 18th
1869	Battle at Summit Springs effectively ends Indian wars in area
1872	Union Pacific Julesburg Branch to Denver begun
1876	Colorado becomes a state
1881	Union Pacific Julesburg Branch to Denver completed
	Burlington & Quincy Railway to Denver completed
1883	Platte & Beaver Canal completed
1884	Fort Morgan Canal completed
	Fort Morgan platted by Abner S. Baker
	Fort Morgan Times established
1887	Fort Morgan incorporated as a city
1889	Morgan County formed with Fort Morgan as county seat

W 61 | W 60 | W 59

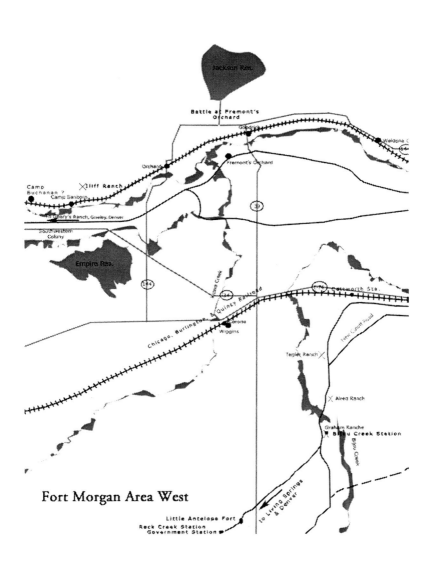

Fort Morgan Area West

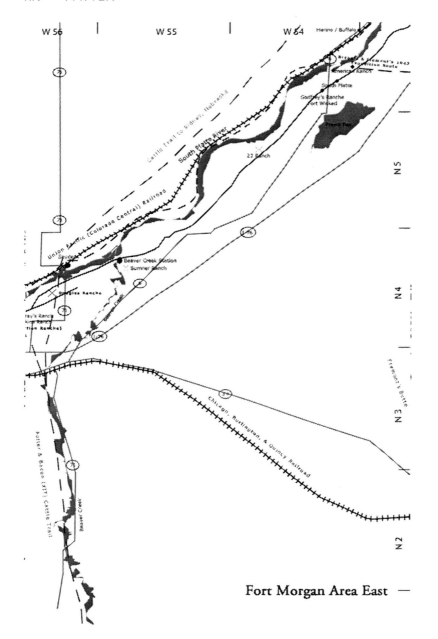

Fort Morgan Area East —

Chapter 1

Introducing Fort Morgan

Fort Morgan, Colorado lies on I-76, 80 miles east of Denver in the northeast corner of the state. Thousands of travelers pass through, stopping for gas or sustenance, heading for the ski resorts or campgrounds of the mountains or adventures further west. And this has been Fort Morgan for hundreds of years, a place of rest and respite, on a journey elsewhere. Settlers moving west in the nineteenth century passed through this junction camping, hunting buffalo, grazing their horses on the grass along the South Platte River. For a road has always been here, a natural road used by Indian tribes on their journeys and it was used by the early explorers of the New World even before a country was formed.

To the casual traveler, the corner of northeastern Colorado looks very much like the flat plains of Nebraska; an empty place, devoid of landmarks, the land stretching out west with a maddening sameness, where a century ago a lone tree served as a landmark. It is a harsh land, where man and animal could die of thirst just miles from the river. This was not a land of interesting rock formations or refreshing lakes, it was a desert prairie. Landmarks are few and far between along the South Platte River Road, but just at Fort Morgan, there is a truly important landmark. At this point, observant travelers of today, just as the travelers of a century past, look west on a clear day and gain their first glimpse of the Rocky Mountains rising from the desert, the distant peaks glistening with snow. After trekking mile upon mile through the same desert, through sand or snow wondering if the journey would ever end, the weary traveler sees Long's Peak and for the first time sees a glimmer of hope on the horizon – the beginning to the end of a journey.

> After we had encamped, towards night, the clouds which had been lowering around the western horizon cleared away, and discovered to us a beautiful bird's eye view of the Rocky mountains. This sight was hailed with joy.... We saw the end of the march – the long-wished-for object of all our hopes. They at first resembled white conical clouds lying along the edge of the horizon. The rays of a setting sun upon their snow-clad summits gave to them a beautiful and splendid appearance[1].

The above quote is from an 1835 report submitted by Colonel Henry Dodge describing the progress of his company of soldiers across the plains. The view has changed little in the 165 years since Dodge's expedition, the mountains still rise from the horizon, teasing the senses; the traveler questioning whether the sight is snowy peaks or cloud formations and much of the land, north and south of the South Platte River remain much as it would have been when Dodge's company marched through. Veering off the well-traveled road north or south ten miles or so, the land as originally laid out by nature still stands, unchanged save for a few fences and cattle, instead of buffalo, grazing lazily in their 100 acre pens. But just along the river, at the place Dodge and his soldiers camped has changed drastically. Visionaries of the west saw farmland where others saw only desert and built a system of irrigation canals and others built telegraphs, railroads, and highways, reaching out, connecting this island in the grass sea to the gold fields of the west and the cities of the east.

Location

Fort Morgan is currently a city with a population of approximately 11,000. The city is located in the northeastern corner of Colorado (N40.25, W103.80) and covers 4.5 miles. The military fort after which the town was named is no longer in existence, but was located on the northern edge of town approximately a ½ mile south of the South Platte River. Fort Morgan is centrally located between Julesburg (a major town on the Overland and Oregon trails) and Denver (a city

"Distant View of the Rocky Mountains" 1820 painting by Samuel Seymour, the painter on Stephen H. Long's expedition west.

emerging with the 1859 gold rush), approximately 90 miles from each.

During the 16th and 17th centuries, the area containing Fort Morgan vacillated between Spanish and French control. In 1800, the French sold a large area of land, containing Fort Morgan to the United States; this transaction is known as the Louisiana Purchase. First known as the District of Louisiana, the area became part of the Nebraska Territory in 1854. At the time, there was tension between the North and South Platte territories and in 1859, the South Platte county attempted to separate itself from the North Platte and secede from Nebraska, seeking to join the Kansas Territory[2]. Instead the area formed unofficially into Jefferson Territory, which was never officially recognized, and then became part of the newly formed Colorado Territory in 1861. While doing business as Jefferson Territory in 1859 and 1860, the land containing Fort Morgan was part of St. Vrain County, but became part of Weld County when Colorado became a territory. In 1889, Fort Morgan became the county seat for the newly formed Morgan County[3].

Fort Morgan lies on the south bank of the South Platte River along what is known as the South Platte River Trail or South Platte River Road. The source of the river is the base of Mount Elbert (between Pike's Peak in the south and Long's Peak in the north), southwest of Denver and drains the highest peaks of Colorado including Lincoln, Long's and Gray's[4]. The river flows north to Denver and the Cache à la Poudre at Fort Collins then veers east onto the Colorado plains until it joins with the North Platte river near North Platte, Nebraska.

The river was known by the Spanish of the 17th and 18th

century as *Río Jesús y María* (River of Jesus and Mary)[5], but was renamed *La Rivière Plat [Platte] or "Flat River"* in 1739 by two French traders, Pierre and Paul Mallet. The name was translated from the Pawnee name for the river *Kits Katus* "flat moving water." The Omaha Indians called the river *Ne braska* or *Ni bthaskake* also translated as "flat water[6,7]." The river was also known as the *Padouca Fork* after the Padouca Indian tribe settled along the river in the 18th and early 19th centuries (however some sources designate the North Platte, rather than the South Platte River as the Padouca Fork.)

Fort Morgan lies on an old Indian trail that follows the South Platte River. This trail was known by the Indian tribes in the area before the Mallet Brother's expedition of 1739. It was referred to as a "natural highway" by the Pawnees[8], with a hard, smooth road following the course of the South Platte River to its source in the Rocky Mountains. In the mid-19th century, the trail became part of the Overland mail route and was variously called the Denver Road, Pikes Peak Trail, California Road, and Platte River Trail/Road. The land beyond the river is desert and the label James Bell, a member of the Long Expedition of 1820, used to describe the area "Great American Desert" likely deterred early settlers.

Three creeks branch off to the south of the South Platte River in the immediate Fort Morgan area. Beaver Creek (also known as *la Fourche aux Castors*) lies fifteen miles to the east of Fort Morgan and Bijou Creek five miles to the west. Bijou Creek was named by Stephen H. Long in 1820 after his guide Joseph Bijeau, a trapper familiar with the area[9]. Kiowa Creek runs west of Fort Morgan approximately 20 miles. These three creeks appear on most early maps of the area and serve as fairly static landmarks. Two additional rivers are closer to Fort Morgan, but are less frequently marked on maps, possibly because they appear dry: Badger Creek branching off to the south and Wildcat Creek branching off to the north.

Historic Overview

From 1864 until 1868 Fort Morgan was a military fort along the branch of the Overland Trail that followed the South Platte River[10]. The military fort started life as a camp, first called Camp Tyler than Camp Wardwell (or Wardell), becoming a permanent fort in July, 1865.

But Fort Morgan's history isn't just linked with a military past; it is linked with the movement west; with the telegraph and railroads - and with gold. When gold was discovered in the Rocky Mountains at the head of the South Platte River, Denver City became the gateway to Colorado's gold fields and Fort Morgan was a central point along the trail leading to Denver. Fort Morgan was placed at a point generically referred to as the "junction[11]." The name "junction" may seem odd as Fort Morgan does not currently appear to lie at a crossroads, but during the gold rush, a "cut-off" road veered off the South Platte River Road over-land to Denver reducing the route by 30 to 40 miles. At this point, a post office and telegraph office was established to relay messages to Denver and it was at this crossroads that the fort built.

In 1912, the Daughters of the American Revolution summarized the history of the fort to congress after marking the old Fort with a monument. Though some of the details cannot be verified, this report provides an overview for the history of the Fort and the surrounding area:

In 1849, when the country west of the Missouri was a vast unknown plain, a sea on whose broad surface no mariner but John C. Fremont had coursed with chart and compass, thousands of brave men threaded the desert prairie and passed on into the rocky defiles of the mountains in a feverish rush for the gold diggings of California. The trail followed the South Platte Valley to Julesburg, there crossing the river and proceeding northwest into Wyoming in ordinary weather, but when the river was high the trail followed the Platte to within a short distance of Greeley, thence going northwest through Virginia Dale, and joining the more traveled route at Fort Steele. Ten years later, in 1859, the chance idler, dropping his pick at a gateway of the Rockies, reawakened the West with the cry of "Gold in Colorado" just as the fever of the California excitement was dying out. The Argonauts of '59 followed the southern or South Platte trail, but very near the present site of Fort Morgan established a "cutoff" by the way of Living Springs to Denver, thus saving some weary miles of travel....

From 1859 to 1864 the Argonauts passed the plot, on which Fort Morgan is built— an unending stream, in vehicles of all kinds, pausing always to camp on the broad plateau, which offered excellent feed or water for the jaded stock. With the exception of the adobe or sod stations, 20 or 30 miles apart along the river, the country was still a wilderness. Indians and buffalo roamed the plains, coyotes bowling on the track of the weak or disabled animals.... The trail the gold seekers wore was from 80 to 150 feet wide, and thousands of cubic yards of earth were worn out of this roadway, which could plainly be seen miles away 25 years later, the gay yellow sunflower blossoms growing high above the sage brush and cactus. To straggle from the trail or fall behind was death to a white man, and in 1864 the Indian became so troublesome that to protect the emigrants and the United States mail service the Government established a military post on the Morgan flats. This was on the brow of the hill above the remains of the old ranch house of Sam Ashcraft, who dispensed "pine knot," "forty red," and other brands of liquid pick-me-ups to the traveler....

The initiatory steps for the protection of the immigrants culminated in Camp Tyler which was established by Gen. Samuel Browne, commander of the Department of Colorado, in 1864. Soon a detachment of "galvanized" troops (rebel prisoners discharged from prison under agreement to enlist under Union officers to fight the Indians under Capt. Williams was called "Camp Wardwell," and in 1866, later some substantial sod and adobe buildings had been erected, it occupied the little tent city. The post was christened Fort Morgan, and the Government took control of the post. The buildings were erected by a detachment of Missouri Cavalry, Lieut. Col. Willard Smith commanding. During its occupancy from one to six companies of cavalry and infantry were stationed here....

It has often been wondered why the fortifications were not built near the river to prevent the Indians cutting off the water supply. Doubtless the wide view from the famous plateau up and down the Platte Valley gave it a strategic advantage, and investigations show that an abundance of good water was furnished the garrison by a well discovered within the stockade itself. L. H. Corniorth, of Denver, describes the buildings at the fort as being surrounded by an earth embankment 5 feet high, and the cannons, two 3-inch rifled Parrott guns, as mounted in two elevated rooms at the northeast and southwest corners of the enclosure....

The fort was the scene of activity until 1868, when the building of the Union Pacific Railroad and the decrease of immigration overland lead to its abandonment. It was occupied occasionally until 1870. Then the buildings began to be rifled of their timbers to supply lumber for the houses and barns of sheep and cattle men who inaugurated the second era in the history of our town and county....[12]

Fort Morgan Area

This book is about Fort Morgan and the geographical area immediately surrounding Fort Morgan. Events outside this area are included only when they directly impact Fort Morgan. For the purposes of this book, the Fort Morgan area is defined, somewhat arbitrarily, as lying approximately 30 miles either side of the town (approximately one day's travel on horseback) and includes the modern towns of Brush, Goodrich, Hillrose, Merino, Orchard, Snyder, Weldona (Weldon), and Wiggins (Corona). This history also includes major landmarks on the Overland Trail which are no longer evident on modern maps: American Ranch, Godfrey's Ranch (Fort Wicked) and Beaver Creek Station east of Fort Morgan and Bijou Creek Station and Fremont's Orchard to the west of Fort Morgan.

This history of the Fort Morgan area will start with the journeys of early explorers, fur trappers and traders and the migration of the various Indian tribes through the area. The references are somewhat vague and at times it is known only that these individuals or tribes were in the northeastern corner of what is now Colorado. During the gold rush, many travelers wrote of their journeys through the plains to the Rocky Mountains. Using landmarks, it is possible to focus on the events and impressions of the travelers as they passed through the Fort Morgan area. Sometimes the notes were mundane, but other times journals were filled with wonder or fear. The Overland mail and the Pacific Telegraph wind through the Fort Morgan area in the 1860s moving west to connect the continent and the history and events in the Fort Morgan area are a microcosm for events taking place all across the country.

The history of the military fort comprises a greater part of this book. Though the fort existed as a military establishment for only four years, it was central to the Indian wars in the area. Rather than isolated from major events of the time, Fort Morgan was connected with the Sand Creek Massacre and tangentially with the events taking place in the Civil War (The War of Rebellion) and even Custer's defeat at Little Big Horn.

The fort would be abandoned in 1868, but Fort Morgan again became central as the Union Pacific and the Chicago, Burlington & Quincy railroads connected at this point. The town of Fort Morgan will of course be discussed, but only its rise from the grasslands, emerging as a center of agriculture defined by the cattle industry and the irrigation canals. With the establishment of the town and Fort Morgan as the county seat, this history will end; leaving the modern history of the city of Fort Morgan for others.

∞

Chapter 2

Early Explorers & Traders

In the 17th century, the French and Spanish took control over vast tracts of land in the new world and both countries set out almost immediately to explore their new lands. Rumors of explorers, traders and trappers in the area of the South Platte River are documented as early as 1659[13] and in 1706, there were rumors of French *voyageurs* illegally crossing into Spanish lands, which at the time included the Fort Morgan area, to trade with the Pawnees. In 1720, an expedition led by Captain Pedro de Villasur left Santa Fé determined to find and evict the French from Spanish lands[14]. Villasur traveled north to the Río Jesús María (South Platte River) and then east into what is now Nebraska. There is some speculation as to exactly where he came to the river. Since the records of the expedition are lost and there were few landmarks regardless it can only be said that Villasur and his troops encountered the river somewhere between Fort

Morgan and the Nebraska border[15]. Villasur may have been one of the earliest explorers through the Fort Morgan area, but his journey would end abruptly a few days later. Where the North and South Platte Rivers join, Villasur's company was attacked by Pawnee and all but a few of the Spanish explorers were killed[16].

Route to Santa Fé

Many early explorers along the South Platte River were fur trappers and traders looking for a route through the wilderness to the Spanish city of Santa Fé. One of the earliest expeditions was made by two French trappers, Pierre and Paul Mallet. With a small company, the brothers set out from Fort de Chartres near St. Louis on May 29, 1739[17]. The company included Phillippe Robitalle, Michel Beslot, Joseph Bellecourt, Petit Jean David, Manuel Galien, and Louis Moreau (or Morin)[18,19]. The Mallet brothers traveled along the Missouri and Platte Rivers into Spanish territory. The Mallet brothers translated the Omaha name for the Platte River, *Nithbaska* or "river that spreads out in flatness," to *La Rivière Plat* or "flat river[20]." The brothers' exact route is unclear, but apparently the Mallets travelled along the South Platte River and then at some point veered overland striking the Republican River[21]. Their southwesterly course and the mention of the mountains possibly places the crossing near the Fort Morgan area. The Mallet brothers successfully reached Santa Fé on July 22, 1739[22].

The journeys of two other traders through the area are known only from the journals of Zebulon Pike. Pike himself did not travel along the South Platte River, but along the Arkansas River and then south to Santa Fé. However, once reaching Santa Fé, he wrote of encountering James Purcell and Baptiste La Lande, travelers who may have journeyed through the Fort Morgan area a few years earlier.

James Purcell set off from St. Louis in 1802 on a trapping and trading mission. He spent three years in what is now eastern Colorado[23] encountering many hostile Indians and arrived in Santa Fé in 1805. Pike wrote of Purcell (Pursley) in his journal noting the extraordinary discovery Purcell made in the Rocky Mountains – a discovery that would later define Colorado:

> …[James Purcell]'s employer dispatched Pursley [sic] on a hunting and trading tour with some bands of the Paducahs and Kyaways [Kiowa], with a small quantity of merchandise. The ensuing spring they were driven from the plains by the Sioux to the mountains which gave birth to La Platte…. He assured me that he had found gold on the head of La Platte, and had carried some of the virgin mineral in his shot-pouch for months; but that, being in doubt whether he should ever again behold the civilized world, and losing in his mind all the ideal value which mankind have stamped on that metal, he threw the sample always. He had imprudently mentioned it to the Spaniards, who had frequently solicited him to go and show a detachment of cavalry the place; but, conceiving it to be in our territory, he had refused…[24]

Shortly after Purcell traveled through the plains, another party of traders set off from St. Louis. Baptiste La Lande, a trader of Creole descent born in Louisiana, along with Jeannot Metoyer, Joseph Gervais and Laurent Durocher were sent by William Morrison to trade along the South Platte River and if possible, explore a route to Santa Fé[25]. La Lande did reach Santa Fé, but to his employer's annoyance he settled there rather than returning with the proceeds of his trading mission[26].

Zebulon Pike explored the Arkansas River through what is now Colorado and veered southwest into New Mexico just as Lewis and Clark were exploring the northern states to the Pacific Ocean. A third explorer set off a decade later to ex-

Map of Long's expedition to the Rocky Mountains [Excerpt]. 1823.
Note: Fort Morgan is located near the junction of the Padouca or South Fork of the Platte and the Bijeaux Creek.

plore the middle of the country. This explorer would choose to follow the course of the South Platte River directly through the Fort Morgan area.

Long's Expedition

Major Stephen H. Long set off in 1819-1920 to explore the central plains of the Louisiana Purchase. His company included Captain John R. Bell and John Biddle journalists; Lieutenants James D. Graham & William H. Swift, topographers; Edwin James, botanist, geologist, and physician; Thomas Say, zoologist and ethnologist; Titian R. Peale, naturalist; Augustus Edward Jessup, geologist; William Baldwin, physician and botanist, and Samuel Seymour, artist[27,28]. This was intended as a scientific expedition, but it was also part of a larger military project surveying possible locations for posts to protect fur traders and assess the Indian population and threat[29]. Long set off from Pittsburg, Pennsylvania on May 5, 1819, arriving in St. Louis in June. On June 14 1820, the party was joined by two French guides, Joseph Bijeau dit Bissonet (or Bissonette) and Abraham Ledoux (or Ladeau), trappers who at the time were living amongst the Pawnee. Bijeau was familiar with the languages of various tribes and the men knew the area well[30]. Bijeau (1778-1836) had worked as a fur trapper for Manuel Lisa and Jules DeMun and Auguste P. Chouteau out of St. Louis, showing up in the company records as early as 1806[31]. In 1815-1817, he was among the 21 trappers arrested by Spanish troops for illegally trading in Spanish lands and had been imprisoned for a short time in Santé Fé[32]. Long's party arrived in the Fort Morgan area on June 27th and camped near Fort Morgan on June 30th:

> ...Crossed the point of a range of sand bluffs, between it and the river is grove of scattered cotton wood trees, where is the remains of an old Indian fortified camp - the defense consists in a number of logs and pieces of drift arranged so as to form an oblong pin, being about 9 by 12 feet at the base, raised about 5 feet and partially covered...our interpreter informs us that a party of 8 or 10 Indians in such a place of defense would keep off a party of a hundred if attacked...the besieged party fireing [sic] thro' the apertures purposely left open in constructing the work.... On examining the Indian fortified camp last evening, there was found three small sticks each about 6

feet long, peeled of the bark, on each of them was fastened three leather thongs at the distance of 6 inches apart commencing from the small ends of the sticks. There was also found 16 buffalo skulls, fifteen of them arranged forming the circumference of a circle, the other was placed in the centre, on which was painted 30 black stripes & a small half circle. These were explained to us by our Guide & interpreter, Bijeau as follows - The stripes and marks on the buffalo skull, and the arrangement of them, signify that the place was last occupied by a war party of the Pawnee Loups returning from the Spanish frontier - the sticks, that they had taken 3 scalps....

Thursday June 29th...the atmosphere during the fore noon was very hazey [sic], so that objects at a distance appeared singular and very different from they were in reality. I was in advance of the party and for the distance of at least two miles, observed an object in front of me, which I took to be an Indian on horseback...so strong was my impressions, that I even imagined I could distinguish the tracks of his horses feet.... I have reason to believe my sight & imagination was in this instance deceived by the effects of hazey [sic] atmosphere....

Friday, June 30th. At 8'oclock, being on an elevated part of the prairie, in order to cross near the heads of some deep ravines - we discovered a blue strip, close in with the horizon to the west – which was by some pronounced to be no more than a cloud – by others, to be the Rocky Mountains. The hazy atmosphere soon rendered it obscure – and we were all expectation and doubt until in the afternoon, when the atmosphere cleared, and we had a distinct view of the sumit [sic] of a range of mountains – which to our great satisfaction and heart felt joy, was declared by the commanding officer to be the range of Rocky Mountains – a high Peake [sic] was plainly to be distinguished towering above all the others.... The whole range had a beautiful and sublime appearance to us, after having been so long confined to the dull uninteresting monotony of prairie country...the prairie, a barren gravel and sand plain, having but little vegetation.

Engraving by Samuel Seymour "View of the Rocky Mountains on the Platte 50 Miles from their Base" 1823.

The mountains present a beautiful appearance, their tops, and the valleys leading from them, as they appear to us, filled with snow....[33]

Long's first view of the mountains was made just west of Fort Morgan near Bijou Creek, named for the expedition's guide, Joseph Bijeau. The "high peake" mentioned was supposed by the expedition to be the "highest peak" described by Zebulon Pike (Pike's Peak), but was not. It would later be named Long's Peak for Stephen H. Long[34].

The Long expedition would push through to the Rockies, turning south and then back east along the Arkansas River. The results of the mission were disappointing. On maps the area was labeled the "Great American Desert" and Long concluded that "…this extensive section of country…is almost wholly unfit for cultivation, and of course uninhabitable…want of timber, of navigable streams, and of water for the necessities of life render it an unfit residence for any but a nomad population[35]." On many counts, Long was wrong.

Trading and Fur Trapping

In the early 19th century, various fur trapping companies set up posts along the front range of the Rocky Mountains in what is now Colorado: Bent and St. Vrain (Fort Lookout), Sublette and Vasquez, Fort Jackson, and Fort Lupton[36]. Trappers working for these companies went out into the wilderness to trap beaver and buffalo or to trade with the various native tribes living in the area[37].

It is difficult to track the movements of the trappers as there is little written evidence of their travels, but a few were known to have traveled along the South Platte River and likely through the Fort Morgan area. In 1812 William H. Ashley of the Rocky Mountain Fur Company along with a young Jim Beckwourth traveled up the South Platte[38]. In May 1827, Albert G. Boone set off from the foothills with furs and traveled down the South Platte River to St. Louis. In April of 1831, John Gantt led 70 men across the South Platte river and in 1836, Andrew Sublette took furs east through the area followed in 1838 by Peter A. Sarpy and Henry Fraeb. Other traders who possibly traded with Indians in the Fort Morgan area were Robert Newell in 1836-7, Antonio Montero in 1839-40, Sir William Drummond Stewart and William L. Sublette in 1843, Kit Carson, Oliver Perry Wiggins, James Beckwourth, and Ike Chamberline in 1846 and Kit Carson again in 1847[39].

Trapping was a lucrative business, but it held many dangers. In 1816, Jean Baptiste Champlain a trapper with the St. Louis Missouri Fur Company who had been working in the area of the Rocky Mountains since about 1809 began to have problems with the local tribes[40]. He sent part of his company over the Rockies and Champlain with ten men headed onto the plains along either the South Platte or the Arkansas River. Over the next few months, Indians killed all but Champlain, Ezekiel Williams, and Porteau[41]. Williams eventually reached St. Louis, but Champlain did not. The story of the missing trapper was the subject of the 1847 book *The Lost Trappers* by David Coyner.

William Henry Ashley, a fur trapper and owner of the Rocky Mountain Fur Company, regularly explored the western frontier trading with various Indian tribes. On November 3, 1824 Ashley set out from Fort Atkinson with a company that included Tom Fitzpatrick, Zacharias Ham, James Clyman, Robert Campbell, Moses ("Black") Harris, Baptiste La Jennesse, LeBrache, Dorway, and Clement (or Claymore), and James P. Beckwourth (Beckwith)[42]. It was the height of winter and the going was difficult. Ashley's party traversed the Fort Morgan area at the end of December, 1824 stopping at Fremont's Orchard on January 1, 1825 to recuperate[43]:

…The morning of the [December] 26th was cloudy and excessively cold. At 3 o'clock in the afternoon it began to snow and continued with violent winds until the night of the 27th. The next morning (28th) four of my horses were so benumbed with cold that they were unable to stand, although we succeeded in raising them on their feet. A delay to recruit them would have been attended with great danger, probably even to the destruction of the whole party. I therefore concluded to set forward without them. The snow was now so deep that had it not been for the numerous herds of buffaloe [sic] moving down the river, we could not possibly have proceeded. The paths of these animals were beat on either side of the river and afforded an easy passage to our horses. These animals were essentially beneficial to us in another respect by removing (in their search for food) the snow in many places from the earth and leaving the grass exposed to view, which was the only nourishment our horses could obtain. We continued to move forward without loss of time, hoping to be able to reach the wood described by the Indians before all our horses should become exhausted. On the 1st January, 1825, I was exceedingly surprised and no less gratified at the sight of a grove of timber, in appearance, distant some two or three miles on our front. It proved to be a grove of cottonwood of the sweet-bark kind suitable for horse food, situated on an island, offering among other conveniences, a good situation for defense. I concluded to remain here several days for the purpose of recruiting my horses, and made my arrangements accordingly. My Indian friends of the Pawne [sic] Loup deputation, believing this place to be nearly opposite to the Arapahoe and other Indian camps on the Arkansas determined to proceed hence across the country. They prepared a few pounds of meat and with each a bundle of wood tied to his back for the purpose of fuel, departed the following morning on their mission. Being informed by the Pawneys [sic] that one hundred of my old enemies (the Arikara warriors) were encamped with the Arkansas Indians, and my situation independent of that circumstance, being rendered more vulnerable by the departure of the Indians, who had just left us, I was obliged to increase my guard from eight to sixteen men. This was much the most severe duty my men had to perform, but they did it with alacrity and cheerfulness as well as all other services required at their hands; indeed, such was their pride and ambition in the discharge of their duties, that their privations in the end became sources of amusement to them. We remained on this island until the cottonwood fit for horse food was nearly consumed, by which time our horses were so refreshed as to justify another move forward. We therefore made arrangements for our departure and resumed our march on the 11th January.... From this last mentioned island, we had a clear and distant view of the Rocky Mountains bearing west, about sixty miles distant[44].

Fur trapping was only one source of income, the other came from trading goods with native tribes living in the area. Robert Newell (AKA Doc Newell), employed by the Bent and St. Vrain Company, travelled extensively throughout the Colorado plains in 1836-1837[45]. Newell kept detailed records of the transactions from his trip. On one occasion, tobacco, axes, glasses, guns, knives, cloth, beats, gunpowder and balls were exchanged for 77 [buffalo] robes and 29 pieces of meat[46]. Collecting the goods and hides however was only part of the job. The profits came from selling the goods back east.

On the 26th of April, 1840 E. (Elias) Willard Smith and his party set off from Fort of Sublette and Vasquez sailing up the South Platte with a load of furs heading for St. Louis. It made sense to the fur companies to use the river's power to sail the heavy loads east, but the South Platte River was very shallow and Smith's boats were often caught on sand bars. At this point, the boat would be unloaded, pushed off the sandbar, and then reloaded. In the end, the company waded alongside the boats, pushing them nearly 300 miles[47]. Two years later, another trapper Jean Baptiste Charbonneau would attempt to replicate Smith's journey with even less success.

Charbonneau (Charbonard) was a well-educated and well-traveled trapper. He was the son of Toussaint Charbonneau and Sacagawea, who accompanied Lewis and Clark on their expedition. Jean Baptiste himself had famously traveled west with Lewis and Clark as an infant slung on his mother's back. In the 1840s, Charbonneau was sent by the Bent and St. Vrain Company[48] with a boat-load of buffalo hides to sell in St. Louis. David Lavender described the scene:

[In the] spring of 1842, as men at the other Platte forts had done before, company employees under Baptiste Charbonneau built shallow draft boats, perhaps of pine timber sawed in a pit or perhaps of buffalo hides shrunk tight over willow frames and waterproofed with tallow. The trip was unmitigated hell-the very name Platte means shallow water. Stranded almost hourly on sand bars, Charbonneau's dry-land sailors, mostly Mexicans, floundered into the muck and tried to wrestle the boats ahead. Brute force failing, they unpacked the cargo and lugged it by hand downstream to the next navigable water. They made forty-five miles. Then the shrinking stream stranded them entirely. Philosophically Charbonneau made camp on a wooded island, named his exile St. Helena, and settled down to wait for whatever came next[49].

The island Charbonneau settled on was near present-day Orchard, Colorado about 15 miles west of Fort Morgan and what happened next was that Charbonneau received visitors.

Fremont's First Expedition

In June 1842, Captain John C. Fremont set off on his first expedition from St. Louis under orders to explore the "frontiers of Missouri and the South Pass in the Rocky Mountains, and on the line of the Kansas and Great Platte rivers[50]." Fremont was accompanied by Charles Preuss, a cartographer; Lucien B. Maxwell, a professional hunter; Baptiste Bernier, Honore Ayot, and Basil Lajeunesse, trappers; and four additional men who had been fur trappers in the area. Also accompanying Fremont was a party of three

Major General John C. Fremont.

Cheyennes who they met at the fork and who said their village lay up the South Platte River[51]. Where the river forks,

Fremont divided his company; he and a small party took the South Platte River Road and Christopher "Kit" Carson and the rest of the party set off along the North Platte River. The going was rough and Preuss and Bernier were sent back to the main party after only a day's journey.

Fremont entered the Fort Morgan area on July 7th camping about 20 miles east of Fort Morgan at Beaver Creek[52]. The journey along the South Platte River had been uneventful, but the next day would be anything but boring. Early on

Indian Buffalo Hunt. Published in Frank Leslie's Popular Monthly *magazine 1883.*

July 8th, the company came upon traces of Indians and soon the company found themselves surrounded and in fear of their lives:

> Journeying along, we came suddenly upon a place where the ground was covered with horses' tracks, which had been made since the rain, and indicated the immediate presence of Indians in our neighborhood. The buffalo, too, which the day before had been so numerous, were nowhere in sight – another sure indication that there

were people near. Riding on, we discovered the carcass of a buffalo recently killed – perhaps the day before. We scanned the horizon carefully with the glass, but no living object was to be seen. For the next mile or two, the ground was dotted with buffalo carcasses, which showed that the Indians had made a surround here, and were in considerable force. We went on quickly and cautiously, keeping the river bottom, and carefully avoiding the hills; but we met with no interruption and began to grow careless again.....

There were some dark-looking objects among the hills, about two miles to the left, here low and undulating, which we had seen for a little time, and supposed to be buffalo coming in to water; but...another glance at the dark objects showed them at once to be Indians coming up at speed. Had we been well mounted, and disencumbered of instruments, we might have set them at defiance; but as it was, we were fairly caught...and we endeavored to gain a clump of timber about half a mile ahead.... At first, they did not appear to be more than fifteen or twenty in number, but group after group darted into view at the top of the hills, until all the little eminences seemed in motion, and, in a few minutes from the time they were first discovered, two or three hundred, naked to the breech cloth, were sweeping across the prairie.... [B]efore we could reach the bank, down came the Indians upon us.... Just as he was about to fire, Maxwell recognised the leading Indian, and shouted to him in the Indian language, "You're a fool, G--- damn you, don't you know me?" The sound of his own language seemed to shock the savage, and, swerving his horse a little, he passed us like an arrow. He wheeled, as I rode out toward him, and gave me his hand, striking his breast and exclaiming "Arapaho[53]!"

The Indians proved to a village of Arapaho with whom Lucien Maxwell had lived and traded with a year or two previously. Along with the Arapaho were a band of Cheyenne, about twenty lodges and kin of the Cheyenne accompanying Fremont. When told that Fremont's companions were Cheyenne, "[t]hey seemed disappointed to know that they were Cheyennes, for they had fully anticipated a grand dance around a Pawnee scalp that night[54]."

The Indians were in the area hunting buffalo and Fremont's company sat on the opposite bank of the South Platte and watched the hunt unfold:

The chief showed us his village at a grove on the river six miles ahead, and pointed out a band of buffalo on the other side of the Platte, immediately opposite us, which he said they were going to surround.... In a few minutes the women came galloping up, astride on their horses, and naked from their knees down, and hips up. They followed the men, to assist in cutting up and carrying off the meat.... [We] sat down on the bank to view the scene; and our new acquaintances rode a few hundred yards lower down, and began crossing the river. Scores of wild-looking dogs followed, looking like troops of wolves, and having, in fact, but very little of the dog in their composition.... One party proceeded directly across the prairie, toward the hills, in an extended line, while the other went up the river; and instantly as they had given the wind to the herd, the chase commenced. The buffalo started for the hills, but were intercepted and driven back toward the river, broken and running in every direction. The clouds of dust soon covered the whole scene, preventing us from having any but an occasional view.... We were too far to hear the report of the guns, or any sound; and at every instant, through the clouds of dust which the sun made luminous, we could see for a moment two or three buffalo dashing along, and close behind them an Indian with his long spear, or other weapon, and instantly again they disappeared. The apparent silence, and the dimly seen figures flitting by with such rapidity, gave it a kind of dreamy effect, and seemed more like a picture than a scene of real life. It had been a large herd when the *cerne* commenced, probably three or four hundred in number; but, though I watched them closely, I did not see one emerge from the fatal cloud where the work of destruction was going on....[55]

After the eventful day with the Arapaho, another surprise and more companions would greet the company on the morning of July 9th:

This morning we caught the first faint glimpse of the Rocky mountains, about sixty miles distant [likely 90 miles]...and we were just able to discern the snowy summit of "Long's peak," ("*les deux Oreilles*" of the Canadians,) showing like a cloud near the horizon. I found it easily distinguishable, there being a perceptible difference in its appearance from the white clouds that were floating about the sky. I was pleased to find that among the traders and voyageurs the name of "Long's peak" had been adopted and become familiar in the country....

About 8, we discerned several persons on horseback a mile or two ahead, on the opposite side of the river.... We found them to be two white men, and a mulatto named Jim Beckwith, who had left St. Louis when a boy, and gone to live with the Crow Indians. He had distinguished himself among them by some acts of daring bravery, and had risen to the rank of a chief, but had now, for some years, left them. They were in search of a band of horses that had gone off from a camp some miles above, in charge of Mr. Chabonard [Charbonneau].... About eight miles from our sleeping-place, we reached Bijou's fork, an affluent of the right bank.... Seven miles further brought us to the camp of some four or five whites, (New Englanders, I believe), who had accompanied Captain Wyeth to the Columbia river, and were independent trappers. All had their squaws with them, and I was really surprised at the number of little fat buffalo-fed boys that were tumbling about the camp, all apparently of the same age, about three or four years old. They were encamped on a rich bottom, covered with a profusion of rich grass, and had a large number of fine-looking horses and mules. We rested with them a few minutes, and in about two miles arrived at Chabonard's camp, on an island in the Platte...which he had named St. Helena.... Mr. C. received us hospitably. One of the people was sent to gather mint, with the aid of which he concocted very good julep; and some boiled buffalo tongue, and coffee with the luxury of sugar....[56]

At the place where Jean Baptiste Charbonneau and his family had taken up summer residence was a "fine grove" of cottonwoods which became known as Fremont's Orchard. The next day, Fremont and his company took their leave of Charbonneau and continued west to St. Vrain's fort. Charbonneau continued to wait and enjoy his summer on the South Platte and six weeks later, he had another visitor.

Rufus B. Sage

In September, 1841, Rufus B. Sage, a self-confessed tourist, set out with a group of fur trappers to see the Rocky Mountains[57]. He entered the Fort Morgan area on August 29, 1842, just over a month behind Fremont. Sage, like Fremont and Long before him, noted the view of the Rocky Mountains in the area of Fort Morgan. Sage also noted the buffalo and the remains of an Indian village, likely that of the Arapaho encountered by Fremont a month earlier, and Sage also met Charbonneau:

A few miles above Beaver Fork, we obtained a distinct view of the main ridge of the Rocky Mountains with the snowy summit of Long's Peak…. They appear like a pile of dark clouds just rising from the verge of the horizon, and could be identified only by their uniform and stationary position….

From the time of first entering the buffalo range till we reached Bijou creek, our entire course was beset with dense masses of those animals, which covered the river bottoms and prairies in all directions, as far as the eye could reach…. A few miles above Beaver creek we passed the site of a recent Indian encampment, where was yet standing the frame-work of a medicine lodge, erected by the Cheyennes and Arapahoes in the performance of their religious rites and ceremonies. This was made of light poles, describing an amphitheater with a diameter of some fifty feet. In form it was much like the pavilion of a circus, and of sufficient dimensions to contain several hundred individuals....[58]

A ride of ten or fifteen miles...brought us to a camp of whites, in the employ of Bent and St. Vrain, occupying a small island in the Platte. They were guarding a quantity of robes with which they had attempted to descend the river, but were unable to proceed further on account of low water. I was much gratified at here meeting an old acquaintance, with whom I had passed a portion of the previous winter upon White river. The camp was under the direction of a half-breed, named Chabonard [Charbonneau], who proved to be a gentleman of superior information. He had acquired a classic education and could converse quite fluently in German, Spanish, French, and English, as well as several Indian languages. His mind, also, was well stored with choice reading, and enriched by extensive travel and observation. Having visited most of the important places, both in England, France, and Germany, he knew how to turn his experience to good advantage. There was a quaint humor and shrewdness in his conversation, so garbed with intelligence and perspicuity, that he at once insinuated himself into the good graces of listeners, and commanded their admiration and respect....[59]

Sage moved on and eventually so did Charbonneau.

Whether the river rose sufficiently for him to continue his journey or alternate transportation was sent from St. Vrain's fort is unknown, but Charbonneau and his company were gone by the time Fremont returned.

Fremont's Second Expedition

Setting off again from St. Louis, Fremont and company, which included Theodore Talbot, Thomas Fitzpatrick, and William Gilpin (later the first territorial Governor of Colorado), made their way in 1843 across the Great American Desert and over the Rocky Mountains this time into Utah, Washington, and California. On this expedition, Fremont started down the Republican River and then crossed over prairie to the South Platte River. The going was difficult and there was little water. Theodore Talbot wrote of the arid journey:

...Mr. Fitzpatrick left us in search of water...early in the evening we reached a pond of the most execrable water, halting here for a while we let those of our animals drink that would, and then journeyed on in hopes of finding better. About 8 oclock [sic] we found some ponds in which the water was not quite so nauseous, and there we camped. These ponds or wallows are formed by the buffaloes wallowing, an amusement they are fond of. When any rain falls, it is collected in these places, and here the buffalo come to drink and stand during the heat of the day; adding their own excrements to the already putrescent waters. This compound, warmed for weeks in a blazing sun and alive with animalcules, makes a drink *palatable* to one suffering from intense thirst. O, that some over-dainty connoisseur might taste of it![60]

A few days later, the party encountered the South Platte River. Fremont was likely following an established trail northwest from the Kansas boarder and encountered the South Platte just east of Fort Morgan possibly near what is now called Fremont's Butte. Fremont noted the refreshing scene:

> Crossing the summit of an elevated and continuous range of rolling hills, on the afternoon of the 30th of June [sic] we found ourselves overlooking a broad and misty valley, where, about ten miles distant, and 1,000 feet below us, the south fork of the Platte was rolling magnificently along, swollen with the waters of the melting snows. It was in strong and refreshing contrast with the parched country from which we had just issued; and when, at night, the broad expanse of water grew indistinct, it almost seemed that we had pitched our tents along the shore of the sea....
>
> Travelling along up the valley of the river, here 4,000 feet above the sea...we caught a far and uncertain view of a faint blue mass in the west, as the sun sank behind it; and from our camp in the morning, at the mouth of Bijou, Long's peak and the neighboring mountains stood out into the sky, grand and luminously white, covered to their bases with glittering snow[61].

Charbonneau was no longer on his island in the Platte, but near where the trapper was met a year earlier, Talbot tells of meeting another unexpected friend:

> This morning, the atmosphere being very clear, we for the first time caught a glimpse of the far distant peaks of

the Rocky Mountains. The whole range stood forth in bold relief against the surrounding sky, a succession of stupendous masses, all clothed in pure white mantles and linked together, forming a rigid and impenetrable barrier of cliffs piled on cliffs, each in eager rivalship, ambitiously pointing towards the highest heavens. The coming sun soon cast his golden veil upon them, and we turned away to seek relief from the dazzling refulgence of his reflected rays!...

We took our road partly in the river bottoms, and occasionally we mounted the bluffs beyond as we saw prospect of better travel. The whole country is here overrun with the prickly pear or cactus and the dwarf sunflower. About noon we discovered three Indians; after hovering round camp for sometime they ventured in. They proved to be of the Blackfeet who reside with the Arapahoes, and one was an old friend of Fitzpatrick's. They told us that a portion of the Arapahoe village was on the South Fork a few miles above, trading with the Sioux: the other part had crossed over to the Arkansas River, where the main body would soon follow in quest of the buffalo which had become scarce in this vicinity. We had hardly made preparations for our evening camp when 40 or 50 warriors came down from the village to visit us....

We were accompanied by many Indians in our travels today. Among others a handsome young Indian came dashing up to Fitz. And cordially shaking his hand expressed in the best English terms, the great delight it gave him to meet Fitz, with a thousand kind interrogatories, as to his health, purpose, &c. We were much surprised at this unusual Indian salutation until we heard its cause explained. It seems that Fitz. returning from the Rocky Mts in the year 1831 found this young man, then but a little boy with (I think) 2 other children alone on the prairie and actually starving to death. In a sudden attack of the enemy they had become separated & lost from their parents and friends who had fled.... [A]lthough the poor orphans were suffering the keenest pangs of hunger and cold, they still endeavored to conceal themselves from the newcomers. But they were unable to elude Fitzpatrick's keen eye.... He had advanced very close when to his utter astonishment he found that his imaginary enemy was no other than a helpless little boy. He drew him forth more dead than alive, but soon succeeded in calming his groundless fears. On looking farther the other children were brought to light. Their wan faces too plainly told their pitiable situation. Taking compassion on them Fitzpatrick relieved all their wants and carried them to a place of safety. He was so much pleased with the one first found that he resolved to carry him to St. Louis, whither he was journeying. The youthful savage received the name of "Friday" from his new master who in time became much attached to his protégé. Arrived at St. Louis, Friday was sent to school and soon acquired a knowledge of the English language. He remained several years among the whites, occasionally making a trip into the Indian country with his patron. On one of these excursions he accidentally entered an Arapahoe village....a woman rush[ed] up clasped him fervently in her arms, claiming him as her lost son....[62]

Indian village. Sketch published in the Journal of the U.S. Cavalry Association 1904.

Friday, Fitzpatrick's protégée remained on the Colorado and Wyoming plains, leading a peaceful band of Arapaho through the tumultuous decades to follow. Friday refused to fight the whites, even at the height of the Indian wars of the 1860s and was active in trying to broker a peace between the whites and the Indian tribes on the plains[63], but for now, the plains tribes and the exploring whites met as friends.

Bryan's expedition

In 1856, Francis T. Bryan a Lieutenant of the Topographical Engineers was sent to survey the area around the Republican and Platte rivers. He set-off from Fort Riley on June 21st. In his party included John Lambert, Henry Engelmann, and Charles Larned[64]. On his outgoing trip, he went to Fort Kearney and up the Platte taking the north fork to Laramie. Returning, his party came south along the Cache a la Poudre and then traveled eastward along the South Platte River Road coming into the Fort Morgan area on Wednesday, September 10th 1856.

Bryan noted the "burial" of Indians in the branches of a small grove of trees. Later travelers would also note the sight indicating that the confluence of Beaver Creek and the South Platte River was a place of some significance to the tribes in the area. Bryan's journey through the Fort Morgan area was uneventful save for the death of one of the company, Frederick Bortheaux on Sunday, September 14th. The burial of Bortheaux, the first recorded in the Fort Morgan area, occurred near the place where later Fort Wicked would stand. After the burial, the company struck off overland likely along the same trail Fremont traversed in 1843[65].

Military Moves West

Long, Fremont, and Bryan were military officers, but their expeditions were primarily scientific and they were not accompanied by troops. As early as 1835, however, military troops entered the South Platte area and in the 1850s, the first conflicts with the Indians heralded the Indian wars to come.

In May 1835, Colonel Henry Dodge led three companies (A, C, and G) of the First United States Dragoons across the central plains to the Rocky Mountains along the South Platte River. The three companies were led by Captains Lancaster P. Lupton, Matthew Duncan, and Lemuel Ford. Lieutenants Enoch Steen, Terrett, Wheelock, and G. P. Kingsbury (journalist), Major Dougherty (Indian Agent), Captain Gantt (Indian trader and guide), and Dr. Fellows (surgeon), also accompanied Dodge[66].

Dodge's Dragoons entered the Fort Morgan area in mid-July, camping at Fort Morgan on July 16th:

> ...entered upon a high prairie, and came to an old deserted Indian camp, supposed to have been lately

occupied by the Arepahas [sic] The poles of the medicine
lodge were still standing, and some of the emblems of
their worship, such as buffalo heads, painted arrows, &c.
After we had encamped, towards night, the clouds which
had been lowering around the western horizon cleared
away, and discovered to us a beautiful bird's eye view of
the Rocky mountains. This sight was hailed with joy by
the whole command. We saw the end of the march – the
long-wished-for object of all our hopes. They at first resembled white conical clouds lying along the edge of the
horizon. The rays of a setting sun upon their snow-clad
summits gave to them a beautiful and splendid appearance[67].

A couple of soldiers chronicled the journey. Though some
of the details and mileage disagree, there are commonalities,
especially the thrill at seeing the mountains for the first time.
Sergeant Hugh Evans of Company G wrote:

...We halted & encamped in a beautiful situation
where late in the evening we could look and behold visible to the natural eye the high white snow tops which
appeared like the lowering white clouds just raising above
the horizon; all eyes were open to curiosity and runing
[sic] to catch a glimps [sic] of this wonderful structure of
nature - though the sight was distant and glimering [sic]
yet it was sublime and beautiful[68].

The purpose of Dodge's trip was to talk with the chiefs of
the various plains tribes[69] and many councils, though none in
the immediate Fort Morgan area. Relations with the Indians
were peaceful for the next couple of decades, but this was to
change. With the finding of gold in California, a large num-

bers of emigrants and gold seekers flooded onto the plains and confrontations with the various native tribes were in evitable.

The Cheyenne Expedition was a military operation not designed to explore the region or talk peacefully with the Indian tribes, but to encounter the Cheyenne and possibly, as one source noted, to provoke a battle. Leading up to the expedition, there had been conflicts with the Cheyenne especially in the vicinity of Forts Laramie and Kearney. The Cheyenne Expedition began at Fort Leavenworth on the May 18, 1857 with six companies of the 4th U. S. Cavalry under the command of Major John Sedgwick traveling south along the Santa Fé trail and three companies of the 6th U. S. Infantry under the command of Colonel Edwin Vose "Bull" Sumner traveling north to the Platte river and onto Fort Laramie along the north fork. The two regiments circled around the edges of Cheyenne country[70] meeting on the South Platte River on July 7, 1857 at what Colonel Sumner named Camp Buchanan just west of Kiowa creek on the South Platte River. Camp Buchanan became the first established military camp in the Fort Morgan area.

Preparations began for a lighter force of six companies of cavalry, under the command of Major Sedgwick, and three companies of infantry under the command of Captain Ketchum, to move eastward along the South Platte river to engage the Cheyenne Indians[71]. The Cheyenne Expedition marched through the Fort Morgan area in mid-July, camping near the place where only a few years later Fort Morgan would be built. The expedition encountered no Indians on their journey along the South Platte River, but at Beaver

Creek, there were signs of recent habitation:

> ...scattered along the banks of the South Platte, were a few trees that had been used as a burial site by a band of Cheyennes the previous year. Probably they were Ridge People, a band that regularly camped and hunted in the country between the Republican and South Platte. At least one tree burial was visible, and near the river they found a tripod consisting of three old lodgepoles (the remains of a burial lodge), from which were suspended some bloody blankets and skins. On the ground beneath were the bones of a human body with some of the cartilaginous matter still attached. At one side, staring toward the remains of the body, were a number of buffalo skulls set in a line. One of the civilian packers with the column said the bones were those of a young Cheyenne chief named Young Antelope, who had died or been killed in the vicinity the previous summer. That afternoon Sumner's command made camp seven miles beyond Beaver Creek. Timber along the river had given out almost entirely, and the mountains to the west had faded from view....[72]

After leaving the Fort Morgan area, Colonel Sumner struck out overland and into Kansas where he would find what he sought, a battle with the Cheyenne Indians on July 29th on the south fork of the Solomon River. A few years later the battles between the military and the Indians would find their way to Fort Morgan.

∞

Chapter 3

Tribes of Northeastern Colorado

Native Americans lived and hunted near Fort Morgan long before the first whites explored the area, but the tribes were migratory, moving with the seasons, or at the whim of the government or a hostile tribe. The first reported tribes in the Fort Morgan area were the Apache and the Padouca in the 16th and 17th centuries. Early in the 18th century, the Comanche and the Pawnee controlled eastern Colorado with the Kiowa taking over by the end of the century. By the 19th century, the Sioux, Arapaho and Cheyenne were the predominant tribes in the area.

In the early 19th century, Fort Morgan was part of the Indian Territory, created in 1825 for the protection of various tribes, but by the middle of the 19th century, as more emigrants moved west and land became more valuable, the

Indian Territory was compressed[73]. The Laramie Treaty (or Fitzpatrick's Treaty) of 1851 between the U. S. government and the Sioux, Cheyenne, Arapahoe, Crow, Assinaboines, Gros-Ventre Mandans, and Arrickaras[74] defined the lands given to the tribes. The treaty in part read:

> The territory of the Cheyennes and Arapahoes, commencing at the Red Butte, or the place where the road leaves the north fork of the Platte River; thence up the north fork of the Platte River to its source; thence along the main range of the Rocky Mountains to the headwaters of the Arkansas River; thence down the Arkansas River to the crossing of the Santa Fé road; thence in a northwesterly direction to the forks of the Platte River, and thence up the Platte River to the place of beginning[75].

The Laramie Treaty placed the South Platte River squarely in Cheyenne and Arapaho territory, but the river wandered through prime hunting ground and within the decade would also become a major highway to the Colorado gold fields making it a center of conflict[76].

At first, the Indians generally avoided or traded amicably with the whites, but the influx of emigrants threatened the Indians' way of life. The settlers hunted or chased away most of the buffalo and chopped down the already scarce trees for firewood. The settlers also brought with them diseases for which the Native Americans had no immunity; Small Pox in particular ravaged many tribes. As the tribes became destitute, unable to feed themselves, they were reduced to a reliance on government subsidies or even begging for food. The frustrated tribes blamed the whites for their problems[77].

In 1865, an attempt was made to move the Cheyenne and

Arapaho off the land granted them in 1851, but the whites had little understanding of tribal politics. Many of the plains tribes had a long history with their neighbors, sometimes allies and other times bitter enemies. Black Kettle, a Cheyenne chief, summed up the problem:

> Yesterday you spoke of a reservation north of the North Platte, or south of the Arkansas. North of the North Platte has once been given to the Sioux to my knowledge; south of the Arkansas has been given to the Comanches and Kiowas. To place them [Cheyenne] on the same ground would be to make prisoners of us, or like going out of one fire into another[78].

The whites only understood that the Indian stood in the way of progress.

Migration though Northeastern Colorado

Many mid-western tribes migrated through what is now northeastern Colorado and likely had a presence in the Fort Morgan area. Generally, tribes moved into the area for a period of 50 to 100 years and then when supplanted by a dominant tribe, migrated south.

The history of tribal migration is sketchy and filtered through the eyes of white writers. Two early sources documented tribes in the 19th century: Captain Meriwether Lewis' *Delineations of the Manners, Customs, Religion, &c. of the Indians, compiled from Various Authentic Sources, and Original Documents, and a Summary of the Statistical View of the Indian Nations* which was included as part of the published account of the *Travels of Capts. Lewis & Clarke* published in 1809 and Samuel Griswold Goodrich's 1852 *History of the Indians of*

North and South America. Annual reports submitted to the Commissioner of Indian Affairs also provided some written documentation of the tribes on the Colorado plains though the documentation was at times biased or confused. The white authors did not always understand the distinctions between tribes and tribal names were not codified until the mid-19th century.

Padouca

One of the earliest tribes documented in the Fort Morgan area was The Great Padouca Nation. There is very little information about this tribe, but the Platte River on maps as early as 1684 carries the name Padouca (Rivière des Parouke), presumably for the predominant tribe of the area[79]. The Padouca appear to have lived on a large area of the plains covering modern day Colorado, Kansas, Nebraska and southern Wyoming[80] and villages of Padouca are noted on maps directly in the Fort Morgan area. In 1815, there were reportedly 1000 Padoucas (300 warriors) living along the Padouca River (South Platte),[81] but the tribe seems to have disappeared sometime during the 19th century.

Some scholars conjecture that the Kiowa[82] are the descendants of the Great Padouca Nation, but it is difficult to confirm this assertion[83]. Others speculate the Padouca became part of the Comanche tribe[84] and still others equate Padouca with the Apache[85,86]. An alternate theory is that the Padouca tribe at some time split into the various plains tribes known as Apache, Kiowa, Crow, and Arapaho[87].

Plains Apache & Comanche

The Apache were in the area of the South Platte River as early as the 16th century, though as mentioned previously, the references to Apache may instead refer to the Padouca[88]. The Apache obtained horses from the Spaniards and "armed with lances, mounted Apaches expanded over the southern plains after 1620"[89]. By 1719, the Apache controlled the plains between the Red and South Platte Rivers[90]. The tribe at this time was allied with the Spanish and a number of Apache accompanied Villasur on his fateful expedition into Pawnee territory. Later in the 18th century, Apache power declined and their relationship with the Spanish became strained[91]. Early in the 18th century, Comanche attacks moved the Apache out of the South Platte area and the Comanche took control over a vast tract of land covering Kansas, Oklahoma, New Mexico, and Texas[92,93]. The Mallet brothers, following the Missouri and Platte Rivers in 1739 noted arriving at the mouth of the "River of the Comanches" which was likely the junction of the North and Platte Rivers[94]. A 1777 Spanish map of the area reportedly labeled the area east of the Rocky Mountains as the "Unknown land of the Comanchis [Comanche]" and goes on to describe the tribe:

Comanche warrior.
Published in Western Wilds, *1877.*

This nation is very warlike and cruel. It has made

itself master of the buffalo plains from the land of the Yamparikas to the province of Texas. It is very skillful in the handling of horses. It has dispossessed the Apache Nation of all its lands, becoming master of those as far as the frontier of the provinces of our King. These two said nations are those which for many years have been in a continual state of war against this kingdom, the one from the north and east, and the other from the south and west, and have brought about such panic that they have left no towns, cities, or ranches of the Spaniards unattacked[95].

Similarly, Goodrich described the tribe as a

...very warlike tribe, traversing the immense space of country extending far north and south, east and west, from the Red River to the Pacific Ocean. They were long the dreaded enemy of the Spaniards, as they now are of the Mexicans, on whom they make frequent incursions, and bear off prisoners, especially female children, whom they adopt and marry.... The Camanches [sic] have fought many a bloody battle with their enemies, and have always succeeded in preserving their independence. They particularly excel in catching and taming for use the wild horses of the plains, and form a terrible cavalry in war, particularly as they are able, in a moment, to throw themselves over to the opposite side of the horse, so as to be screened from their enemy, while they can shoot their arrows, either over or under the horse's neck, with such force as to pierce through a buffalo. They also carry, in war, a shield, and a lance of fourteen feet in length, which they use with great effect[96].

The Comanche fought with other tribes of the plains including the Pawnee, but it was likely the Kiowa who pushed the Comanche south of the Arkansas River[97].

Pawnee

The Pawnee tribe in the late 17th and early 18th century likely occupied, or at least had a presence, in the area surrounding Fort Morgan along the South Platte River, but by the time explorers and fur trappers came into the area, the tribe had positioned itself primarily in Nebraska and Kansas. A large village was reported as early as 1719 at the fork of the Loup and Platte River (southwestern Nebraska)[98] and it was here that the Pawnee attacked Villasur's Expedition. However there was

Pawnee scout 1874.

evidence of the Pawnee venturing west. In 1820, Long's Expedition came across a recently abandoned camp along the South Platte River east of the Fort Morgan area:

It was constructed of such broken half-decayed logs of wood...intermixed with some skeletons of bison recently killed. It is of a circular form, enclosing space enough for about thirty men to lie down upon. The wall is about five feet high, with an opening towards the east, and the top uncovered. At a little distance in front of the entrance of this breastwork, was a semicircular row of sixteen bison skulls, with their noses pointing down the river. Near the centre of the circle which this row would describe, if continued, was another skull marked with a number of red lines. Our interpreter informed us that this arrangement of skulls...were designed to communicate...that the camp had been occupied by a war party of the Skeeree or Pawnee Loup Indians, who had lately come from an excursion against the Cumancias, Ietans, or some other western tribe. The number of red lines traced on the painted skull indicated the number of the party to have been thirty-six; the position in which the skulls were placed, that they were on their return to their own country. Two small rods stuck in the ground, with a few hairs tied in two parcels to the end of each, signified that four scalps had been taken[99].

The Pawnee were staunch enemies of the Arapaho, Cheyenne, and Sioux and the animosity between the Pawnee and their neighbors was used to the advantage of the military who employed Pawnee scouts during the Indian Wars of the 1860s and 70s[100,101]. Pawnee fought alongside the U. S. military against the Cheyenne in a number of battles including the 1869 Battle of Summit Springs near Sterling, Colorado[102]. The Sioux and Pawnee remained at war for most of the 19th century with the Sioux eventually defeating the Pawnee in the 1870s[103].

The distinguishing characteristic of the Pawnee, at least to the whites, seemed to be their hair:

The men cut their hair close, except for a tuft on the top…which they plait as a valued ornament, the removal of which is disgraceful…. Over their shoulders is thrown a loose buffalo robe, dressed and warn with the hair inward. A girdle, close tyed [sic], an inch wide, encompasses their body, to which is attached their breech clout. Their mocasins [sic] are made of elk or deer skins[104].

To this day, many features of the landscape north of Fort Morgan are named for the Pawnee including the Pawnee National Grasslands, Pawnee Buttes, Pawnee Hills, Pawnee Valley, and Pawnee Creek hinting at the history of the tribe in the area.

Kiowa & Wetapahato

The Kiowa also had a presence along the South Platte River controlling the area in eastern Colorado from about 1775 until 1815[105]. The Kiowa were described as wearing "their hair long, in three plaits, hanging down the back. The

Kiowa chief, Two Hatchett

other two, from behind each ear, hanging front, decorated with beads and buttons[106]".

At this time, the Wetapahato and Kiowa appear to be linked, but retained individual identities[107]. In William Clark's 1805 census of Indian tribes, he counts the Wetapahato and Kiowa together estimating 70 lodges, 200 warriors, and about 700 total

Wetapahato and Kiowa[108]. In 1819, it was reported that there were a total of 3000 Kites, Wetapahatos, and Kiawas [sic] combined with 1000 warriors and placed on the Padoucas branch of the Platte River[109]. Most likely, the Wetapahato were subsumed into the Kiowa, but not all researchers agree. Some note that "Wetapahato" was a Sioux name for the Kiowa[110] or another name for Pawnee[111]. Still others assert the Wetapahato were Plaines Apache and became part of the Comanche[112], or are related to the Padouca[113].

In the early 19th century, the Cheyenne and Kiowa battled for the land around the South Platte River and by 1815 the Cheyenne had succeeded in pushing the Kiowa tribe south out of the South Platte River area[114,115]. The map from Long's 1820 expedition does not label Kiowa Creek which lies just west of Bijou Creek, though the creek is labeled as such on Fremont's 1842 map. Kiowa Creek may have taken its name from the predominant tribe of the area, but another possibility is that the creek was named for a famous battle between the Kiowa and the Cheyenne which took place in the mid-1830s. The Kiowa were traveling through eastern Colorado on their way to trade with the Crow when they were overtaken by a group of Cheyenne hunters[116]. The story of the battle was told by George Bent, a Cheyenne half-breed. He noted the battle occurred at Scout Creek later known as Kiowa Creek:

> The Kiowas were moving across an open plain when they saw the Cheyennes making towards them.... The Kiowas retreated slowly toward this creek, where their women and children were already engaged in digging pits in the sand and making breastworks to fight behind. The Kiowa warriors would retire a short distance, then turn

and face the Cheyennes, checking their advance. One Kiowa man on a fine white horse was very brave. Again and again he took his lance and charged right through the Cheyenne lines. In one of these charges he struck a Cheyenne named Man Above with his lance such a hard blow that he knocked Man Above right off his horse. As they were nearing the creek, this brave Kiowa came back again and charged right in among the Cheyennes; but this time they shot him with arrows, and he turned and rode slowly back toward the Kiowa lines, but dropped his lance and fell from his horse before he could reach his friends. The rest of the Kiowa warriors lost heart as soon as they saw this brave man fall, and they at once retreated into the timber.... The Kiowas now hid behind these breastworks and fought off the Cheyennes. Our men made several charges, attempting to drive the Kiowas out of their defenses, but the position was a very strong one, and all the Cheyenne efforts to reach their enemies failed. The Cheyennes then turned their attention to the Kiowa herd and succeeded in cutting out a large number of animals.... After the Cheyennes had run off all the horses they could get at, they gave up the fight and withdrew[117].

Culture Clash

With the western gold strikes of the mid-19th century, white settlers began arriving in droves into what had traditionally been Indian land. At this point, the Cheyenne and Arapaho and to a lesser extent the Sioux were dominant on the plains of northeastern Colorado. Though distinct tribes, the Arapaho, Cheyenne, and Sioux had formed a strong alliance in the 1820s and were in conflict with the Kiowa, Ute, Comanche, Pawnee, and Plains Apache[118,119]. The tribes at first did not direct hostilities towards white emigrants, but continued attacks against enemy tribes. An Indian agent in 1847 reported:

> The Chyennes [sic] claim this river [South Platte] and the surrounding country, without any definite or defined limits; and, together with the Aripohoes [sic] and Sioux, occupy indiscriminately the whole country along the eastern base of the Rocky mountains, from the northern frontier of New Mexico up to the Missouri river, without regard to lines or limitations of boundary; and sometimes they extend their war and hunting excursions across the mountains, into the country of the Snake and Utawa Indians – as well as south into New Mexico, east down the Arkansas, Kansas, Platte, and Missouri, to almost the very boarders of our western settlements[120].

In 1860, the Indian Agent at Fort Kearny reported eight full scale attacks on the Pawnee by war parties of Sioux, Cheyenne, and Arapaho. Feeling obligated to protect the Pawnee, the agent attempted to broker a peace between the warring tribes, but to no avail[121].

The relationship between the native tribes and the whites was at first peaceful, marred only by a few individual groups, but the mounting cultural conflicts lead eventually to full out war with the United States military. Much of the conflict was centered on the Platte and Arkansas Rivers and the land in between covering parts of Colorado, Wyoming, Kansas, and Nebraska.

Sioux

For the most part, the Sioux were located north and west of the South Platte River, but because of their alliance with the Cheyenne and Arapaho, bands often ventured along the South Platte River. The Sioux, sometimes called Lakota or Dakota, divide into numerous bands: Teton (prairie dwellers), Oglala

Sioux chiefs photo by Edward S. Curtis, 1905.

(scattered), and Brulé (burnt thighs). Fremont met a band of Oglala near Bijou Creek on the South Platte River in 1843 on their way to visit the Arapaho[122].

Conflicts between the Sioux and white explorers began early and would continue for nearly a century. Lewis' description of the Sioux was unequivocal:

> These are the vilest miscreants of the savage race, and must ever remain the pirates of the Missouri…. Unless these people are reduced to order, by coercive measures, I am ready to pronounce that the citizens of the United States can never enjoy but partially the advantages which the Missouri presents…they never fail to plunder, when in their power. Persuasion or advice, with them, is viewed as supplication, and only tends to inspire them with contempt…[123]

The Sioux were not just in conflict with the whites, but also with neighboring tribes. Goodrich described the political situation and the vast lands of the Sioux in the mid-19th century:

The powerful nation of the Sioux, or Dahcotahs, occupy the region west of the Mississippi…though the main body of them are found on the Upper Missouri…[they] have always been great warriors…. They have ever been at war with the Chippewas, and are the mortal foes of the Osages, whom they have greatly reduced, and who hold them in great dread…. They have conquered and destroyed vast numbers of their red brethren, and have swept the whole region extending from the banks of the Mississippi to the mouth of the Great Platte, together with the plains that lie to the north, between the Mississippi and the Black Hills. They form six distinct tribes, comprising about 28,000 souls, subsisting chiefly on buffalo's meat and the wild fruits of the forest…. The Missouri branch roam over the plains between [the Missouri] and the Rocky Mountains[124]."

Black Hawk, an Oglala Sioux chief once boasted to U.S. government officials that "These lands [from the South Platte to the Arkansas Rivers] once belonged to the Kiowa and the Crows, but we whipped these nations out of them. We met the Kiowas and whipped them, at the Kiowa Creek, just below where we are now [Laramie]. We met them and whipped them again and the last time at Crow Creek[125]."

During the Indian Wars of the 1860s, the Sioux raided along the Platte River in Nebraska and along the North Platte River in Wyoming, with an occasional foray along the South Platte River into Colorado Territory[126]. There are mixed reports as to how active the Sioux were in the raids along the South Platte River. In some reports, the Sioux are portrayed as friendly Indians who were sometimes caught in the crossfire and at other times, Sioux are portrayed as hostile, allied with war parties of Arapaho and Cheyenne. After the Sand Creek Massacre, however the Sioux joined with the Cheyenne and Arapaho to exact revenge and raided posts along the Platte River.

Arapaho & Cheyenne

When gold seekers arrived in Colorado, the Arapaho were centered on the Colorado plains. The tribe had moved south from Minnesota and the Dakotas at the end of the 18th century as the Sioux took over the northern territories and by 1800 were in Colorado[127]. One of the tribe's favorite campgrounds was at the relatively lush confluence of the South Platte and Beaver Creek about 15 miles east of Fort Morgan. In the winter months, the Arapaho moved to the more sheltered foothills to avoid the harsh winters on the plains[128].

Goodrich described the Arapahos as "…brave, thrifty, and hospitable people. They derive their name, which signifies *dog-eaters*, from fattening and eating that animal[129]." They were also described as "generally well formed, slim and tall, with good countenances. They wear their hair long, collected on the forehead into a large roll, which serves as a protection to their eyes from the bright rays of the sun…. They are a warlike people, and often making predatory and murderous excursions on their eastern and northern neighbors[130]." Margaret Cole, writing about the Arapaho chief Left Hand, described defining characteristics and a brief history of the Arapaho in the Colorado area:

In physical characteristics the Arapahoes resemble their neighbors very closely. In stature they were rather inferior to the Missouri Indians, but much like them.... A distinctive feature of their tribal custom was the tattooed breast. They gave great attention to the hair, which they permitted to grow to great length, sometimes even increasing its length by the use of false hair. Their clothing was like that of the tribes farther north, but contained in addition blankets and other articles obtained from the Spaniards. The Arapahoes were exclusively a wandering tribe, living in skin tents, and during the period of the fur trade numbered about 2,500 souls. With most of their neighbors, except the Utahs and Pawnees, they were at peace. In the early years of the trade they were very hostile to Americans, but in 1832 Captain Gant, of the firm Gant and Blackwell, established a trading post in their country on the Arkansas river and succeeded in gaining their confidence. After that time they were uniformly friendly to the whites. While not aggressively warlike, they were good fighters, and were held in high respect by their enemies. They were a brave, candid and honest people, and were much less given to beggary and thieving than were most other Indians.... The Arapahoes were an important tribe to the traders, and their country was always one of active opera-

Arapaho Scabby Bull.

tions. Not only were they good fur producers, but they were accomplished traders themselves.... Many posts were established in their country upon the headwaters of both the Arkansas and the South Platte[131].

The Cheyenne, like the Arapaho, migrated into Colorado from the north as the Sioux took over their territories in Minnesota and the Black Hills. From 1730 to 1780, the tribe

Cheyenne chief. Photo by Edward S. Curtis 1905.

lived in North Dakota along the Missouri River[132]. Cheyenne elders remembered moving into the South Platte area around 1825 in response to attacks by Gros Ventres and Blackfeet and the expansion of the Sioux[133]. In his book on the Cheyenne, Stan Hoig noted that "[n]o written accounts of their early conquests exit, but Mandan robes decorated with symbolic artwork often include depictions of battles with the Cheyenne warriors[134]." By the early years of the 19th century, both the Cheyenne and Arapaho were in Colorado living in peaceful coexistence.

The Cheyenne consisted of five soldier bands: Dog, Fox, Smooth Elkhorn, Swift's Tail, and Strong Heart (also called Crazy Dog and Bow String[135]). The Dog Soldiers especially became known to the whites during the conflicts of the 1860s. The Cheyenne were allied with the Arapaho and the Sioux, and at war with the Kiowa, Comanche, and Pawnee[136].

Goodrich described the Cheyennes as

> ...a fine race of men, scarcely a man in the tribe being less than six feet in height. They are said to be the richest in horses of any tribe on the continent, living, as they do, where the greatest herds are grazing on the prairies; these they catch in great numbers, and vend to the Sioux, Mandans, and other tribes, as well as to the fur-traders. They are described as dexterous horsemen and fierce warriors, having carried on an unceasing contest with the Pawnees and the Blackfeet[137].

Pawnee history tells of a battle in the 1830s with the Cheyenne and Arapaho a few miles northeast of Fort Morgan at Pawnee Buttes[138]. Again in 1852, the Cheyenne, Arapaho, Sioux, Apache, and Kiowa[139] fought a bloody battle with the Pawnee near the head of Beaver Creek. Eight Cheyenne warriors were killed including the beloved chief Alights-on-the-Cloud. The death of this great warrior shook the Cheyenne. Little Robe, a Cheyenne Dog Soldier whose son had also been killed that day[140], carried the Cheyenne pipe of mourning to the allied tribes, who met to plan a retaliatory attack against the Pawnee. The meeting took place at the mouth of Beaver Creek[141]. The chiefs met and ultimately declared war on the Pawnee, though subsequent attacks were unsuccessful[142].

During their time on the plains, the Cheyenne lived in lodges or *tipis* which could easily be packed up and moved to a new camp or hunting ground. The lodge was made of buffalo skins stretched across wooden poles. The size of the lodge was based mainly on how rich the family was as larger structures required more horses to move them. The edges of the lodge were weighted with stones, especially in winter, which accounts for stone circles sometimes encountered on the plains. Some of the lodges were colorfully painted with symbols[143]. In 1809, Lewis wrote of the Cheyennes that they "wander in quest of the baffaloe [sic], having no fixed residence. They do not cultivate. They are well disposed towards the whites, and might easily be induced to settle on the Missouri, if they could be assured of being protected from the Sioux[144]."

But the relationship with the whites would change. In the middle of the 19th century, the buffalo population started to wane and the whites emigrated onto the plains in growing numbers[145]. Following the Treaty of Fort Wise in 1851, the U. S. government began providing subsidies and supplies to the tribes and even attempted to introduce the Cheyenne and Arapaho to the idea of farming. William Bent, a trader in the southern plains of what would become Colorado Territory, was a friend of the Indians, the Cheyenne especially as his wife was a member of that tribe, and was sent by the U. S. government to give out subsidies and talk with the Cheyenne about the possibility of settling down to an agricultural life. In 1859, he set off from St. Louis and found a large body of Cheyenne camped at the mouth of Beaver Creek on the South Platte River[146] near Fort Morgan. After returning from his meeting, he wrote an optimistic report about the possibility of inducing the Indians to a less nomadic lifestyle which would also reduce contact with the white emigrants. However there were dark undercurrents in William Bent's report – predictive of the troubles that lay ahead[147]:

This country is very equally divided into halves by the South Platte. A confederate band of Cheyennes and Arapahoes, who are intermarried, occupy and claim ly the half included between the South and the North Platte.... I had a full and satisfactory interview with the Cheyenne and Arapahoe...I submitted to them the wish of the department that they should assume a fixed residence, and occupy themselves in agriculture.... Being Buffalo Indians, they require dwelling-houses to be constructed for them.... They ask for pay for the large district known to contain gold, and which is already occupied by the whites, who have established the county of Arapahoe and many towns. They further ask annuities in the future for such lands as they may cede and relinquish to the government....

The Cheyenne and Arapahoe tribes scrupulously maintain peaceful relations with the whites and with other Indian tribes, notwithstanding the many causes of irritation growing out of the occupation of the gold region, and the emigration to it through their hunting grounds, which are no longer reliable as a certain source of food to them. These causes precipitate the necessity of immediate and sufficient negotiations for the safety of the whites, the emigrant roads, and the Indians. Regulations, strictly enforced, are essential in the granting of licenses to trade with the Indians....

A smothered passion for revenge agitates these Indians, perpetually formented by the failure of food, the encircling encroachments of the white population, and the exasperating sense of decay and impending extinction with which they are surrounded. To control them, it is essential to have among them the perpetual presence of a controlling military force.... The concourse of whites is therefore constantly swelling, and incapable of control or restraint by the government. This suggests the policy of promptly rescuing the Indians, and withdrawing them from contact with the whites...anticipat[ing] and prevent[ing] difficulties and massacre....[148]

The massacre William Bent foretold would come soon enough. In 1864, white soldiers and the Cheyenne would clash at Fremont's Orchard, about 15 miles west of Fort Morgan. This battle would set off a series of events, including the Sand Creek Massacre and the retaliatory attacks along the South Platte River, leaving thousands of whites and Indians dead. These attacks lead to the building of a fort at the Junction — a fort that would later be called Morgan.

∞

Chapter 4

Rush for Gold

The source of the South Platte River which so lazily flowed past Fort Morgan held a secret – a sparkling secret that would reignite the embers just dying down in California. In 1858, in the mountains where the riv-

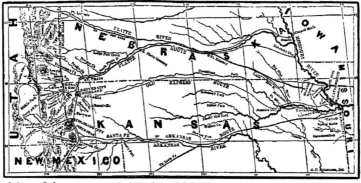

Map of the routes to Colorado gold fields. Published in the Chicago Press and Tribune, *1860.*

er originates and merges with Cherry Creek, William eberry "Green" Russell acting on rumors he had heard from the Cherokee, began prospecting and found gold. Russell wasn't the first to hear rumors of gold in the Rocky Mountains. Zebulon Pike published rumors of gold after meeting James Purcell (or Pursley) in Santa Fé in 1807, but not until Russell's finds were reported a half century later did prospectors being surging into the Rockies in hopes of riches. Gold fever flared again. The cry was "Pikes Peak or Bust[149]!"

An estimated 100,000 people swarmed to the Rocky Mountains in the spring of 1859 in what became known as the "great stampede:"

> ...The golden vision flitted before their eyes, and obscured all else. Money was borrowed; lands were sold or mortgaged; other property sacrificed; wife and children placed upon a scanty allowance to live upon the hope of future abundance; and fathers, brothers, and sons were *en route* for Pike's Peak. Banners floated, revolvers were flourished; the pick and pan were ostentatiously displayed as emblems of future and certain acquisition; and light and merry hearts sang or whistled along the westward roads.... [T]he great mass were inconsiderate, rash, and reckless, with indifferent teams, poor, crazy wagons, and almost without harness. A large number of men actually harnessed themselves to hand-carts, as beasts of burden...some undertook the journey with wheelbarrows, while not a few hazarded the entire trip...on foot, lugging their tent-poles and scanty supplies upon their shoulders. Such a scene is not witnessed once in a century[150].

Prospecting in mountain streams was not the only way to

Emigrant Train across the Plains. Published in Colorado *by Frank Fossett, 1876.*

find gold. The prospectors needed supplies and some stationed themselves along the routes to sell goods and make their fortune. Until this point, there had been no major settlements in the Great American Desert, but as more and more gold-seekers poured into the area, the streets of Denver City were full, not just of miners, but store owners selling goods and supplies.

The majority of the "Fifty-Niners" or "Pikes Peakers" used the South Platte River Road as their highway to the west[151]. In 1860, the *Rocky Mountain News* reported emigrants coming to Denver at a rate of about a thousand a day. "They come in long trains, or singly, pouring in from the Platte road, and the cutoff, in an almost endless stream[152]". This was the picture of the trail leading through Fort Morgan during the height of the Colorado goldrush:

It is doubtful if there was another section of country on the face of the globe over which, in the '60's passed so much traffic by ox, horse and mule team. A goodly portion of the travel for 200 to 400 miles was along the right or south bank of the South Platte.... At times there was hardly an hour but what, as far as the eye could reach, there appeared to be almost a solid train of moving, white-covered wagons, or as they were then more familiarly termed "prairie-schooners"[153].

South Platte River Trail

The South Platte River Road had sometimes been used during the California gold rush of 1849 when the weather was poor along the Overland Trail, which followed the North Platte River, or when the northern trail was under Indian attack. Travelers followed the South Platte River to the mouth of the Cache a la Poudre and Fort Latham and then turned north through Virginia Dale, joining the northern route at Fort Steele. Ten years later, the South Platte River Road would again host hopeful prospectors, this time seeing the sparkling gold at the foot of the Rocky Mountains.

At the start of the Colorado Goldrush in 1859, the trail was very much in a wilderness with great buffalo herds roaming the plains. The landscape was sparse and a single tree could serve as a landmark. Only isolated sod or adobe stations placed 20 to 30 miles apart along the river marked man's claim on the land. The journey was difficult and many reports of travelers note the skeletons of oxen, horses, and even fellow emigrants strewn along the road[154]. But on the trail, somewhere between Beaver and Bijou Creeks where Fort Morgan would later stand, the weary travelers saw hope in front of them, in the form of mountain peaks rising from the flat desert:

…"The mountains! The mountains!" was shouted from one end of the train to the other. Each team was stopped, and a reserved demijohn of "pure Bourbon," that had been hid away in the boiler, was produced, and congratulations were exchanged *ad infinitum*. Soon the whole chain of mountains were visible, looking like a group of heavy clouds belting the horizon. The sight was pleasing, for we could now see the end and aim of our journey, and we experienced about the same feelings that the mariner does, when "land ho!" is proclaimed from the mizzen-top, after a long and stormy voyage across the main. For days and days, the dreary open plain had stretched out before us, until lost to view in the sky; but now, the high snow-clad peaks and lofty ridges of the mighty mountains stood out to mark our progress....[155]

The South Platte River Road was one of three routes to Pikes Peak, the other routes were farther south along the Arkansas River or along the Smoky Hill Route. The distance from Leavenworth, Kansas to Denver City was 750 miles along the Platte River, longer than both the Arkansas River (550 miles) or the Smoky Hill (600 miles) routes, but the South Platte route, despite the sand and the length of the journey, was seen as the easier route and was the route advocated by many guidebooks of the day[156,157]. For instance, of the thirteen routes described by Allen in his 1859 guidebook, ten utilized the South Platte River Road[158]. One of the most popular guidebooks of the time was written by Smith and Oakes who also advocated the South Platte River Road and provided helpful suggestions as to how best to prepare for the journey, descriptions of the route, and what to do when encountering Indians:

> ...the nearest and most practicable route is by way of the south side of the Platte and South Platte rivers, following mainly the course of these streams.... The country traveled is comparatively *level* and the road unusually

straight.... Another advantage is that by far the greater portion of the distance between the mouth of Platte and Cherry creek is over a regular and much traveled emigrant road; which cannot be mistaken, and on which teams are met with almost every day....

The tribes of Indians likely to be met on this route are the Pawnees, the Sioux, the Cheyennes, and the Arapahoes. These tribes are at present on friendly terms with the whites; and if properly treated will probably remain so. The less emigrants have to say to Indians the better. If they are met, and manifest a friendly spirit, extend to them the usual salutation and pass on, manifesting no fear, and as little emotion of any kind as possible. If you make a trade with an Indian, and he is not satisfied, trade back, without hesitation. The principal danger of collision arises from meeting a *war party*. In a war party, there are no squaws and the braves usually are on horseback. In approaching an emigrant train they frequently ride as though they were about to make a *charge*, when, in reality, they are only excited by curiosity. If they should stop a train, and demand presents, they will usually leave after receiving a little tobacco or flour, or something of that kind. Should this fail, and there is danger of collision, the best weapon that can be used is an ox-goad or whip. Let some stout man, without paying any attention to their weapons, seize his whip and thrash away at them, and they will run much sooner and faster than if a dozen were killed. The proper plan for each emigrant train is to select one of their number to act as Captain, and let it be his duty to do all the talking with the Indians.... If these rules are observed, there need be no apprehension of difficulty with any of the Indians....[159].

The *Merchant's Magazine* published in January 1861 also described the route along the Platte River to Denver City, but their route includes a mention of the "cut-off," a road that left the South Platte River Road at the Junction (later Fort Morgan) and went overland to Denver City saving 30 or 40 miles of travel.

Fifty-Niners

Emigrants setting off for the gold fields were a diverse bunch. Many embellished the canvas of their wagons with slogans such as "Pikes Peak or Bust," or "Ho for the Pike Mines[160]." Albert D. Richardson, a newspaper correspondent wrote letters describing his journey from Kansas to Denver along the South Platte River Road in 1860. He wrote of the mass migration across the plains including the trials and the hardship encountered generally by the emigrants:

The emigration by the road from Omaha is quite as heavy as that by the route we have followed, and the valley of the Platte, as far as we can see, is white with "prairie schooners." Passengers from Denver by the express coaches state that they have met from 800 to 1,000 wagons per day. They speak of business as somewhat dull in the towns at the Gold Region, as the great majority of the winter population is absent, in the mines. As yet, we have met less than a dozen wagons of returning emigrants; but there will soon be a backward stampede....

The intelligence of the killing of several Pony Express riders creates some apprehensions among the emigrants; but thus far all the savages on this route are peaceable toward the whites, though we have met several war parties of the Sioux, on their way to scalp or be scalped among the Pawnees. We have encountered comparatively few returning Pike's Peakers, as yet, though we occasionally see a party of them, looking like the very last roses of summer, and breathing out all sorts of maledictions against the new El Dorado. The westward emigration continues enormous - far surpassing anything ever before witnessed upon the plains. While we were stopping two hours for breakfast, the other morning, more than two hundred wagons passed us; and a short time after, ascending a high bluff, I saw the green valley of the Platte, for many miles both before and behind us, teeming with the busy life of thousands of hopeful pilgrims. Tottering age and unconscious infancy - poverty and wealth - manhood and womanhood - and almost every nation in the world, were represented in the motley throng.... There is something very impressive about this uncontrollable movement westward, which from remotest antiquity has impelled the human race toward the setting sun, and which now, on a great wave of human life, is bearing commerce and American civilization to our farthest frontier, and founding a new empire at the base of the Rocky Mountains.

Among the emigrants whom we have encountered are several delicate, "lily browed" Chicago ladies; an unfortunate lady from Omaha, so reduced by recent rheumatic fever that she cannot walk alone, but is compelled to ride upon a bed; and a baby, who left the Missouri river at the extremely callow age of two weeks! We have passed about a dozen handcarts, and perhaps half as many emigrants on foot-domestic Atlases, with their little worlds upon their shoulders....

Many of the emigrant wagons bear quaint inscriptions, like- "I'm off for the Peak-are you?" "Good bye, friends; I'm bound to try the Peak"; "The eleventh commandment: Mind your own business"; "Ho! for California!" etc: Supplies of all kinds are extremely high along the road. Raisins command 75 cents per pound, cheese 50c, and other articles are in proportion. The blacksmiths upon the route charge $4 per animal, for shoeing....

During the last week, we met about a dozen wagons a day, of returning emigrants. Some of the "go-backs" told the most lugubrious stories about the mines, asserting that there was little or no gold; others thought the diggings rich, but that quartz crushing alone would prove profitable. We encountered one emigrant on foot, alone, and without a cent of money, who had started to walk back to Leavenworth-665 miles!....

There has been some sickness on the road. A few days ago we passed a handcart party of four men. Three of them were drawing the cart containing their whole "outfit," and the fourth member of the company quite low with dysentery. Mr. G. Hopkins - a merchant from Dubuque, Iowa, who left the river in very poor health died of the same disease, on the 8th inst., and was buried by the roadside, near Lamb's station, seventy-five miles east of this city, at the junction of the "cut-off" with the old Platte road [near modern town of Fort Morgan]. A package sent out by his family arrived a few hours after his death. On the same day, a party of Chicago emigrants found the corpse of a child, wrapped in a white blanket, in a secluded spot, on an island of the Platte. The skull was broken in, and the clothing stiff with blood, and there had evidently been foul play. The body was somewhat decomposed, but the dress and form seemed to be that of a girl, five or six years old. They buried the remains on the bank of the river, three miles west of Beaver creek - endeavoring to mark the spot, so that it can be identified hereafter. The neck was encircled by a string of beads. The circumstances leave little room to doubt that the defenseless little child was murdered.

A few evenings before reaching the end of our journey, our great tent presented a novel appearance. It was filled by our own company and several visitors from neighboring camps, and enlivened by songs, and the strains of a violin. The never-wearisome, ever-amusing "Arkansaw Traveler" opened the entertainment, and was followed by many of the popular melodies of the day, in which all present who had music in their souls most heartily joined. It was a strange, impressive spectacle, to see that group of swarthy, sunburnt men, clad in the rough habiliments of the plains, lying upon the ground like a party of pirates or smugglers in their cave, while a single candle threw a dim, flickering light upon their features. As the songs called for changed from gay to grave...[161]

The way was hard and many had given up everything to make the westward journey. Many never made it to the sparkling gold fields of the Rockies.

"Go Back, Young Man"

The gold rush of 1859 incited nearly 100,000 people to

uproot and "stampede" west in hopes of easy wealth. But becoming rich wasn't going to be easy. Those who set off early in 1859 found provisions scarce and the gold fields still covered in snow making mining impossible. One source estimated that one-third of those who set out for the gold fields of Colorado never made the mountains and another third arrived, but turned around almost immediately setting off for home[162]. There were various names for those who returned home, traveling eastward along the same trails as the hopeful prospectors heading west: "turnarounds", "backsliders", "gobacks", "second thinkers",

Busted by Thunder. Published in Beyond the Mississippi, *1869.*

"humbuggers", "croakers", and "stampeders":

> Some went nearly through, others half-way, but by far the larger number only a short distance into the Territory, encountering severe rains, snow-storms, and other hardships and exposures.... [T]he malcontents started for home, many of them begging their way, and all carrying the most doleful reports of "no gold," "humbug," famine,

murder, etc.... Pike's Peak banners were exchanged for pictures of "the elephant," and other emblems and mottoes of defeat equally significant. Party after party was turned back in succession, til eventually almost the whole mass had set their faces toward the rising sun; and even the few who had the fortitude to persevere had to haul down the Pike's Peak flag, and hang out for "California," to protect them from insult and injury....[163]

The go-backs changed their slogans from "Pikes Peak or Bust" to "Busted by Gosh!" or "Pike's Peak humbug," and chanted "Hang Byers and D. C. Oakes. For starting this damned Pike's Peak hoax[164]." The go-backers blamed the men who written the guidebook that had fired them up with promises of gold. But once gold was confirmed, the eastbound "go-backers" turned once again. Given new hope, the despondent again turned west.

Freighters

Not all travelers across the plains went in search of gold – at least not the kind that sparkled in the creek waters, they were freighters, bringing goods to the west and returning east with empty wagons to be filled again. The trains could be anywhere from 25 to 100 wagons and emigrants, especially in the dangerous times of the Indian Wars traveled with, or near, trains of freight for protection. Trains traveled slowly, only one to two miles per hour or fifteen to twenty miles per day. An article published in *The Merchants' Magazine and Commercial Review* in 1861 describes freighters on the trail:

...[Wagons] consist of a four-wheeled body, made in the most substantial manner, and carrying a huge box, of a tapering shape, much like a flatboat, some sixteen feet long at the top and twelve at the bottom, four feet wide and five feet high. The whole is surmounted by a double cover of sheets of osnaburg, resting on a succession of bows. These immense structures, "facetiously denominated prairie schooners," are made to carry from five to seven thousand pounds each.... The draught animals in most general use at this moment are oxen...grass fed, and unaccustomed to any kind of shelter—two most essential qualities while doing freighting service on the Plains. Their work is hard and treatment bad; and hence, like the stage horses of Eastern cities, they are soon used up. Two seasons are all they are expected to go through.... Horses are seldom used for pulling heavy loads across the Plains. Mules, however, are extensively employed, owing to their great powers of endurance. As five yoke of oxen cost no more on the frontiers than one pair of good mules, only the United States government (in the transportation of military stores) and the wealthier among the freighters, that find an object in making quick trips, can afford them.

One teamster for each wagon is attached to the train. Under his charge there is one yoke of oxen or one pair of mules for every thousand pounds of freight. From four to ten extra hands further accompany each train, to fill possible vacancies and do all work not strictly coming within the province of the driver. One or more so-called mess wagons, carrying cooking and eating utensils....

The whole—drivers, cooks, extra hands, oxen, mules, and wagons—is under the supreme command of the "wagon or trainmaster"... vested with authority...accorded to officers of vessels at sea.... They are all men of great physical vigor and undaunted courage, ready resolution and tireless execution. They know how to command and how to enforce obedience. But not all their characteristics are equally laudable. They can swear worse than Turks; they love whisky; they never shrink from a fight; they are experts in the use of bowie-knife and revolver; they are often guilty of barbarous tyranny, and abuse their subordinates as cruelly with words and deeds as our ocean captains and mates. The oxwhip and bullets are frequently resorted to by them as means of preserving discipline.... [T]he "crews"...consist mostly of desperadoes and villains from all parts of the globe—fighting men, border ruffians, escaped convicts, unpunished thieves and assassins; in short, the moral scum and dregs of both the East and West enl-

Ox-drawn train across the plains. Published in the Illustrated London News, *1887.*

ist.... Such is *the personnel* of the caravans launched every spring upon the Plains....

[T]he regular routine of freighting life is strictly enforced. Long before daylight every morning the whole camp is aroused by the guards. Reluctantly the sleepers crawl out of their tents and wagons.... [Breakfast consists of] bread baked in pans and pregnated with a superabundance of saleratus, boiled rice and beans, fried bacon, and, perhaps, dried apples, form, together with "flapjacks," and an undefinable concoction passing for coffee.... [T]he command of the wagon-master to "drive up" is heard. The teamsters all sally out to assist the night herders in getting the animals within the elliptical enclosure denominated "corral," nightly constructed out of the wagons, with an opening at one end. The quadrupeds being all crowded between the vehicles, ropes are stretched across the inlet, and all hands go to work saddling, harnessing, yoking, chaining. For a short time the utmost uproar and confusion then predominates. The drivers belch forth oaths and curses in furious succession. Their lashes, fists, and feet belabor the animals most mercilessly. In return the mules rear and kick, and the oxen butt and balk. Distressed braying and lowing sound on all sides.... At last the commander-in-chief gives the sign of readiness by mounting his mule, and before sun-up the whole of the caravan is moving along the road.... [T]he jarring and creaking of the wagons, the reverberations of cracking whips, and the incessant "gee-ho's" and "ho-haw's" of the teamsters will be carried through the rarified atmosphere...the train rises gradually into sight, just as ships

appear to emerge from below the horizon. The whole being in view, the shining white of the covers and the hull-
like appearance of the wagons produces a striking resem-
blance to a fleet sailing, with all Canvass spread, over a
seeming sea...[165]

Travelers' Diaries

Many travelers kept diaries; some recorded the minutia of
life while others were more poetic. The way the emigrants
spoke of the land, whether it impressed them or depressed
them, breathes life into the arid soil. The following diary en-
tries are snapshots of life traveling through the Fort Morgan
area. For most, not much happened, but a few had adventures
they were likely to remember throughout their lives.

The earliest travelers set off for the Rocky Mountains
even before it was certain there was gold. Confirmation came
late in the summer of 1858 and anyone setting off after that
point would face the cold winter of the plains and arrive
when little gold could be prospected so most left for the gold
fields as soon as possible the following spring. One of the earliest emigrants was E. H. N. Patterson traveling to the gold
fields of the Rocky Mountains in April and May of 1859.
Patterson (pen name Sniktau) was an experienced journalist
from Illinois. He began his journey in March of 1859 and
noted his arrival at Beaver Creek on May 28:

Our day's travel has been somewhat monotonous and
tedious, being over a broad plain covered with little else
than cactus and wild sage of a dwarf variety.... About
noon we passed a cluster of eleven trees on the opposite
side of the river – a welcome sight, these lonely cotton-

woods! Saw a number of boats – four or five – going down the river today; they make pretty good time, averaging three men in each, the current being about five miles an hour, and a channel of two or three feet being easily found. If they meet a rise in main Platte, they may make a successful voyage down, otherwise the shoal water in that stream will occasion much vexation and delay. At twenty miles distant we reach Beaver creek – a running stream very much resembling the Platte, on a much smaller scale; the banks are steep, but the crossing is not difficult.... Some of the boys have an idea that they saw the Rocky mountains this evening – perhaps it was only a cloud....

May 29. Sunrise reveals a peak of the mountains, covered with snow, standing out in bold relief against the sky, far off in the West....

May 30. Five miles over hard gravel roads brought us to a handsome little creek of clear, sparkling water [Bijou], slightly impregnated with sulpher and alkali.... Authorities differ as to what is the name of the stream we just passed, whether it be Kiowa or Bijou; I will therefore call it Kiowa [sic]. After crossing it, we ascend to the table land again, where we have, for five miles, a hard gravelly road, very trying on the feel of the cattle.... We strike then five miles of desert – deep sand – and reach the brow of the hill, whence, by taking the right hand road, we strike the river in a short distance, at a Cottonwood grove, known as Carson's Point.... Two miles further on, still over deep sandy roads, partly, brought us to Fremont's Orchard, where we have lots of wood, but no good grass. There is excellent pasture two miles above, but our cattle were very much fatigued with their long, hot, dusty trip that we had to traverse today.... Fremont's Orchard is a lovely grove of young thrifty cottonwoods and occupies a nice level area of some eight acres, entirely destitute of undergrowth, whilst the trees present the appearance of having been set out with almost the regularity of an orchard.... The lofty range of mountains, covered far down with snow and far up with dark forests, have loomed up ahead of us, all day, like some Titan sentinel set to guard this sterile waste, against the kindly influences of any angel messenger that mercy might send to bless the land and make it productive[166].

Patterson did not note meeting any Indians, but most of the other travelers did. Relations appeared friendly and most of the natives were traveling with their families rather than gathered for attack.

Helen E. Clark and seven others left Plano, Illinois in April following her father and brother who had made the trip to Denver a year earlier taking the Santa Fé or Southern route. Helen mentions passing O Follers [O'Fallen] Bluffs on June 2, 1860 and Fremont's Orchard on June 14th. The following excerpt begins between these two landmarks:

June 7. Thurs. Camped near an Indian village so we have plenty of company, begging & trying to sell moccasins. One squaw said she had dirt in her eyes and we gave her a wash dish and water and cloth. She washed herself and then her papoose and he cried loudly and it sounded more civilized than anything else we had heard. There was a very bashful young Indian who could not find courage enough to ask for anything so Mother filled a plate of victuals & he began to eat. When he had finished he strung his meat on a weed and got up. Another young one – a warrior – came up smiling enough and hands Edward his tomahawk, which served the purpose of pipe & so he points down into the bowl and said – smoke. He was quite intelligent and talkative, almost as soon as he came in an old Indian came in from the other fire, he shook hands – as they all do – and wanted to know if I was Mother's papoose and Edward too, she told him yes, he pointed to the warrior and said HE was HIS papoose and talked quite loudly....

June 8, Fri. I awoke by the cry – "The cattle are all gone", and on listening find they have gone into the Bluffs. The boys go after them. I got up feeling not very well This is a very cold morning. Edward gets back with the cattle.... Tom has begun to have some of the comforts of Job – went hunting over the bluffs yesterday and wore moccasins and today he is sore footed enough. We this morning followed round the bluffs a mile or so and then came into the sand hills. The sand is very deep but the hills are not so high as those we crossed yesterday.... Mother is not very well today...[she] has a foreboding something is going to happen. She asked us how we would feel if when we got there Father should be dead. For my part I cannot imagine any such thing as real.... Tonight we camp near the wigwams which are inhabited by Mexicans and squaws, too. We daily meet teams on the return, there has been a great many teams pass for a few days. We have seen but one dead ox till this week, since when there are quite a number....

Mon. 11ᵗʰ... Find middling good roads, pass a stage and two Indian camps. Stop for dinner and drive the cattle toward the river – they get to a slough and the cattle most of them, run in and begin to drink. It was the strongest kind of alkali and the men ran after them as hard as they could & had to take the horses to go after them, and they yoked them right up to feed them fat bacon and I guess that will keep them straight. This is the first difficulty we have had of the kind as we have been very careful....

14ᵗʰ. All feel better. Yesterday we drove 18 miles and passed Fremont Orchard & Fremont hills too, I guess, judging by some steep ones we came down. Came down one big hill into one of the most picturesque place one can imagine – the river filled with islands on one side and on the other were steep bluffs.... Fremont Orchard is a beautiful grove of trees that appear to stand in rows, it looks more like home to see the trees close by. Come over a very large sand hill and Mrs. Wimple and I went down the side to the bank and found a beautiful road and shade but we had just got to the teams again when we came to an alkali stream which we went around by a path on the mountain to where we camped for dinner on the Platte and a tribe of Cheyennes came along with their dogs & ponies, some of them have this year's colts saddled for the papooses to ride. Some of the prettiest ponies for only ten dollars, but they won't take any thing but silver dollars and we have nothing but half dollars. It is a very large tribe, we see one squaw 80 years old, she laughs at my bloomers. We afterward see her lugging a great bundle of wood as large as two men ought to take....[167]

In the early years, the Indians were a source of interest, amusement, or annoyance for the travelers, but soon relations deteriorated and the journey across the Colorado plains would be filled with fear. A confrontation between the United States military and a group of Cheyenne near Fremont's Orchard over supposedly stolen cattle in April of 1864 would lead to attacks along the South Platte River and massacres of whites and Indians alike. This confrontation would also lead to the establishment of a military camp along the South Platte River Road at the Junction. This military camp would later become Fort Morgan.

Few of the travelers reported direct attacks, but many reported evidence of the violence on the plains. Emma Shepard Hill, a girl of 13, wrote of her family crossing the plains in the summer of 1864, amidst the Indian uprising. Emma's party was not attacked by Indians, but the fear in her narrative is palpable. She initially speaks of camping at Fremont's Orchard, but it is likely she is mistaken and the camp was at Beaver Creek:

> At Fremont's Orchard [sic], where we camped one night, just as the sun was setting, we saw, off in the west, Long's Peak—nearly two hundred miles away. We did not see it again for many days. Near Fremont's Orchard [sic] a road branched from the main line, called the "Cutoff." This road, I believe, saved something like eighty miles of travel. Many of the men wished to take this road, and my father, being anxious, in his helpless condition, to make as quick time as possible, and his teamsters being willing, decided to go with the small number who were

taking this route. We were told that Indians in large numbers had been seen on this road very lately; but, in disregard of this warning, about sixteen men left the main road and the larger train, and took the Cut-off....

It was a clear, moonlight night, and we traveled until about ten o'clock, the five miles lengthening into ten—and still no water. Earlier in the day one of the mules being driven on our family wagon had become sick, and an extra mule, sometimes ridden by one of the men, had been put in the sick mule's place. Now our other mule gave out entirely and refused to go another step. Many others were in almost the same condition; but the majority of the men were determined to go still farther. Mr. Smith asked Pierson if he was afraid to stay with the wagon until he could come back after it, offering

Emma Shepard Hill, 1864

to exchange places with him; but Pierson declared his willingness to stay; and so the matter was settled.

It now seems a wicked thing to do—to take common freight and leave the human. But we must remember that these men were answerable to someone for the freight in their wagons, and they also were tired with the journey and anxious to get on. Why Mr. Smith—who, since my father became sick, had taken the lead in our affairs when it was necessary—did not think to leave one of our own freight wagons instead, I can only account for by the probability that my father ordered him to go on with the rest. Just how it came about I could never quite understand; but that wagon, containing my sick and helpless father, my little brother, who had grown worse and was now delirious, and my mother, together with the driver, Pierson, was left there in the middle of the road, with nothing to hide it from the full view of any creature that might be abroad that night. My sister and I begged to stay; but my father would not listen to it, nor would the men in the train. We afterward heard them say that enough were left for the Indians to scalp without us.

This night I shall never forget. The scene is indelibly stamped upon my memory: the brilliant light of a full moon; the white road stretching before and behind to the horizon; the long train of wagons moving silently and slowly; and the one wagon, containing all that was dear to us, growing smaller and fainter in the distance.

We had driven probably something over two hours, when, on looking back, we saw a dark object against the sky. To our excited minds it seemed to grow larger and larger, and soon took on the form of mounted men. At last the tramp of hoofs was really heard, and we quickly formed in corral, every man standing ready with his gun. I was again put down between boxes and covered with a robe. My sister also was hidden in the same manner. As the tramping came nearer, Mr. Smith thought of the driver, Pierson, and, when within hailing distance, called out his name and was answered by him. When he came alongside, he was asked why he left the wagon. He replied: "I am not a heathen, and if there is water to be had, I am going to have it for my mules." Some of the men expressed regret that they had not fired while they still thought him an Indian. The fact was that he had become so frightened, when the others were out of sight, that, with all my mother's pleading, he would not stay....

And what of my mother during this time? When we saw her again, she told us that, soon after we left, Mr. Pierson reloaded the gun, took all the ammunition he could carry, and then began unhitching the mules. She did not dream he meant to desert her, until he mounted one of the mules and rode away. She implored him to stay, or at least to leave her the gun; but he was deaf to all her entreaties. She watched him out of sight, and then crept into the wagon. The sick mule was still tied behind, and Mr. Pierson, in his haste to get away, did not notice it; but now, finding his mate gone, the mule began to bray, keeping it up at short intervals. In the stillness of the night he could be heard for miles around. Mother did not think to untie him and let him follow the others, and father was too sick to notice. Every time the mule brayed, mother would get out of the wagon and scan the horizon, expecting every moment to be surrounded by Indians; then would kneel and pray to her Heavenly Father for help and protection; then climb into the wagon and lie down by the others for a little while. Thus, praying and watching, expecting every moment to be her last, she passed the time, until, after one unusually loud and protracted braying, she saw horsemen approaching. Feeling now certain that the end had come, she prayed that God would take care of her daughters, and, commending herself and those loved ones with her once more to Heaven, she crept in beside them. When the men — for it really was Mr. Smith and party—were within hailing distance, they called her name; but when they reached the wagon, she had fainted....

Looking back through the years, I realize more and more the bravery of those four men. They were not interested in us, and we had no claim on them, except that of common humanity; and yet they risked their lives for strangers. Surely the Good Father above held us all in His kind keeping that night[168].

A lot happened in the area in the months following Emma's trip: hundreds of Cheyenne were massacred at Sand Creek and the Indians retaliated by attacking ranches along the South Platte River. The military responded by sending in soldiers to establish posts and escort emigrants and the mail over the plains. Francis Crissey (Frank) Young wrote of his travels in 1865 across the plains just months after Indians had raided ranches all along the South Platte River Road. Young's company travelled through the Fort Morgan area on Easter Sunday and learned the shocking news of President Lincoln's assassination - just two days after it occurred. The excerpt of Young's journey begins the day he arrives at the American Ranch (near present-day Merino), lately attacked and burned:

SATURDAY, *April 15th*... As I have noted before, one must be "in it" to realize the full beauty of the early hours of a fine day on these high Plains — it is very difficult to invest one with a full appreciation of it by any attempt at description...the plain between the bluffs and our side of the river at least three miles wide, and covered with a pretty carpet of green; and there is nothing ahead of us to obstruct our view for eight or ten miles, while if we turn for a glance behind, we find the same clear sweep of vision for as great a distance down to the eastern horizon. It is a noble natural highway, and we put the miles behind us at a great rate all the morning. By noon we are at the American ranche — or what is left of it — for this was one of last January's battle-fields, and there are indications of the work of the gentle savage all around it. He was here to the number of perhaps two hundred on the 16th of January, while poor Morrison, the rancheman, had but three men with him to help protect his family and property. The odds were too heavy against him, and it is only a week or two ago that the soldiers found his body in the Platte, close by, with seventeen arrows in it (he was missing for some weeks after the fight); while there are four graves across the road, about two hundred yards from the house, where his three defenders sleep beside him. His wife and children were carried away prisoners.

The red men were forced to pay something for their victory, however, and a part of the price lies here, in the road to this day — a dead Indian, flat on his back, with lustreless [sic] eyes staring at the sky, his right arm cut off at the elbow, both legs off and lying by his side, his body gashed and mutilated — a ghastly testimony to the ferocious hatred engendered in the Plainsman against him and his kind by their barbarous warfare of the past year. Several other red victims of the Morrison fight fell near him, and were carried off on the plain and buried by the soldiers who came after; but for some unexplained reason this fellow was left sprawling in this horrible fashion in the middle of the trail, to be driven over, and kicked, and cut up, and made the object of execration of every passing pilgrim. Two miles beyond, and on the same or the next day in January, the same band of savages, or a part of it, attempted to repeat their experiment of cleaning out the ranche and starting a little cemetery for the white man by the roadside, but they soon found they had caught a Tartar, and after getting a little taste of his quality they declined to make any closer acquaintance. This was at Godfrey's ranche.

Godfrey is something of a "character," and his house is peculiar in construction, like its master. He is, like Jack Morrow, one of the traders of the Plains, and his big storehouse, built of adobe, and deep and spacious, is

Mutilated remains at American Ranch following January, 1865 attack.

packed full of goods for the pilgrim trade. He long ago fo-
resaw the necessity of being in good condition for
defence, and in the floor of his building, perhaps half-way
back from the entrance, he shows us a trap-door, covering
a shallow shaft from which runs a tunnel underground to
a "dug-out" at the rear of his house — and this he had in
reserve as a place of retreat for his family, should such necessity ever arise in a scrap with the red men. In front of
the building, ten feet away, he had built an adobe stockade five or six feet high, protected by angles at the sides,
and pierced for rifles. The whole structure he calls "Fort
Wicked," which is indicated by a small painted sign on
the front of the house, near the top. Here, on the day
mentioned, he had three men with him behind the stockade, while just inside the front doorway of the main
building were his wife, daughter, and two or three other
women, who kept the men supplied with ammunition,
and attended to their other wants. In this way the brave
little garrison not only stood off the whole band without
loss to themselves, but made vacancies in the lodges of
several of the warriors. There is a pretty story (true, also,
but thrilling as any fiction) of Godfrey's fourteen-year-old
daughter rushing out during the fight with a bucket of
water, drenching the fire which the Indians had started in
a nearby haystack in the hope of destroying the house,
and getting back safely to cover through a storm of arrows
and bullets. After a hard and a losing fight of several
hours, the red devils gave it up as a bad job, and returned
to the American and other ranches to the eastward, to
complete their work of destruction, and to gather in any

plunder that might have escaped them the previous day. Godfrey, though not boastful, seems quite proud of his victory, the story of which is now known to every pilgrim and in every cabin on the Plains; and well he may be, for his foes were fifty to one. He is, and always will be, one of my frontier heroes. I have only one little bit of a grudge against him. Our drivers say the stock need some hay, and I buy a few armfuls of the precious feed from him, for which he charges me twelve cents a pound. These figures seem innocent enough at first, but when, after a little mental arithmetic, I discover that this is at the rate of *two hundred and forty dollars a ton,* I am somewhat staggered, and begin to suspect that perhaps the old man isn't living out here in the Indian country entirely "for his health."

For five miles beyond Godfrey's, we neither meet nor see one living thing in our afternoon drive, and then we pass a little adobe about fifteen feet square, the occupant of which is a very dirty-faced man, apparently living there alone. What his daily work is, if he has any, or why he should be all by himself in this exposed and defenceless fashion on the war-swept Plains — these are riddles as incomprehensible to us as is the fact that he doesn't treat himself to an occasional bath, or at least get some of the outer coats of dirt off his face, with the Platte river flowing wide and free a hundred yards away. Another five-mile stretch brings us to Beaver Creek station, and three miles more, all through a country entirely bare of settlement, to Beaver Creek ranche, where, to our amazement, we are obliged to cross a tollbridge and pay a toll of three dollars for our two wagons, "to help keep the road in order between here and Julesburg!" We regard this as a swindle, but at the same time accept it as an indication that we'll soon be getting "out of the wilderness," for, irritating as tollroads and their charges generally are, one always associates them in his mind with settled communities and civilization. We drive down into the fine bottomland between the house and the Platte, and make camp a quarter-mile from the river, after a day's work of twenty-eight miles — the longest drive, with the exception of one day with an exactly similar record, that we have made on our entire journey.

Just before coming into camp we at last enjoy our first view of the Rocky Mountains. It is rather curious and novel, though not very thrilling. As the sun is dropping in the west, we see a little to the south of it two small, dark-colored pyramids which seem to be just peeping over or resting on the horizon. The one next the sun, which is twice the size of the other, we are told is the summit of Long's Peak, and by the road the distance to it from our camp is a good hundred and fifty miles. As we approach them we shall now "raise" them rapidly, and in a day or two we may expect the whole range to gradually come into view.

Sunday, April 16th...Easter Sunday...we have still a fine level sweep of open country in front of us, the width from bluffs to river being three or four miles. We cover eleven miles over this fine road by eleven o'clock, which is "express" speed, and take a nooning at Douglas ranche. Six miles beyond this, without incident, we reach Junction ranche, and not far away are the ruins of old Fort

Morgan, one of the trading posts of the "thirties." There is a telegraph station at the ranche, and the operator horrifies us with the news that President Lincoln and Secretary Seward were assassinated in Washington on Friday evening. We get just the briefest telegraphic account, with no details, and that makes it all the more a subject of wonder and of general speculation by the whole train. Two miles beyond, at Junction stage station, we come upon another camp of Colorado boys, and also upon a problem, which creates more or less discussion. From this point there seem to be two roads to Denver; that is our present road continues to follow the windings of the river, and the distance is just one hundred miles, while, by leaving the Platte at this point and running off southwesterly straight across the country, the other, called the "Cutoff," is twenty miles shorter. The latter fact is somewhat tempting, but there prove to be some weighty arguments on the other side, so we conclude to stick to the stream that has been so pleasant a companion for three hundred miles, and we continue on for a couple of miles further to where Bijou creek, a little tributary, empties into it from the south, and here we make a pleasant camp. The old Platte during the afternoon has been narrowing down considerably, and is not more than two hundred yards wide at our campground, while at the opposite side of it the bluffs have suddenly come nearly down to the bank.

Monday, April 17th...quite a bend here, and we leave it [river] for a few hours and cut "across lots" to save a mile or two, striking it again about noon at a point opposite Fremont's Orchard, which at the time of the great

Pathfinder's first pilgrimage through here, twenty-odd years ago, was a fine grove of cottonwood trees; they are somewhat thinned out now, although no one seems to know why. We stop here for a leisurely nooning. During the afternoon we pass several eastbound wagons; and a few soldiers quartered in a log cabin by the roadside, and between five and six make camp a quarter-mile from the river at Sony Point, or Kempton's ranche. After our first view of the summits of Long and its twin peak night before last, the mountain range yesterday gradually pushed up above the horizon in a very irregular and eccentric way – by sections, as we travelled slowly toward it – and by night we still had only about the upper half of it in sight, although perhaps nearly all its length had come into view; but this morning the whole magnificent stretch of hills seemed at once bound to clear the plain and rise before us in all their majesty – one hundred and fifty miles in length of dark blue range in front, and behind and above them the line of eternal snow, glistening in the glorious sunlight and resting on a background of a sky of such deep blue as none of us have ever seen before....[169]

Sarah Raymond Herndon wrote of the domestic life on the trail in a series of letters published in the *Rocky Mountain Husbandman*. Her family traveled by wagon with the Kerfoot family, a family of twelve. The excerpt below begins the day before she saw the mountains for the first time, likely just downstream of Beaver Creek:

Wednesday, June 28. Cash [Kerfoot] is on the sick-list today. I trust it will not prove to be anything serious. I greatly fear Mr. Kerfoot's family are destined to have considerable sickness before this trip is ended. They have such a sameness of diet, and it is so poorly cooked I fear the result. When we started on this trip not one member of the family had ever prepared an entire meal; they had always had a houseful of servants to cook and do everything else for them. The first two or three weeks Neelie and her mother tried to learn to cook, and mother and I tried to teach them. It takes great patience to learn to bake in stoves out of doors; they heat red-hot so quickly, and cool just as suddenly; they must have careful attention all the time. They made several failures baking light bread, and, giving it up in disgust, settled down to biscuit that are hard as brick-bats, when cold, bacon, coffee, and beans – when we stop long enough to cook them. They were well supplied with fruit at first; the canned fruit was so easily served that it is all gone. They have dried fruit, but think it too much trouble to cook.... The wind blew so all afternoon that we could not ride horseback. The roads are smooth and hard as asphalt, result of rain yesterday and the wind to-day....

Wagon train on the prairie. Published in Woman on the American Frontier, *1876.*

Thursday, June 29. We could see the mountains, as the sun was sinking behind them; they were plainly visible though one hundred miles away. It does not seem possible they are so far away…. They look very much as I have imagined mountains would appear in the distance…. We crossed a small stream to-day that was bridged and had to pay fifty cent toll for each wagon [Beaver Creek]; the ford had been spoiled, or we could have crossed without the bridge.

Friday, June 30. We stopped at noon where the road forks, the left-hand road goes to Denver [the cut-off]. Mr. and Mrs. May, and Mr. and Mrs. Kirkland and children took the left-hand road, as they are going to Denver. Mr. May's brother, George, goes on to Montana on horseback; he will leave us in the morning and depend upon reaching stations, or emigrant camps, for food and shelter nights. I do hope the Indians will not get his scalp. We have been feasting on antelope, the first that any of our party have killed. It is fine, much better than venison…we do get so tired of cured meat. We see no game except antelope and jack rabbits. The great herds of buffalo – that we read about – have not been in sight as yet. Mr. Morrison's four-horse team ran away this afternoon with Mrs. Morrison and the children in the wagon. I had been riding with them since noon, had just left the wagon. When all the horse teams were driven out of ranks and down to the river for water the lead horses took fright at an ant-hill – the ant-hills are big as chicken house – and started to run. There were several men near who caught and stopped them just as the forewheel went over the bank of the river. Mr. Harding was driving; he tried to rein them away from the river but they were right on the verge when stopped, one moment more and there would have been a serious accident. Mrs. Morrison did not scream nor try to jump out, neither did she allow the children to, but sat quite still and acted like the sensible woman that she is....

Saturday, July 1. We were awakened this morning at the first peep of dawn by the sound of the bugle call. Soon the teams were hitched, corral broken, and we were journeying to the crossing of the river, where we were driven into corral again. While we were getting breakfast the men were raising the wagon-beds and fixing them upon blocks as high as the wheels, and binding them tight with ropes to the coupling poles and lower parts of the wagons, ready to ford the river. They had a top-heavy appearance, as if the least jolt would topple them over. Some of the women were very nervous about riding in wagons set upon stilts, and felt quite certain somebody would be drowned. Wagons were crossing when we drove into corral, of course we had to wait our turn – first come, first served. Some enterprising young men have the blocks and ropes there to rent, at a very reasonable hire, too, for they might have asked what they would, we had no choice but to use them. The river is half a mile or more wide, about half way over there is a large freight wagon stuck in the quicksand, just below the track of the wagons; it has been there since yesterday; it is slowly, slowly sinking and cannot be gotten out. It has been unloaded and left to its fate, it seems a signal of distress to warn drivers to keep farther up the river and avoid the quicksands.... Wagons have been crossing all day, and this evening we are a considerable town of tents and wagons; more than two hundred wagons within sight on the north side of the South Platte, at the eastern extremity of Fremont's Orchard – though why it is called an orchard I cannot understand, for there is certainly no fruit about it, mostly quaking-asp and cottonwood.... We will stay here over Sunday, and hope to have religious services to-morrow as there are several preachers with us.... Cash is much better, able to be out, though quite pale and weak. The mountains looming up in the distance seem to be the goal to which we are tending, and now we seem to make some progress every day for we are certainly nearer than when we first saw them on the twenty-ninth of June. Before they came in sight we did not seem to make any progress, but traveled day after day after day, and seemed to camp at night always in the same place; there was such a sameness in the landscape. In the early morning when the sun shines upon the snow-capped mountains the effect is thrilling; they seem to be the great altars of earth raised up to Heaven for the morning sacrifice.

Sunday, July 2. It is wonderful, wonderful to behold how this town of tents and wagons has sprung up since yesterday morning when there was no sign of life on this north bank of the South Platte, and now there are more than one thousand men, women and children, and I cannot guess how many wagons and tents. The wagons have been crossing all day, the last one has just been driven into corral at sunset. I was sitting on the bank of the river watching with anxiety the wagons as they ploughed through the deep waters for the ford has washed out and the wagons go in much deeper than when we crossed yesterday when a gentleman came and introduced himself as Dr. Howard, physician for the McMahan train. He said, "Miss Raymond, I have known you by sight since we camped at Kearney, and now as I have an errand for an excuse I hope to become better acquainted." I could not

Crossing the Platte by Albert Bierstadt Published in Harpers Weekly, *1859.*

imagine what his errand could be…"Miss Raymond, I have been directed to your wagons for the best and most wholesome bread that is baked on this road. Captain McMahan's nephew, Robert Southerland, has been very sick but is now convalescing and needs nutritious and wholesome food to help him gain strength. I came to ask you for a piece of good bread." Of course I gave him a loaf, and said, "Come get more when that is gone." He thanked me profusely.

There has been no serious accident nor any lives lost, although thousands of cattle, hundreds of horses, and more than a thousand human beings have crossed the river since yesterday morning. Oh, for the pen of a Dickens to describe this wonderful scene, which no one ever has or ever will see again, just as it is. The moon is at the full and shining brightly as there is not a cloud in the sky, the camp-fires do not glow as they do dark nights. The men are building a great bonfire in the middle of our extemporaneous town. There is to be a praise and thanksgiving service for our safe conduct through the deep waters and our protection from the Indians. The people are beginning to gather near the bonfire and I must go, too. Later. Our service is over; it was grand, the singing of the old familiar hymns by so many voices spontaneously was inspiring, the talks by five or six ministers of different denominations were full of love for the Master, and brotherly love for every one. An invitation was then given for all who had enlisted in the service of the Master to come forward and shake hands with the preachers, thus testifying for Christ....

Monday, July 3. The scenes in this great expanse of low, level land on the north side of the Platte in the early hours of this morning is hard to describe. Corrals and camps here, there and everywhere. Cattle and horses being driven into corrals to be harnessed and yoked, men and women cooking by camp-fires and on stoves, everybody seemed to be in a great hurry all was animation and life, men riding after horses, oxen and mules; yelling, hallooing and calling, but not a profane oath did I hear. Among so many children, we rarely ever hear a child cry, and never hear a woman scold. Our train was the third to break camp and file into the road this morning. The place that knew us yesterday will know us no more forever. Our town of tents and wagons that was teeming with life this morning is this evening deserted, silent, and uninhabited...[170]

Some travelers through the Fort Morgan area during the Indian Wars were attacked. Agnes Miner tells of traveling along the South Platte River Road in the turbulent year of 1867. She briefly mentioned traveling through Fort Morgan and her party took the cut-off road to Denver where they would encounter Indians. The soldiers stationed at the fort would come to the rescue. The following excerpt from her journal begins at Wisconsin Ranch, just east of Sterling:

...Just before reaching Wisconsin Ranch we saw a stage coach coming from Denver. On the stage was a young man who had come out to repair some telegraph lines that the Indians had cut. While talking to the driver and this young man we saw the coach coming on its way to Denver, and since the roads were narrow we had to hurry on. We soon heard shots and turning saw the coach coming down the hill just as fast as the horses could travel. The other coach turned around and followed. The young telegraph operator had been killed. They said it seemed as though the Indians came right out of the bluffs. Following this there was no more trouble with the Indians until after we left the soldiers at Fort Morgan. We camped that night at Steven's ranch sixty-five miles from

Denver. We put our horses in the barn, thinking they would be safe there. We slept in the house. About 12 o'clock we heard a shot and saw a light in the barn. There was much excitement in camp. Our Captain had given orders that anything moving should be shot. The man on guard crawled along and told the Captain that something was moving. The Captain raised on his elbows and fired. Something jumped into the air. They found it was an Indian. Upon investigation we found our horses had been stolen. We could see the Indians all along the horizon...we expected an attack at daybreak... A few minutes after this Indian was killed, we heard the coach from Denver coming.... Father wrote a telegram asking for help and gave it to the driver to send from the first telegraph station. When the word reached Fort Morgan the next morning, a few soldiers hurried out. Among them was a young brother of General Philip Sheridan [Michael V. Sheridan, then in command of Fort Morgan].... We traveled along, reaching living Spring before sundown. A sad company, we were expecting never to see the rising sun again....[171]

Towns sprang up first along the foothills and then along the route connecting the Rocky Mountains to "The States." The white emigrants had arrived, pushing progress onto the plains in their quest for gold.

∞

Chapter 5

Communications West

With the discovery of gold in the Rocky Mountains, the small town of Denver City began to grow and would soon become an important center of commerce. But at the time gold was discovered the city was

THE DENVER, SALT LAKE AND OREGON TRAIL, 1865.

Overland trail stations along South Platte River. Published in Across the Plains in '65, *1905.*

an island in the Great American Desert, disconnected from both the east and the west; the Oregon Trail running 150 miles to the north through Laramie, Wyoming and the Santa Fé Trail laying more than 200 miles south. The South Platte River Road through Fort Morgan would soon became the primary link between the growing population of Denver and "The States" via stage, mail, telegraph, and eventually railroads.

Overland Mail

COC&PP express stamp from Denver City, C.T.

The first mail to Denver arrived in 1859 carried by the Leavenworth and Pike's Peak Express Company owned by Russell, Majors and Waddell. Initially, the company tried sending coaches west to Denver along the Republican River, but in May the company bought the Utah mail contract from John M. Hockaday which sent mail west along the Oregon Trail and to consolidate their operations, the route to Denver was switched to follow the South Platte River[172]. By the end of the summer coaches were running consistently and more importantly twice a week[173].

In February, 1860, the Leavenworth and Pike's Peak Express Company became the Central Overland California and Pike's Peak Express Company and began operating an express service over the Oregon Trail. This express service known as the Pony Express traveled from St. Joseph, Missouri to Sacramento, California in just 10 days. The short-lived Pony press, while famous, was fabulously expensive and sent the company into bankruptcy. In March, 1862, Ben Holladay bought the Central Overland California and Pike's Peak Express Company and renamed it the Overland Stage Line[174]. At the same time, Holladay bought the Western Stage Company, which had been operating a competing mail service from Council Bluffs to Denver along the South Platte River[175]. The first of Holladay's express coaches traveled along the South Platte River to Denver reaching its destination on September 12, 1862 where it received a grand salute from the canons at Camp Weld[176]. In October of 1864[177], Holladay changed the route to include the Cut-off at the Junction (Fort Morgan) which separated from the South Platte River Road and went overland directly to Denver cutting 40 or more miles from the journey. Mrs. Taft recalled her journey to Denver in one of the Overland Stage coaches in 1862:

...travelers going to "Pike's Peak" were obliged...to choose – by stage coach, ox team and horse or mule team. The stages were Concord coaches, hung on thorough-braces, which were two hung straps made of leather and fixed to a framework, one on each side upon which the body of the coach was fastened. By them all jolting was presented and in going over rough places gave a rocking motion – which made folks who were inclined that wey [sic] thoroughly seasick – but for most people was an easy and pleasant motion.

The time was six days from Atchison [Kansas] to Denver – about seven hundred miles – traveling day and night. They carried mail. On the inside was room for nine passengers. The fare was $75 to Denver until the Indian trouble began, then it was $175. The baggage limit was twenty-five pounds, besides which the traveler, for his own comfort, took a pair of blankets or a buffalo robe and a supply of good things to eat (and sometimes to drink.)

The coaches were drawn by four horses which were changed every ten or twelve miles at "swing stations." They stopped at the "home stations" for meals, which cost $1.50. The menu was decided upon by the stage company and consisted of bread, meat, beans, dried ap-

Overland mail coach.

ples, coffee and the "four seasons." Sometimes there were potatoes and, as I remember, canned milk... The quality of the meal depended upon the cook. A good cook's reputation as such was known for miles....

There were three seats in the coaches and room for three people on each seat. Lucky, indeed, was the passenger who secured a corner on the back seat. If one did not mind riding backwards, the next most desirable places were the two corners on the front seat. The use of the middle seat was optional, unless there were more than six passengers aboard. The back of this seat was a brad strap of very thick leather and could be removed. It was a case of first come, first served; the seat you engaged was yours, and woe betide the poor mortal who must take the middle seat and stay there sitting bolt upright for six days and nights....

At first, until the Indian troubles began in '64, all wagons were driven independently. After that all wagons were stopped by the U. S. military at Fort Kearney coming west, and Camp Wardwell (now Fort Morgan) going east, until there was a number of armed men considered sufficient for their own protection; then they were allowed to proceed. At first a dozen men were considered enough, but later the number was increased to fifty.... I have known of two such companies meeting, one coming west and the other going east, that were an hour and a half in passing....[178]

In the mid-1860s, David A. Butterfield ran a competing mail service up the Smoky Hill Route to Denver[179], but in 1866, Holladay took over the Butterfield Overland Dispatch Company and the two major overland lines consolidated forming the Holladay Overland Mail and Express Company[180]. The Overland would eventually be taken over by Wells Fargo & Company and the line moved to the Smoky Hill Route, but by this time, the railroads were moving in and age of the stage was coming to an end[181].

Stations

The first stations along the trail were built by the Leavenworth and Pike's Peak Express Company in 1859 both for the comfort of the passengers and to keep and care for the horses and drivers. When Holladay took over the route, he used some of the established stations and built others. The Overland Stage Line, which included the section of road along the South Platte River, went from Atchison, Kansas to Placerville, California, a distance of 1913 miles. There were 153 stations along the route an average of about 12.5 miles apart. The stations placed along the route allowed passengers to stop for a meal or to stretch their legs as tired teams were exchanged for fresh ones. Frank Root, a young messenger for the Overland mail, traveled along the route frequently and noted his general impressions of the stations:

> There was a remarkable similarity in many of the stations built along the Platte on the stage route.... Most of the buildings were erected by the stage company, and usually they were nearly square, one-story, hewn, cedar-log structures, of one to three rooms. When constructed with only one room, often partitions of muslin were used to separate the kitchen from the dining-room and sleeping apartments. The roof was supported by a log placed across from gable to gable, by which poles were supported for rafters placed as close as they could be put together, side by side. On these were placed some willows, then a layer of hay was spread, and this was covered with earth or sod; and, lastly, a sprinkling of coarse gravel covered all, to keep the earth from being blown off. The logs of which most of the first stations were constructed were procured

in the cañons south of the Platte, in the vicinity of Cottonwood Springs, in the southern part of western Nebraska. Nearly all the "swing" stations [a station where there was no family living – only a stock tender] along the Platte-in fact, over the entire line-were similar in construction and closely resembled one another. A number of the "home" stations, however, differed somewhat in several respects, being two or three times larger, and provided with sheds, outbuildings, and a number of other conveniences....[182]

Beaver Creek along with Valley Station (Sterling) and

TABLE OF DISTANCES BETWEEN ATCHISON, KAN., AND PLACERVILLE, CAL.

Between stations.	NAMES OF STATIONS.		From Atchison.	Between stations.	NAMES OF STATIONS.		From Atchison.
	ATCHISON .... Kan.			20	Bijou .... Colo.		553
10	Lancaster..........	"	10	16	Fremont's Orchard.	"	569
14	Kennekuk..........	"	24	11	Eagle's Nest	"	580
12	Kickapoo	"	36	12	Latham	"	592
13	Log Chain	"	49	15	Big Bend...........	"	607
11	Seneca	"	60	17	Fort Lupton	"	624
12	Laramie Creek	"	72	15	Pierson's	"	639
12	Guittard's..........	"	84	14	DENVER	"	653
10	Oketo	"	94	11	Child's.............	"	664
11	Otoe............. Neb.		105	12	Boon's	"	676
11	Pawnee	"	116	18	Little Thompson ...	"	694
14	Grayson's	"	130	8	Big Thompson......	"	702
10	Big Sandy.........	"	140	16	Laporte	"	718
14	Thompson's........	"	154	10	Boner..............	"	728
14	Kiowa	"	168	12	Cherokee..........	"	740
12	Little Blue........	"	180	12	Virginia Dale......	"	752
13	Liberty Farm	"	193	15	Willow Springs .... Wyo.		767
15	Lone Tree.........	"	208	15	Big Laramie........	"	782
10	32-Mile Creek	"	218	14	Little Laramie......	"	796
12	Summit............	"	230	17	Cooper Creek......	"	813
13	Hook's............	"	243	11	Rock Creek	"	824
10	Fort Kearney......	"	253	17	Medicine Bow......	"	841
10	Platte Station	"	263	8	Elk Mountain......	"	849
11	Craig	"	274	14	Pass Creek........	"	863
15	Plum Creek	"	289	16	North Platte	"	889
15	Willow Island......	"	304	14	Sage Creek........	"	903
14	Midway............	"	318	10	Pine Grove........	"	913
15	Gilman's	"	333	9	Bridger's Pass.....	"	922
17	Cottonwood Springs	"	350	10	Sulphur Springs....	"	932
15	Cold Springs......	"	365	11	Waskie.............	"	943
14	Fremont Springs ..	"	379	13	Duck Lake........	"	956
11	Elkhorn...........	"	390	12	Dug Springs	"	968
14	Alkali Lake.......	"	404	15	Laclede	"	983
12	Sand Hill	"	416	12	Big Pond..........	"	995
11	Diamond Springs...	"	427	14	Black Buttes.......	"	1009
15	South Platte......	"	442	14	Rock Point........	"	1023
14	Julesburg......... Colo.		456	14	Salt Wells.........	"	1037
12	Antelope	"	468	14	Rock Spring.......	"	1051
13	Spring Hill........	"	481	15	Green River.......	"	1066
13	Dennison's.........	"	494	14	Lone Tree........	"	1080
12	Valley Station	"	506	18	Ham's Fork.......	"	1098
15	Kelly's............	"	521	12	Church Buttes.....	"	1110
12	Beaver Creek......	"	533	8	Millersville........	"	1118

Mileage and stations between Atchison and Placerville on the land stage. Note: Mileage may have been adjusted to make stations appear more evenly spaced.

Fremont's Orchard were designated as eating stations or "home" stations while Junction [Bijou Creek] was a "swing" station.

In addition to the Overland stations, a number of stores and hostelries appeared along the route catering to the needs of the passing trains. These stores were not officially part of the Overland Stage line, but not all travelers along the route were passengers of the stage company. Many potential prospectors soon learned they need not go as far as the Rocky Mountains to find their gold.

American Ranch

Travellers passing through the Fort Morgan area on the Overland stage would first pass the American Ranch approximately 30 miles east of Fort Morgan on the south bank of the river near present-day Merino, Colorado. American Ranch had many names in its short life including Kelley's (or Kelly's) Ranch, Murray & Kelley's Ranch, and Morrison's Ranch[183]. In addition to being a post office and stage stop,

American Ranch, 1861.

American Ranch supplied groceries and provisions to passing emigrants. "'The American Ranche, a Home for the Weary,' had its card regularly in *The Huntsman's Echo*, announcing that it 'Keeps constantly on hand a supply of Groceries and Provisions, Garden Sauce – Can fruit of all kinds, Liquors, Cigars, Corn, Oats – and, in fact, everything to please the Emigrant'"[184].

During the Indian Wars of 1864 and 1865, the ranch was attacked by Indians on numerous occasions. In the summer of 1864, the station keeper at the American Ranch, William A. Kelley grew concerned and wrote to Governor John Evans:

> Having finally become uneasy at the repeated presence of Indians near my place, I have thought it proper to inform you of the fact.... [Y]esterday [I] started out, thinking to kill an antelope. When about 3 miles from home, suddenly saw about 16 Indians riding furiously toward me. I immediately started for home, they pursuing and firing upon me repeatedly; but having a good horse, I made my escape unharmed. I think if there were troops stationed along the road it would give a feeling of greater security to both settlers and emigrants. Our lives and property appear to be in great danger[185].

Kelley was right to be concerned. The first Indian raid on the American Ranch occurred in July of 1864 and was attacked again and burned in August of 1864. William Kelley resigned from the Overland Stage Company and moved his family to Denver – a decision that likely saved his life.

In September 1864, a new family, William and Mary Morris (in some sources Morrison[186] or Morrissey[187]) arrived and the ranch was quickly rebuilt. The Indian attacks escalated and the American Ranch was again destroyed by Indians in January of 1865. This time, the station keeper, Morris and his men were killed and his wife and children taken by Indians.

The bodies of the Indians killed in the attack became symbols of the anger the emigrants felt. At one point, the bodies were reportedly placed in a small graveyard near the ranch, but Sam Ashcraft and a group of other local ranchers threw the bodies into the road where passing travelers mutilated them[188]. Frank Root arrived at American Ranch a month after the attacks and was confronted by the gruesome sight:

> ...On our arrival at the station, one of the dead Indians, with only one leg and one arm, was standing up against the south-wall of the burnt building, while the other, with arms cut off at the elbows, stood against the paling surrounding a grave only three or four rods distant. Both Indians were practically in a nude condition, nearly every article of clothing having been stripped from them. They were frozen stiff, and their bodies had been horribly mutilated. Both had been scalped, apparently in genuine aboriginal style, but whether by white men, or an enemy belonging to the scalp-lifting fraternity, can only be surmised. Slices of flesh from different parts of their bodies had also been cut off and carried away as souvenirs. Each had an eye gouged out and an ear cut off, several fingers had somehow disappeared, and one was minus his nose. (A driver suggested he had evidently been poking his nose into other people's business.) The entrails of one were visible...

The passengers, after making a thorough inspection, were unanimous in their belief that they were "good Indians" [dead Indians]. All hoped that, if any more, of the "noble red men" were encountered on the trip, we would find them as quiet and peaceable as were these[189].

After the attacks in January of 1865, the American Ranch was abandoned, but Godfrey's Ranch took the name "American," and the post office continued until 1867[190].

Godfrey's Ranch: "Fort Wicked"

Two miles west of the American Ranch was Godfrey's Ranch named for Holon Godfrey. The ranch later became known as "Fort Wicked" after Godfrey successfully staved off an Indian attack in 1865. Originally, Holon Godfrey traveled the South Platte River Road in 1960 along with thousands of other prospectors on his way to the promised gold but, at this time there were many "go-backers," travelers returning from the gold fields disappointed and disheartened so instead Godfrey settled along the route and opened a store selling groceries and baked goods[191]. Soon he was joined by his wife Matilda and children Cuba, Nettie, Carey, and Allen[192]. Godfrey's Ranch was on the Overland Trail, but was a private establishment and not an official mail or stage stop until after the American Ranch was destroyed in 1865. Godfrey's Ranch was on the south side of the river near the modern-day South Platte River Bridge on Highway 6. A historical marker is placed approximately three miles west of Merino, Colorado[193,194].

Godfrey's Ranch was attacked by Indians in January 1865 in the same series of attacks that destroyed the American

Ranch and killed the stationkeeper. The siege and the successful defense of the ranch became something of a legend. A correspondent for the *New York Tribune* wrote of Godfrey and the raids in January of 1865 that gave his "Fort" its name:

> The Indians...encircled the ranche of Hallen [sic] Godfrey, a native of Western New York, but an old resident of the Indian country. I supped with him a few nights ago, and had his story from himself. He gave it with a degree of modesty and candor that stripped the popular history of the affair of some of its romance,

Fort Wicked. Published in Harper's Weekly, *1866.*

but that he gave it truthfully there could be no doubt. He is an intelligent, keen-eyed and brawny-armed man of over 50, and makes no pretensions to the heroic; but he does pretend to protect his little store of whisky, tobacco, and canned fruits, and notions, and his wife and children, and more than that, he does it. He has a sod fortification running along the south and west sides of his ranche, and extending out some six feet front and rear, so as to protect two sides of the building, and command the other two. His fort is but a sod wall, six feet high, with loop-holes, but it is an infinitely better fortification than the science officers of Fort Sedgwick have to protect that post.

One hundred and sixty warriors attacked the Godfrey Ranche, but as it was defended, they exhausted Indian strategy to reduce it. There were but four men and then women in the ranche, but they had several guns each, and plenty of ammunition. The Indians first formed a circle about the ranche at a distance of 400 yards, and endeavored to draw Godfrey's fire so as to get his range; but he never pulled a trigger until he had an Indian within 200 yards. "My favorite double-barrel ain't sure at over 200 yards," he informed me, and he said that he had no ammunition to waste. Judging that they could not accomplish anything without a direct attack they selected 30 of their fleetest riders and they charged to within 30 yards of the ranche in single file, and each one fired, and wheeled at the nearest point. They made several such charges, each time selecting different loop-holes for their fire; that they harmed no one, and one or more of the charging 30 fell in every charge. Finally, they abandoned the direct attack and fired the grass at various points, hoping to get his ranche on fire. At one point they had forced the fire close to the stable, but Godfrey could reach the endangered corner under cover, and he extinguished the fire. Sixty balls struck the corner of the stable where he was working, but he managed to protect himself and escape unharmed. The siege was maintained with occasional charges, until night, which they were glad to abandon the ranche, and leave their dead behind them. Wherever a dead Indian lay, Godfrey kept special watch, knowing that they would exhaust every effort to get their dead off the field; but he shot several who attempted to remove their fallen comrades, and they finally surrendered their dead braves as trophies for the victor.

They gave Godfrey, the euphonious sobriquet of "Old Wicked," and since then he is known only by that name. His ranche is called "Fort Wicked," and his actual name of Hallen Godfrey is almost forgotten. He is now expecting another raid, as do all the ranchemen on the line, and he is the only man I have found whose face occurs to brighten as he speaks of the probability of "another brush" with them, as he calls it. I made a careful examination of his armory. It contains eighteen rifles, from the old hunter's to the most improved Spencer and Sharpe. All are loaded, and ready for the combat at the moment's warning. When we arrived it was nearly midnight, and the old man was on guard himself in front of his ranche, armed with a Spencer rifle. Night or day his ranche is never without a sentinel and surprise is impossible. The general belief of the ranchemen is that when the Indians do come, they will not molest "Old Wicked"....[195]

Godfrey was a colorful character and many wrote of him and his family:

My last letter closed with the arrival of our party at Godfrey's ranche...about midway between old Julesburg...and Denver city. As this is a noted place and its proprietor a "character," I propose to dwell a while. "Old Godfrey," as he is called by travelers and himself when he is at his ranche, and "Old Wicked" when he is on his travels, is a man about sixty years of age, above the average stature, well built and firmly knit, his hair iron-gray, his eye keen and undimmed, his shoulders slightly bent by time, hardships, and wounds received from the Indians who are his only near neighbors, and who never visit him to take tea or drinks socially, but always do call when they think their forces large enough to take his cattle, his goods, or the scalp of the old veteran, or of some or all of his family. His watchfulness has thus far thwarted them and protected his household treasures; but they often run off his stock, and he as often succeeds in getting even with them. The ranch is built of adobe, the walls being two feet thick; the apartments are the dining room, for travelers, a kitchen, two or three lodging rooms, and a large room used for a sitting, wash, and store-room – the floor being rough boards. In this room are also the arms and ammunition used in defending his home from the frequent attacks of his neighbors aforesaid.

His family consists of his wife, a frail, patient looking woman, a daughter about eighteen, and three sons. These form the corps reserve, while one or two hired men assist in guarding against surprise and doing the work about the ranche. Outside of the house, and ten feet from it, are the fortifications, which completely surround it. The walls of defense are built of sod taken from the surface of the prairie, being about two feet thick at the bottom and one at the top, the height being five feet; near the top loop holes are frequent, affording range in all directions. Through this wall, opposite the front door, is an opening about three feet wide, and bags of sand lying near to barricade the same if required.

The Indians, who have often by treachery and open attack tried to destroy this fort and murder its occupants, have a wholesome fear of the determined Godfrey and his brave family. They hate him with a bitter hate, and declare they will yet have his hair, and Godfrey delares [sic] that they shall not.... Thus the pioneers of our country live in perils and dangers constantly without aid or sympathy from the government which ought to afford them sure protection[196].

By 1869, the steady stream of gold prospectors was gone and the "fort" closed and Godfrey turned his attention to cultivating the land.

Beaver Creek Station

Beaver Creek Station was located about 15 miles east of Fort Morgan[197,198] near present-day Snyder, Colorado. The station was located at the confluence of the South Platte River and Beaver Creek, the first stream since Fort Kearney that needed to be forded by the travelers. In 1860, a toll bridge was erected over Beaver Creek[199,200] and each vehicle was charged up to $1.50 for passage, half price if returning east, and loose stock was charged 3 cents per head. A man on horseback was charged between 10 and 25 cents[201]. Beaver Creek Station was built sometime in 1860-1861[202]and was a "home station" where passengers on the Overland stage stopped for a hot meal. In 1861 the station keepers were J. H. Stephens (or Stevens[203]) and James A. Moore, famed rider for the Pony Express who set a record for completing a round trip ride of 140 miles in 25 hours[204].

In 1863, Fitz Hugh Ludlow, along with artist Albert Bierstadt, traveled on an Overland stage up the South Platte River Road to Denver describing in great detail his journey in his book *The Heart of the Continent*. Ludlow described his impressions of the Fort Morgan area (Junction) and especially of Beaver Creek Station:

> For twenty-five miles beyond Spring Hill [Station], we rode through a solitude broken only by one station-house, a few antelope, and innumerable jackass-rabbits.... About day-break we drew up at Beaver Creek Station, five hundred and thirty-three miles from Atchison, and a hundred and twenty from Denver. The station consisted, as usual, of a single house with the company's stables and corral attached, and is situated about three miles east of the Beaver Creek laid down on the maps. The light was vague when we first stopped, but sufficient to reveal a picturesqueness in the immediate landscape which set my heart bounding, after the experience of the past two

Sketch of Beaver Creek Station in A Trip to Pike's Peak and Notes by the Way, *1858.*

days.... The Platte had made a concession to our rebellious aesthetic sense, by sending out from the main channel, where it crept eastward, some forty rods north of the house, a sinuous lagoon terminating in a marsh near the road. All along the borders of this still but living water, the grass was green and thick even to rankness, and its high banks bore a profusion succulent weeds....

As the sun grew nearer the horizon, this pleasant feature showed to better advantage. They eye rested on the broad borders and patches of living greenness.... We were all seated on or in the wagon, when our scarred driver pointed westward across the Plains, now all aflood with the gold of the risen sun, and said "There are the Rocky Mountains." I strained my eyes in the direction of his finger, but for a minute could see nothing. Presently sight seemed adjusted to a new focus, and out against the bright sky dawned slowly the undefined shimmering trace of something a little bluer. Still, it seemed nothing tangible. It might have passed for vapor effect on the horizon, had not the driver called it otherwise.... They are made out of the air and the sunshine which show them. Nature has dipped her pencil in the faintest solution of ultramarine, and drawn it once across the western sky.... I confess...that my first view of the Rocky Mountains had no way of expressing itself save in tears....[205]

Edwin Legrand Sabin wrote a fictionalized account of life on the Overland Trail entitled *On the Overland Stage*. In the novel, the protagonist, a young boy Terry Richards, travels along the route as a cub driver and spends time as a station keeper at Beaver Creek. Though a novel, Sabin prided himself on historical accuracy and included detailed descriptions including one of Beaver Creek Station:

[The station] sat here by itself, in a lonely stretch of flat country, on the south side of the stage road. Just across the stage road was a crooked slough; and beyond the slough was the South Platte River.... The station house was a low building of sod walls three feet thick, and sod roof. It had one room, divided off by muslin partitions into dining-room, bedroom, and kitchen. The muslin broke the view, but that was about all. Anybody could hear right through it, and the shadows cast on it were very funny, from the other side. The ceiling was muslin, also, to keep the dust from sifting down. The floor was clay. There were three small square windows, one beside the door and one in the center of either side wall, closed by wooden shutters instead of glass panes. The dining-room or living-room had a fire-place and large flue; the kitchen had a rusty stove and chimney; the bed-room had several bunks softened with hay mattresses and blankets; there was a rough board table to eat from, and hand-made chairs and stools with seats of cowhide. On the wall hung a shot-gun and an old smooth-bore musket.... The corral was of poles, and the stable, at the end of it, was of rough-hewn cottonwood logs, chinked after a fashion but pretty airy, under a dirt roof. There was a well, from which the water was drawn by a bucket and windlass. The water was only seepage water, and tasted rather flat, but it was wet....about the best station on the road! On a clear day you could see the Rocky Mountains, like clouds, a hundred miles west; the slough was full of ducks and the brush was full of rabbits; two stages passed through every day and stopped for meals, news from Denver was only twenty-four hours old, and a sod house was the warmest and the coolest kind of a house, winter and summer. Indians could not burn it, either. It was a regular fort. For the 'privilege' of living on such luxury he was paid $60 a month, as station-keeper, and got a profit from the meals, as cook...[206]

Though reportedly destroyed in the Indian raids of 1865, Jack Sumner, a guide and trapper, apparently took over the old Beaver Creek Station in 1871[207] after returning from accompanying John Wesley Powell on an expedition down the Colorado River[208].

In the 1870s, when the flow of emigrants had stopped and the mail no longer traveled up the South Platte River, the area quieted down and the remaining settlers switched their attention from selling goods to the emigrants to cattle and crops.

The Junction (Fort Morgan) & Bijou Creek Station

The next stage stop was Bijou Creek Station[209] located at or near the Junction, the name given to the area along the South Platte River Road that now contains the town of Fort Morgan.

Junction was located approximately 15 to 20 miles west of Beaver Creek[210] near the confluence of Bijou Creek and the South Platte River and lay almost equidistantly between Julesburg and Denver. Junction was so called as it was the point at which the trail diverged: the South Platte River Road continuing west along the river and the Cut-off route veering overland southwest directly to Denver. The Junction was many things, a post office, a telegraph office, a swing station for the Overland Stage, and later a military outpost, first called Camp Wardwell and later Fort Morgan. Fort Morgan became a central military outpost during the worst of the Indian Wars along the South Platte when emigrants and the mail required military protection from raiding Indians. The fort also accommodated stores and shops allowing travelers to purchase goods or make repairs. Patrols were sent out from the fort and wagons were organized into trains for protection before being released to continue their westward passage. Later, two railroads would be built, one on the north bank of the river and the other on the south bank, making Fort Morgan a railroad junction as well.

There is much confusion about the ranches and stations located at the Junction. Bijou Creek station and Bijou Creek Ranch are often interchanged with references to Junction House, Junction Ranch(e), Junction Station and Post Junction[211]. Even after the military arrived and a fort was established, the area continued to be referred to generically as the "junction." More specifically, Junction House appears to be the point at which the Cut-off trail separated from the river and the latter pair (Junction Ranch and Junction Station) apparently lay approximately 2 miles apart. Additionally, a number of ranches in the area served as stage stops and trading posts which were sometimes referred to by the name of the proprietor and sometimes referred to loosely as either Junction House, Junction Station, or Junction Ranch(e).

Samuel Plummer Ashcraft (Ashcroft) established a ranch at the Junction in 1861[212,213] and traded with the Indians dispensing "pine knot," "forty red," and other brands of uor[214]. Ashcraft was married to a Sioux woman[215] and traded with the various tribes in the area so he was well placed to aid the cavalry during the Indian wars serving as a guide and interpreter. He rode with the soldiers many times during 1864 and was at the Battle of Sand Creek. His trading post was located approximately two miles northeast of the fort along the bank of the South Platte River[216]. In 1866, Ashcraft was granted a homestead near Greeley[217] and rancher, Mark V. Boughton took over Ashcraft's ranch having lost his previous ranch at St. Vrain[218,219]. In 1866, Boughton expanded his operation buying out Charley Williams' Sutler's store located at the fort[220].

Frederick Lamb, an Englishman, was the station keeper at the Junction for the stage company in 1861[221] living with his wife Caroline and children Elizabeth, Thomas, F. (Frederick?), and Ella[222]. There is some disagreement as to where Lamb's ranch was located, one source placing the ranch six miles east of the Junction Cut-off[223] and another placing the Lamb ranch at or near Ashcraft's[224]. The Western Stage Company also maintained a trading post and station operated by William McMackin only a couple of miles from Lamb's[225,226]. Also in the immediate area of the junction was Murray's Ranch (formerly Douglas Ranch), run by the Murray Brothers, John and Michael, seven to nine miles northeast of the Junction[227] and Perkin's Ranch established by Elisha (Si) and Margaret Perkins about two miles north of Brush. There is evidence that at one time or another each of these ranches were referred to as the "junction."

The fort as well as the mail and telegraph stations closed

in 1868[228] and the land around the Junction was given over first to pasture in the 1870s and then, with irrigation in the 1880s, to farm land. In 1884, the town of Fort Morgan was established on the land formerly known as the Junction.

Fremont's Orchard Station

Travelers choosing to continue west along the river rather than take the Cut-off at the Junction had one further choice to make: whether to go through deep sand beds or avoid the sand beds by climbing and descending a steep bluff. The sand between Bijou Creek and Fremont's Orchard stretched 8 to 10 miles and was so heavy that trains could only move a few feet at a time[229]. Another danger was the alkali springs that make the water foul for the cattle to drink[230,231]. Fitz Hugh Ludlow described his difficult journey along the South Platte River Road to Fremont's Orchard. He referred to being on the Cut-off, but as the cut-off route by-passed Fremont's Orchard, it is likely he is referring to the road that ascended the bluffs to avoid the sand:

At Junction, the next station west of Beaver Creek, we left the Platte, and took a cut-off to Fremont's Orchard, twenty miles across a succession of high sand-hills, on which the sun pelted and the dry hot wind blew more mercilessly than anywhere on our previous journey…one might as well look for water in an ash barrel as anywhere along the cut-off…. But for the misery of a parched tongue, a throat like a glass-house chimney, lips cracked by the alkali atmosphere, and the lassitude of a perfectly shadeless ride on the hottest day of the season, I should have enjoyed the new nature…. From the time we left

Junction till we struck the Platte again, we seemed to be in a new zone, both botanically and zoologically.... We found on the long sand-hills which we now had to climb, a greater variety of plants than we had discovered all over the comparative level between O'Fallon's bluff and Beaver Creek.... Less apparent to the eye, but abundantly sensible to feeling, were the minute buffalo-gnats, which at intervals during the past three days had much annoyed us along the Platte, but now became a nuisance justifying imprecation. As if we had not enough to suffer from parching heat and thirst, mules tired to death, deep sand, and a surly driver, these pestilent little creatures swarmed around our heads and into our hair, stinging us on neck and scalp like so many winged cambric needles dipped in aqua-fortis.... The last three or four miles of our way led us through a series of arroyos, or deep channels...their shape, and the successive terraces of their banks, suggests a series of water-courses only recently dried up.... They are, all of them, larger than the channels laid down on the maps as creeks, and, to all appearance, might as well discharge some water from the plateau...yet their thirstiness is a matter of ages, not of years[232].

After the difficult journey, Fremont's Orchard was a welcome sight. It was not a true orchard in any real sense, but a grove of cottonwood trees that on the sparse plains was a delightful surprise. Fremont's Orchard, near present day Orchard, Colorado was named for John Fremont[233] who explored the area in 1842 and wrote of the grove in his journal. Fremont's Orchard appears to have been a natural meeting place where traders and Indians met to exchange goods. A mail station was established at Fremont's Orchard in 1863 and a military camp in 1864[234].

Writing in his journal in 1859, Patterson described Fremont's Orchard as "a lovely grove of young thrifty cottonwoods and occupies a nice level area of some eight acres, entirely destitute of undergrowth, whilst the trees present the appearance of having been set out with almost the regularity of an orchard...."[235] But a couple of years later in 1865 Cauthorn reported the orchard had succumbed to the emigrants:

> Nooned at Fremont's Orchard... The orchard is of low, scrubby cottonwood and in the formation of the trees resembles an old abandoned apple orchard. Those who were acquainted with this road years ago, say that at one time these trees formed a beautiful grove and were an inviting camping ground, but when necessary the beautiful must give way to the useful, and the wood man's axe has disposed it of its dignity and nothing of its former self is left except a few trees and some stumps close to the ground[236].

The "orchard" has long since disappeared under the farmland of Northeastern Colorado.

The next station west of Fremont's Orchard was Eagle's Nest then Latham, where coaches turned either south towards Denver or crossed the Platte and joined the Overland Trail to Salt Lake City. For travelers going to Denver, the stations were: Big Bend Station, Fort Lupton Station, and Pierson Station[237,238] before reaching Denver City in the foothills of gold country.

The Cut-Off

The South Platte River Road led travelers almost due west along the river to the confluence with the Cache la Poudre (near Fort Collins) where the road turned south following the river into Denver. Along this route was some of the most difficult terrain on the trail. The Cut-off was established in 1860 as a short-cut to Denver[239] striking out southwest from the Junction (Fort Morgan) and avoiding the deep sands between Junction and Fremont's Orchard. The route was 30 to 40 miles shorter and was level and much less sandy, but the safety of the river was lost as was the guarantee of water. At least one dry camp had to be made along the route[240]. The Cut-off was variously known as the "Fort Morgan Cut-off", "Junction Cut-off", "Denver Cut-off", "Denver Road," "Beaver Creek Cut-off," "Beaver Creek Road," "Bijou Creek Road," "Bijou Creek Cut-off," "Denver & Bijou Creek Cut-off Wagon Road," "Great Express Route," or sometimes generically as the "toll-road" or "cut-off."

A debate raged over whether the old road along the river or the new cut-off was the best route and every traveler had to make a choice at the Junction based on information passed along the trail. After arriving in Denver, many travelers assessed the route taken. One report, headlined "Pike's Peak Humbug" reported the cut-off as being a "full NINETY MILES LONG, SANDY, Minus Water, save what is alkalized, and is in fact, a nuisance and a humbug[241]!" Another report in the *Western Mountaineer* from Dr. Higinbotham condemned the cut- off:

> ...the road is almost entirely destitute of wood, water and grass.... One man informed us that it took him three

and a half days to accomplish the distance, with a horse team, while another horse team which he was in company with until reaching the "cut off," and which came the old road, got in a whole day in advance of him. This individual was exceedingly indignant with those who induced him to take the "cut-off," he says that what little water there is, is tainted with alkali, and that his horses were injured more by going over this road than by all the rest of the journey out here.... Our advice to emigrants is to avoid that route entirely if they wish to save their teams....[242]

To make matters worse, the Cut-off was a toll-road. Each wagon drawn by two animals was charged $1.00 and 50 cents was charged for carriages drawn by one animal[243] ($1.00 in the 1860s is roughly equivalent to $25.00-$30.00 today)[244] with a 25 cent charge for each additional pair of animals. Loose stock were charged at 5 cents per head with sheep, dogs, and hogs charged at a rate of 1 cent per head. Riders on mules were charged 10 cents[245].

The Cut-off trail began at the Junction, near where the city of Fort Morgan now stands. There is some discrepancy as to exactly where the trail began and its exact route. Some maps place the trail head two miles west of Junction and three miles east of Bijou[246], but other sources place the start of the Cut-off between Fort Morgan and Brush[247] and still others list the trail head east of Brush near Beaver Creek[248]. The disagreement partially stems from the variability of the route. The cut-off trail was also not as clear as the river route and it was easy to become lost. Frank Root, a messenger for the Overland stage traveled the route frequently and yet even he

reported become lost when traveling at night[249]. Reverend T.
K. Tyson had a similar experience along the Cut-off from
Denver in 1865:

>...the night grew intensely dark and a steady rain set
>in. It soon became impossible to see our way, but think-
>ing the horse could be trusted to keep the road, we
>persisted in pushing on notwithstanding the darkness and
>the rain. From the roughness of our way we eventually
>became suspicious that we had missed the road and were
>*lost in the hills!*... Although greatly exhausted, Bro. Potter
>arose from his bed in the wagon and held the reins while I
>groped about over the hills to find the missing trail. Find-
>ing this, we determined to make our way toward the only
>camp-fire in sight, and which seemed like a merciful bea-
>con light to us. Not daring to trust the horses further, I
>led them by the bits, and thus we made our way to what
>proved to be the fire of fellow-campers at the very place
>where we had taken supper.... With the first gleam of
>light we pursued our way, making no stops until we
>reached the junction. I saw with no little amazement the
>winding track we had made in the night. At one place we
>had gone for several rods along the very verge of a preci-
>pice.... On reaching Cut-off Junction we found that our
>friends were being held by the military until at least a
>hundred men and sixty wagons should accumulate, and
>we were just in time to be counted in. It was in the midst
>of the great Indian outbreak of those days, and this pre-
>caution on the part of the soldiery was necessary[250].

With these difficulties in mind, some travelers left a warning: "Gentlemen and ladies will please go the old road d--d

fools will take the Cut-Off!"[251].

However, others preferred the cut-off route. A letter prais-
ing the Cut-off was published in February 1860 in the *Rocky
Mountain News*:

As a great deal has been said in favor of and against
the Denver and Beaver Creek Road — having recently
been over it — permit us through your columns to make a
fair and uninterested statement of what we believe and
know concerning it. First of
all, we will say that it is very
far superior to that of the
Platte. It avoids all those
long stretches of sand,
which are so troublesome to
the worn out teams of the
emigrant, along the old
road. There is but a single
mile of sandy ground on the
whole route, and the ma-
terial is at hand to make this
mile even as good as could
be desired. The road is not
hilly, or rough as has been
supposed, but on the contrary, passes over a beautiful
prairie country, far superior to any we supposed to exist in
this region. The grass is far superior too, and more abundant than along the Platte; indeed, we are satisfied that
there is much farming land along the route, that will
compare favorably with that of Eastern Kansas and Nebraska; while its ranching lands are not equaled by any in

Distance Table Beaver Creek & Denver City.

Platt Junction to—
Bijou creek, (wood and water)	13	miles.
Cottonwood springs (water)	9	"
Station	3	"
Living springs	16	"
Kiowa (wood and water)	8	"
Box Elder Station (wood & water)	9	"
Coal creek (wood)	9	"
Eight Mile creek (wood & water)	3	"
Denver	8	"
Total	**75**	"

Distance by old Platte road 121 miles.

TO EMIGRANTS.

The above is the Great Express Route.
By taking this road you will save 50 miles
in distance and avoid 15 miles heavy sand
and have plenty of wood and water and grass.

Rates of Toll.
One wagon drawn by two animals,	$1,00
do do do four do	1,50
Loose Stock per head	5

By order of the board of County Commissioners.

*Stations and mileage for the
Cut-off route published in the*
Rocky Mountain News, 1860.

this region. The whole prairie, commencing a few miles from Denver, is covered with a fine growth of grass. This road, we find, intersects the Platte road sixteen miles this side of the mouth of Beaver Creek; avoiding the bad road above the mouth of the Bijou; and saving, at least, fifty miles travel. Wood and water are abundant along the whole route. In no place is the emigrant without it for a greater distance than ten miles, while ordinarily it is found much oftener. In this we were greatly surprised, as we had supposed it to be a dry and barren waste. Upon the whole we are perfectly convinced that it is destined to draw nearly all the travel to and from this country...[252]

The Cut-off had some advantages over the river route, but the danger of Indian attacks remained the same regardless of the route taken. John D. Young described a harrowing journey along the Cut-off in 1860:

We stopped at the "cutoff" for dinner and I thought from talking it over so often that there was no doubt but that we would keep to the "old road". There was a vote taken upon it and to my intense surprise the vote was un-animous for the new road with the exception of myself. I told them the disadvantages and probable dangers from hostile Indians want of water and grass and fuel from be-ing deprived of what we suffered so much recently. All would not do. The runner employed by the road told them it was twenty miles shorter and that they thought would make up for all dangers and difficulties. So I had to submit but under protest and we started on our jour-ney.... We camped at evening on a small rivulet called Beaver [sic-Bijou] Creek. The water was about one inch deep and six inches wide but quiet clear and cool. There was also plenty of wood, and a little grass for our animals. We were all nice and comfortable but for the fear of Indians…. We then got up cooked breakfast and once more plunged into the Cheyenne country. About two hours after starting we noticed a single Indian on the right hand side of the road about half a mile distant. At first we did not think any thing of the occurrence but in a short time we found out from his actions that he was a spy probably sent during the night to our camp to ascertain our numbers but on account of making a circle of our wagons which we usually did in a hostile country, he was unable to see our tents or count us in any way so he waited till we got on the road when he could easily do so. We saw him at intervals of about fifteen minutes for about an hour and then he disappeared and for two hours more we could not see a single trace of an Indian. Then it being about noon we camped to provide our dinner. We made a large circle of our wagons…we grew careless, and did not set any guard. We had our dinner cooked and were sitting down on the grass to enjoy it comfortably when all at once like an electric shock came the alarming cry of Indians. Every man jumped instantly to his feet grasped his rifle and pistols and as we looked out between the wagons we saw multitudes of warriors pouring down towards us fast as their horses could gallop from all directions. It seemed as if the very hills sprang suddenly to life. On they came rushing at a gallop up to our very wagons. We then presented our rifles and they suddenly wheeled and turned away out of range of our bullets.

There they stood deliberating whether they should make an attack and there we stood fifty men opposed to more than a thousand of those wide devils the "Comanche" of Kansas. I seen some very white faces among our party but the set teeth and firm grasp on the rifles showed that it was not from cowardice as every man was resolved to fight desperately and before he would lose his scalp to stop the howlings of five or six of the infernal hounds. Each party maintained their position for about two hours without any hostile demonstration from the Indians. We then considered that they would besiege us till night and as we had no defenses they could fall upon us with every advantage in their favor. This would not suit us at all. If we had to fight we would rather have it come in daylight...so ten of our number brought in our horses harnessed them up to the wagons and made all ready for a start. The other forty still kept the rifle on the cock.... [W]e divided ourselves half marching on each side of the wagons with our rifle in hand and pistols and knives in

Indians attacking corral, published in Dangers of the Trail *in 1865.*

hand ready for action. The Indians now pressed very closely on to us sometimes so close that we should present our guns at them they would go off again to a considerable distance. They tried to throw us off our guard by pretending that they were not on the "warpath" and offering to trade moccasins buffalo robes and buckskins…. Things continued in the same shape for the next two hours the Indians following us but keeping a respectable distance away. Sometimes…they would rush towards us with whoops and yells and we would expect that our hour had come. They made this feint two or three times…. It was within two hours of sundown and we were afraid they would follow us till night and we resolved to make a charge on them fire a volley and either drive them off or bring on an engagement. Just as we were ready to do this they gave two or three yells and rushed over the bluffs and out of our sight. In five minutes there was not an Indian to be seen….[253]

In 1864, at the height of the Indian troubles along the South Platte, the military ordered that all mail be taken along the Cut-off route which was shorter and easier to defend[254] making Junction even more important and likely leading to the establishment of the fort on this site.

Telegraph

The Pacific Telegraph Act passed by congress in 1860 called for a company to construct the first transcontinental telegraph under government subsidy. Hiram Sibley of Western Union telegraph company won the bid and began to build. To complete the project, Western Union formed two outside companies; the Overland Telegraph Company started from California and built east to Salt Lake and the Pacific Telegraph Company built west from Omaha[255]. The route

Laying telegraph across the plains, in Echoes from the Rocky Mountains.

chosen was that of the Pony Express, along the Platte River to Julesburg and then north along the Oregon Trail. By October of 1861, the two coasts were linked by telegraph wire[256] - but yet again, the residents of Denver had been bypassed.

In 1861, Edward Creighton of the Pacific Telegraph Company proposed a branch line to the citizens of Denver along the South Platte River from Julesburg. The citizens of Denver, not the government would pay for the line. At first, the citizens refused, but demand became so heavy that the citizens of Denver, along with the gold mining cities of Central City, Black Hawk, and Golden, agreed to the contract, raising $35,000 to cover the cost of construction. The telegraph went up at a rate of 15 miles of line per day, a phenomenal speed[257] between August and October of 1863, taking the Cut-off route at the Junction[258]. The cost to send a telegram was also phenomenal. A telegram to New York was $9.10 for 10 words and to Chicago or St. Louis the cost was $7.50[259]. This was equivalent to $130 to $160 in 2010.

Telegraph offices were established approximately 50 miles apart at Valley Station (Sterling), Junction (Fort Morgan), and Living Springs (near Denver)[260]. John W. Ford, who would later report on the massacre of Custer's forces at Little Bighorn[261], was hired as the telegraph operator at Junction and John Haines was at Valley Station. These men were responsible not only for sending messages along the line, but keeping the line active – no easy undertaking in the vast prairie. Telegraph poles would come down during storms and the sandy soil did not serve to anchor the poles well, a buffalo rubbing up against a pole could bring down the line. Later, Indians would purposefully tear down the line[262]. During the Indian Wars of the 1860s, telegraph operators along the line became reporters for the *Rocky Mountain News,* sending eye-witness reports to Denver[263].

This was an active time in the history of Fort Morgan, thousands of settlers traveled through, the telegraph was being built along with buildings for a military fort, and all around there was the threat of attack from the Cheyenne. The west was coming alive and Fort Morgan lay at a crossroads, a junction in a geographical as well as an historical sense. This was a time and a place where the west would change. What happened at the Junction was happening all over the west, and the events were a part of the west – a reaction to what was happening across the country.

∞

Chapter 6

Soldiers & Indians

The town of Fort Morgan is named after a short-lived military instillation built on the site. The fort was in operation from 1864-1868 during the height of the Indian Wars. The fort was never directly attacked by the warring Cheyenne, but soldiers stationed at the fort were responsible for protecting the South Platte River Road and skirmished with the Indians on numerous occasions.

The first soldiers in the area however, were not stationed at Fort Morgan, but near Fremont's Orchard at Camp Sanborn. Soldiers from this camp began the conflict that would lead to the Sand Creek Massacre and nearly a decade of fighting. Later the camp was moved to a more central location along the trail referred to simply as "Junction" or "Junction Station" in military communications of the time after the telegraph station located on the site. The camp continued to be called Junction though the official name became Camp

Wardwell. In 1865, a permanent fort was built which was first called Fort Wardwell and then in 1866, renamed Fort Morgan.

1861-1863: Rumblings

The building of the fort was a direct reaction to the mounting tension between the Cheyenne, Arapaho and white emigrants, tens of thousands of them, flooding into the area on the way to the gold fields of the Rocky Mountains and the growing town of Denver. Freight rumbled across the prairie with supplies for new settlements and some emigrants decided to settle along the route to set up hotels and stores, selling to passing travelers. All this was happening in the middle of prime buffalo hunting ground - land that by government decree belonged to the Cheyenne and Arapaho. The lands granted to the Indians in the Treaty of Fort Laramie in 1851 seemed to be at the time worthless, part of the "Great American Desert." In 1858 when gold was discovered in the Rocky Mountains, the government found that all routes to the gold fields led through Indian territory - the land was no longer worthless.

In 1859, the people living in what later would become Colorado formed a provisional government under the name of Jefferson Territory, but the territorial government was not recognized by the United States as it was still then a part of Indian land[264,265]. A new treaty was needed. The Treaty of Fort Wise signed on February 18, 1861 again limited Indian land. The Cheyenne and Arapaho agreed to give up their lands in what is now northeastern Colorado along the South Platte River and settle on a reservation along the Arkansas

River further south. Peaceful chiefs such as Black Kettle and White Antelope signed this treaty, but not all Cheyenne and Arapaho were happy about giving up their favorite hunting grounds to the whites. For the most part, the tribes ignored the Treaty of Fort Wise and continued to hunt along the South Platte River; moving freely across the plains of Colorado. Later, the tribes would argue the treaty had been a trick and was not endorsed by the tribes.

Just ten days after the Treaty of Fort Wise was signed, Colorado became a territory (February 28, 1861) due mainly to the growing number of white settlers flooding onto Indian lands hoping to strike gold. In June of 1861, William Gilpin, territorial Governor and Superintendent of Indian Affairs in the Colorado Territory, reported that Cheyenne and Arapaho frequently raided the settled regions of Colorado to kill cattle, steal horses, beg and threaten the settlers[266].

In 1862, John Evans became the second governor of the Colorado Territory and began making a bid for statehood. This required more white settlers, settlers who might be frightened away by the Indians. But the settlers were nervous and the Indians were bitter. Governor Evans knew that so long as the Indians were working in small bands, there would be no serious threat to the settlers, but if the tribes were to unite, there could be a full-scale war. He decided to meet with the Indians and sent for the chiefs of a friendly Arapaho band camped near Fremont's Orchard. The chiefs, including Left Hand, met with the Governor and confirmed that the Sioux, Cheyenne, and Arapaho had met and planned to meet again to discuss the situation with the whites[267]. Left Hand reported that many of the Indians were in favor of a war to drive the whites off their lands[268]. Evans warned the chiefs that a war with the whites would likely be a war of extermination for the Indians[269]. Governor Evans then set up talks with the various chiefs from the Cheyenne, Arapaho, and Sioux sending El-bridge Gerry, a trader and an Indian interpreter with a ranch west of Fremont's Orchard, to collect the tribes for a conference. Though he was ultimately unsuccessful, Elbridge Gerry reported his attempt to bring the various chiefs to a conference noting the growing dissatisfaction of the Indians:

> ...[B]y kindness and persuasion...I obtained a positive assurance that their chiefs and headmen, as delegates, should meet.... I proceeded to the Beaver creek, the place where the delegation promised to meet me, arriving there...but found no Indians.... I took the course towards the place where I had left them at their village.... Their numbers had been increased by the arrival of other bands until they numbered two hundred and forty lodges. I called the chiefs together to arrange for our journey.... They then informed me that they could not come to the council, because their children were dying so fast with whooping cough.... [T]hey desired to maintain friendly relations with the whites, but that they would not make any treaty to cede any of their lands until the whole nation north and south were called together to see and hear for themselves.... They said that the treaty of Fort Wise was a swindle; that they who signed it did not understand it.... [T]hey did not want to leave their hunting grounds, and would not.... They admitted that the whites had taken the country on the South Platte, and they did not expect to recover it....[270]

Fearing attacks, Governor Evans wrote to E. M. Stanton, Secretary of War asking for more troops and weapons and permission to raise a militia:

[A]n alliance between the Sioux, Cheyenne, Kioways, Comanche, Apache, and a portion of the Arapahoe tribes of Indians, are of such a character that, taken in connexion with the extensive depredations recently committed on the settlers of Colorado Territory by a portion of these Indians, I am forced to apprehend serious difficulties early in the coming spring. 1st I therefore ask that our military force be not further weakened by the withdrawal of troops from the border. 2d That the first cavalry of Colorado be armed with carbines, their present arms (sabres and pistols) being but poorly adapted to the wants of Indian warfare. 3d That authority be given to the commander of the district to call out the militia of Colorado.... 4th That the troops be stationed at proper intervals along the great routes of travel across the plains, along the Platte and Arkansas rivers, through the country occupied in common by the tribes referred to.... An alliance of several thousand warriors, beginning on the sparse settlements at various points along our extended frontier, as the wild savages propose to do, might sweep off our settlers by thousands, and devastate a large part of our settlements...[271]

The Governor of the Colorado Territory was preparing for war.

1864: Massacres

Governor Evans' predictions of conflicts between the whites and the Indians would soon come true; though it is difficult to know how much was self-fulfilling prophesy. Governor Evans and the U. S. Military expected a fight with the Indians and therefore every minor incident had the potential to explode into a battle. The first battle would be 20 miles west of the present town of Fort Morgan, just north of Fremont's Orchard; a battle that would eventually escalate to the Sand Creek Massacre in November of 1864 and the retaliation by the Indians in January of 1865.

Battle at Fremont's Orchard April, 1864

In the early years of the Colorado gold rush, there was virtually no military presence along the South Platte River Road; the nearest troops were located at Fort Kearny (near Lincoln, Nebraska), Fort Laramie (Wyoming), or Camp Weld (near Denver) – the settlers were on their own.

In January 1864, Company H of the 1st Colorado Cavalry was ordered to Fremont's Orchard approximately 20 miles west of the Junction (Fort Morgan) on the South Platte River Road under the command of Captain George L. Sanborn[272]. Soldiers in Company H were seasoned veterans who had seen action in the New Mexico Territory during the Battle of Glorieta Pass (also known as the Gettysburg of the West). In April, 150 additional troops of Company C under the command of Captain Joseph C. Davidson and 2nd Lieutenant Clark Dunn, joined Company H at Camp Sanborn[273]. The camp was called Camp Sanborn, likely named for its commanding officer as mobile units of the time sometimes were. It was from Camp Sanborn, the Indian wars of the mid-1860s would begin.

On April 12, 1864, a company of about 20 soldiers under

the command of 2nd Lieutenant Clark Dunn set out from Camp Sanborn to find a group of Cheyenne who reportedly stole stock from a local rancher by the name of W. D. Ripley (likely William Riley[274] rather than Ripley). Accounts of that day vary, but in the end, a battle ensued. Lieutenant Dunn reported on the incident from Camp Sanborn on April 18, 1864 already aware of the possibility that his acts could lead to war:

> … [Left] Camp Sanborn, April 12, 1864, to take from the Indians stock consisting of horses stolen by them

U. S. Calvary chasing Indians, 1876.

> from ranchmen in the vicinity of Camp Sanborn, &c., started at daylight, crossing the Platte, and dividing my command, and searching the bluffs on the south side a greater part of the day…. [O]n coming out of the sand hills, I discovered the Indians on the north side of the river, evidently intending to steal a herd of horses and mules grazing near Fremont's Orchard, which belonged to the quartermaster at Denver…. I immediately ordered the gallop and soon intercepted them from the herd… Mr. Ripley…said that they were the Indians, and pointing to

the herd said there was his stock. Feeling the great responsibility that was resting upon me, and not desiring to bring about an Indian war by being the first aggressor, I dismounted, walked forward to meet their chief, and tried to obtain the stock without any resort to violence. After requesting the chief to return the stock, who replied only by a scornful laugh, I told him I would be compelled to disarm his party, at the same time reaching forward as if to take the arms from one of the Indians, when they immediately commenced firing. I ordered my men to return the fire, and after a short time they fled, and I pursued them about 15 miles, when, finding that my horses would soon be worthless in the pursuit, I started toward Camp Sanborn.... My command with me and engaged in the skirmish with the Indians numbered only 15 men, of whom 4 men were wounded, 2 mortally and 2 severely.... [W]e killed some 8 or 10 of the Indians and wounded about 12 or 15 more....[275]

The events of this day would receive no small attention after the Sand Creek Massacre. Many, when asked about the events leading to the massacre, started with Dunn's Battle at Fremont's Orchard. Lieutenant Dunn himself testified about the events under oath a year later and his testimony varies from the original report, especially in reference to the battle line the Indians purportedly formed:

> ...My orders from Captain Sanborn were to recapture the stock taken by them, disarm the Indians, and bring them prisoners to Camp Sanborn. The party of Indians that were driving the stock were driving it very rapidly towards the bluffs when I came in sight of them again, af-

ter crossing the river.... [W]hen I halted my command, and wheeled into line towards the Indians. The Indians also formed in line. They were then about five hundred yards from me down the Platte. I then detailed four men to go with Mr. Ripey in pursuit of the stock, with instructions to get the stock if they could and bring it back without making a fight. I then rode out about one hundred and fifty (150) yards in front of my command and requested that one or two of the Indians come out that I might talk with them. They paid no attention, but marched forward in line to where I was, with their bows strung. My men called to me to come back, that the Indians would kill me; I returned to my command.... The Indians came up to my command with me. I found that my men had their revolvers drawn. I ordered them to return them and dismount, and endeavor to take the arms from the Indians. As soon as they were dismounted the Indians fired upon us. I immediately ordered my men to fire on them in return and mount. We had an engagement there; it must have lasted between half and three quarters of an hour. I had four men wounded, and killed quite a number of the Indians....[276]

The four soldiers injured in the battle were Privates John G. Brandely, John Crosby, Andrew J. Beard (or Baird), and R. E. McBride. Brandley died the morning of the fifteenth and Beard died that afternoon[277].

The Cheyenne had a different report of the Battle, which was told to a half-breed trader by the name of George Bent:

After spending a quiet winter on Beaver Creek, Mad Wolf, along with Little Chief, Bull Telling Tales, Wolf

Coming Out, Bear Man, and ten others, started north to raid in Crow country. As they neared the South Platte they rounded up four mules that had strayed from a white man's herd. Whites were trespassers, unwelcome strangers in this land. The Dog Men thought nothing of appropriating the animals for their own use; the whites owed them this much. That same evening, however, an angry rancher entered their camp, motioning that the mules belonged to him and he wanted them back. The Dog Men made him understand that although they were willing to return the lost animals, they expected a reward for their trouble. Then they sent the white man away, telling him to return the next day with suitable presents. Early the next morning, April 12, the Cheyennes slowly approached the South Platte River. Suddenly, one of them shouted out: "*Ve-ho-e!* Soldiers coming!" Riding hard, fifteen or twenty bluecoats, their pistols drawn, formed in line of battle. The warriors jumped off their slow pack animals and quickly mounted their fleet war ponies, then turned to face the soldiers. A trooper shouted to them, but none of the Cheyennes could understand him. Finally, an officer rode forward, signing that the Indians should throw down their weapons. But before the Dog Men could respond, the soldiers opened fire. Three warriors fell: Mad Wolf, wounded in the hip; Bear Man, shot twice; and Wolf Coming Out, hit in the leg. The lead soldier leveled his revolver and charged Bull Telling Tales, who shot an arrow straight through the man's body, the iron point protruding from his back. As the soldier lay on the ground, Bull Telling Tales sent a second arrow through his heart, then dismounted and cut off his head. At this, the soldiers stampeded in wild retreat. The warriors shot down another man whose horse lagged behind the others.... As proof of the fight and his coup, Bull Telling Tales passed around a blood-stained uniform coat, as well as a pocket watch, pistol, and fieldglass[278].

The Cheyenne account varies from that of Lieutenant Dunn's in a number of ways. The Indians reported collecting stray animals and negotiating with the rancher before the battle. At this time, there were few fences and it is likely stock sometimes wandered away to be collected by passing emigrants or Indians. But as one source noted, "men who had been around the country said that every time a horse or cow strayed out of sight, a greenhorn lost his head and blamed it on the Indians[279]." So, it is possible the Indians recovered the stock without "stealing" them. The ranchman may have involved the military in an attempt to recover his stock without having to reward the Indians. The military account paints the Cheyennes as the aggressors and in the Cheyenne account, the military charged without warning. It is possible that that the fault lay on both sides; the military attempting to take weapons away from the Cheyenne may have been misinterpreted as a hostile act and the Cheyenne responded accordingly to protect their own safety.

In any case, the Battle at Fremont's Orchard signaled the start of the war with the Cheyenne. Over the coming months, Indian would raid along the South Platte River and the military response escalated quickly. This was just the opportunity the military needed to take care of the Indians.

Chasing Indians

Lieutenant Dunn had returned to Camp Sanborn after the Battle at Fremont's Orchard without the sought for stock. So, the following day, a detachment under Lieutenants Dunn and Chase along with Elbridge Gerry, a local ranchman serving as guide, set off to recover the missing stock[280]. But the weather worsened and snow made following the trail impossible and they again returned to Camp Sanborn without having encountered either Indians or cattle[281].

That night, a report came into Camp Sanborn that there had been an Indian attack below Junction at Beaver Creek and two men had been killed[282]. Lieutenants Dunn and Chase set off again with 30 men in pursuit of the raiding Indians. From Camp Sanborn, Dunn's troops went to Bijou Ranch, then to Dry Creek (possibly Badger Creek), and finally to the Junction Ranch where Sam Ashcraft joined the soldiers as a guide[283]. From the Junction, the party went to the ranch on Beaver Creek where the herders were supposed to have been killed, but Dunn found no signs of a struggle, though they did secure about 40 head of cattle[284]. Following Beaver Creek, Dunn found an abandoned Indian camp[285], but at this point, the trail went cold and the soldiers again returned to Camp Sanborn without encountering any Indians or stolen cattle.

After the Battle at Fremont's Orchard, the military began to take the situation in the Fort Morgan area seriously and sent Major Jacob Downing to Camp Sanborn with orders to "...take charge of and give directions in person to the movements against the Indians, and see to it that they are appropriately chastised for their outlawry....[286]" Major Downing arrived at Camp Sanborn on April 18th initially reporting: "...I do not think there is any more danger of Indian depredations at present"[287]. But Major Downing was wrong. Reports of Indian troubles along the South Platte route began flooding into Camp Sanborn. On the 19th, reports were received that a ranch on Beaver Creek had been attacked as well as Morrison's Ranch and another ranch near Junction[288,289] and that Indians were "despoiling property, getting drunk and raising the mischief generally[290]." Dowling immediately took off after the Indians with 60 men searching for the marauding Indians, but found none. Like Lieutenants Dunn and Chase before, he returned without encountering but one Indian[291]. On April 25th, Lieutenants Dunn and Chase again gave chase to a band of Cheyenne who had reportedly stolen horses from Moore and Kelley's Ranch (American Ranch) east of the Junction. They pursued the Cheyenne south for about 25 miles, but having reached a small village of eleven lodges near the Republican River found it abandoned. At this point, possibly fueled by frustration, the Lieutenants destroyed the abandoned village[292].

Panic was taking over in the area and the military was chasing shadows. The settlers may have been frightened, but there is very little evidence that the Indians were escalating attacks. Encounters between whites and Indians had been brief and the injuries mostly minor or unconfirmed. Based on very little direct information, Major Downing decided that all Cheyenne were responsible for the acts of a few:

> I have learned that these depredations have been perpetuated by the Cheyennes, and possibly a few Kiowas...and that the other tribes are peaceably disposed,

and that this party cannot consist of more than 40 or 50 men.... It has been stated that the Cheyennes as a tribe discountenanced the depredations of these men. However that may be, I have as yet been unable to find any of them, and if I find any will punish them for the depredations already committed by members of their tribe....

I have just learned that there are a few lodges of Cheyennes at Gerry's [ranch].... Captain Sanborn, sent him word to notify these Cheyennes to leave immediately, as well as all others who may be on the river, as I intend punishing them for depredations committed by members of this tribe if found on the river. My object is to protect the immigration and get as many together as possible...a command can go to their village and compel them to surrender the depredators, or clean them out[293].

Major Downing was intent on clearing the South Platte of Indians, even if innocent Cheyenne were killed. He hadn't found any Indians so far, but he soon would.

First Blood

The Battle at Fremont's Orchard was likely a product of misunderstanding and fear. The Cheyenne who took the stock likely believed a reward for finding and keeping the errant animals was rightfully theirs and Lieutenant Dunn was under orders to disarm the Indians and likely misinterpreted the situation. But what happened next, both on the side of the U.S. military and the Cheyenne, was no misunderstanding. Fear had escalated to hate.

It is clear from Downing's correspondences of late April that he intended to find and punish the Cheyenne - any

Cheyenne. Punish them for what is unclear. There seems to be an underlying feeling that the Cheyenne had bested the soldiers at Fremont's Orchard and chasing rumors over the next two weeks must have been maddening. Downing centralized his troops at Junction and American Ranch[294], east of Camp Sanborn and it was from here, Downing at last found the Indians he sought.

The first wholesale massacre of an Indian village was not at Sand Creek (which would take place in November), but 60 miles north of the South Platte River at Cedar Bluffs. The name Cedar Bluffs does not appear on modern maps, but it is likely the battle took place on the Cedar River located in the Northeast corner of the Pawnee National Grasslands. At this place, 5 lodges of Cheyenne (approximately 50 Indians) including Bull Rib, Lame Shawnee and Big Wolf camped with their families were attacked by a detachment of soldiers commanded by Major Downing[295]. On May 3, 1864, Major Jacob Downing sent a quick report: "Had a fight with the Cheyennes to-day.... Send me more troops; I need them. The war has commenced in earnest....[296]" Later that day, Major Downing expanded on his report and described how he tracked this particular Cheyenne village:

> ...[May 1st] I captured an Indian in this vicinity whom I supposed to be a Cheyenne spy, and ordered him shot, but upon being informed that he was a half-breed and part Sioux, concluded to spare him upon condition that he lead me to an encampment of Cheyennes, whom I had previously learned had camped near me and committing depredations on the whites.... [A]t about 6 a.m. reached their [Cheyenne's] camp in a cañon near Cedar

Bluffs. Found them prepared for a fight, and I immediately commenced business by intercepting them from their stock, horses, &c., and detailing 10 men to take charge of it, then dismounting Companies Second, Third, and Fourth, to fight on foot…. After a few shots the Indians retreated to a cañon, naturally fortified, and while holding it had great odds against us. I attempted by skirmishing to drive them from it, but my command was too small and their position and numbers greatly against us. I then directed the men to confine their efforts to killing as many Indians as possible, which after a fight of about three hours, they succeeded in killing about 25 Indians and wounding about 30 or 40 more…. If in this affair I had had two mountain howitzers I could have annihilated the entire band. I think artillery will be necessary in all future operations…. In this affair I lost 1 man killed, [Samuel E.] Isner, of Company C, and 1 wounded, Wilcox [either Isaac or Willis], of Company C…. Though I think we have punished them pretty severely in this affair, yet I believe now it is but the commencement of war with this tribe, which must result in exterminating them[297].

There is nothing in the history of the incidents with the Indians that warrants the strong feelings evident in Downing's report. There had been isolated raids along the South Platte River, but nothing that would warrant plans of genocide. In this instance, the military sought out and attacked a Cheyenne village containing women and children, a village that there was no evidence against, no confirmation that anyone in the village had actually committed any theft, vandalism, or murder. Extermination of innocent Cheyenne for the mischief of only a few seems strong, but this report clearly exemplifies the feelings of the times. The U.S. military appeared set on a course of massacre.

A month later, the Indians struck back. On June 11th, Nathan W. Hungate's ranch on Box Elder Creek, thirty miles southeast of Denver was attacked and his wife, Ellen, and his children, Florence aged 6 and Laura aged 3, were killed[298,299]. A first-hand report was sent by the traders who found the carnage. In this report, the Indians responsible were identified as Cheyenne, though other accounts list the attackers as Arapaho[300,301]:

> ...We left this town [Denver] yesterday morning, upon information received that about 40 to 50 mules...had been stampeded in the boldest manner in broad daylight by Indians belonging to the Cheyenne tribe. Mr. Brown's mules were stampeded from Coal Creek, on the main highway from here to the Missouri River, and only 13 miles from Denver. This fact is mentioned to show the boldness of the operation.
>
> Ascertaining that that Indians, after taking a northeasterly direction (for the purpose of misleading pursuit, probably), had turned, and crossed the road near Box Elder Creek, we proceeded to that locality, and thence up that creek about 6 miles, where we met Mr. Johnson coming down, who imparted the startling intelligence that the family of a ranchman named Hungate, living a few miles farther up, had been brutally murdered by Indians, the ranch burned to the ground, and about 30 head of horses and mules driven off. The massacre had occurred on the day previous, some time shortly after noon,

and Mr. Johnson had just assisted a party [from] the mill above in removing the bodies of the murdered woman and children. His statement was substantially as follows;

The party from the mill and himself, upon reaching the place, has found it in ruins and the house burned to the ground. About 100 yards from the desolated ranch they discovered the body of the murdered woman and her two dead children, one of which was a little girl of four years and the other an infant. The woman had been stabbed in several places and scalped, and the body bore evidences of having been violated. The two children had their throats cut, their heads being nearly severed from their bodies. Up to this time the body of the man had not been found, but upon our return down the creek, on the opposite side, we found the body. It was horribly mutilated and the scalp torn off.... [T]he settlers in all that region of country are much alarmed, and justly so; and unless the military in force proceed against the Indians at once all the ranches will be deserted, and much suffering probably ensue[302].

The news reached Denver, frightening and enraging the population. The mutilated bodies of the Hungates were brought to Denver and put on display. The Denver City *Weekly Commonwealth* reported "A Horrible Sight!:"

...It was a most solemn sight indeed, to see the mutilated corses, [*sic*] stretched in the stiffness of death, upon that wagon bed, first the father, Nathan Hungate, about 30 years of age, with his head scalped and his either cheeks and eyes chopped in as with an axe or tomahawk. Next lay his wife, Ellen, with her head also scalped through from ear to ear. Along side of her lie two small children, one at her right arm and one at her left, with their throats severed completely, so that their handsome little heads and pale, innocent countenances had to be stuck on, as it were, to preserve the humanity of form. Those that perpetrate such unnatural, brutal butchery as this ought to be hunted to the farthest bounds of these broad plains and burned to the stake alive.... The deepest feeling pervaded the people of town to-day as they returned from viewing the mangled bodies of this cruelly murdered family. Let us take warning and keep prepared for the future, both in town and in the ranches through the territory, where Indians are wont to visit or pass by.... The men are all ready to join in the pursuit of the atrocious murderers of their neighbors, and will render valuable service in this time of need[303].

The publicity of the Hungate murders may have been politically motivated, trying to move the population to action against the Indians[304]. If this was the plan, it worked. The men of Denver and the mining districts began to cry out for blood and were ready to join a newly forming militia.

Immediately following the Hungate murders, troops were pulled off the South Platte River Road to help guard Denver. Captain Joseph C. Davidson and Lieutenant Dunn, stationed at Camp Sanborn were ordered to find the Indians responsible and not take any prisoners[305,306]. Later in the month Dunn, promoted to Captain following the Battle at Fremont's Orchard, was removed with the rest of Company C to Russellville, a camp near Denver[307]. Almost immediately, the military warned that sending troops to Denver would leave the South Platte River Road exposed[308]. Governor Evans made his first request for permission to raise a militia just three days after Nathan Hungate and his family were murdered[309] and the suggestion to place a camp at the junction (later Fort Morgan) was made a few days later[310].

Indian Raids

After the May attack on the Cheyenne village and the Hungate murders, raids along the South Platte River escalated. An estimated 40 people were killed and nearly a million dollars of property was destroyed[311,312]. Likely, some reports of Indian attacks were exaggerated or misattributed, but there were attacks by bands of Indians, Cheyenne mostly but with the help of Arapaho, Kiowa and Sioux. The battles along the South Platte River were relatively small skirmishes, but fear spread and brought the emigration of the whites to a halt.

The summer raids weren't localized to the Fort Morgan area, but occurred all along the route from Junction through Julesburg and east along the Platte River[313], an essential supply line for Denver314. July 17th was a particularly active day in the Fort Morgan area with Cheyenne attacking Fremont's Orchard, Junction Ranch, Junction Station, Murray's Station, Bijou Ranch, Beaver Creek Station, Godfrey's Ranch, and the American Ranch. John W. Ford, the telegraph operator at the Junction, sent this report to the *Rocky Mountain News*:

> Another raid was made by the Indians last night. They first made their appearance at Bijou Ranch, on the cut-off, about 85 miles from Denver, killing two immigrants and wounding one, probably mortally. They also

Indians attack stage. Published in Massacres of the Mountains, *1886.*

run off 17 head of horses and mules. This same band came directly down the road, and run off all the Stage Company's stock at this place [Junction], and all the station-keeper's horses, two miles below, at the Junction Ranch, kept by Mr. Reynolds. They ran off sixty head of horses from Murray's, the first station below the Junction. They also run off all the stage stock, and killed fifteen head of Murray's finest cattle. The soldiers from Living Springs left the Junction this morning at two o'clock and overtook them about twenty-five miles southeast of here on Beaver creek. Only five Indians were with the stock. These five Indians were killed and nearly all the stock recovered. None of the soldiers were harmed. All of the stage stock was recovered....The women and children are all leaving for Denver. Dead cattle, full of arrows, are lying in all directions. A general Indian war is anticipated. The soldiers under Lieut. Chase, about twenty in number, are here, recruiting their horses. They will start down the road this evening. The excitement is intense....

The stage has just come down and the passengers say that they found two men killed and scalped on the road at

Beaver creek, about a mile about the station. There were eleven Indians came to the station while they were there, and took a pony from the stage barn....

The Indians were lurking in the bluffs between the Junction and Beaver creek.... In the course of the afternoon they killed three men. One of them belonged to a government train, and he was killed near the Junction. The other two were killed eleven miles below. They were out in the bluffs near Beaver Creek hunting cattle..... One horse was stolen from Valley Station last night, but no Indians have been seen in that neighborhood today. There is good reason to believe they have skedaddled[315].

As noted in the above report, the Indians were not just running off stock and attacking ranchers, they were also attacking trains of emigrants on the road. Six Cheyenne reportedly attacked the camp of H. H. and Battea Wentworth who were freighting goods from Topeka to Denver. H. H. Wentworth told the *Rocky Mountain News* about the raid:

...about noon, a party of six Cheyennes dashed in between their wagons and horses.... The horses stampeded...they next plundered the wagon of a family of emigrants camped near.... Following down the road, they attacked four freight wagons on their way up.... Passing the first wagon without molestation, they killed the drivers of the next two and drove the teams away. The young men killed were Wardman Jones, of Golden City, aged 14 years and Philip Rodgers, of Iowa, aged 17. After killing them, the savages scalped and mutilated their bodies most horribly. The driver of the fourth wagon was shot through the body with an arrow, but will probably recover…. The bodies of the murdered boys were brought to the Bijou ranch and properly interred. The emigrants and freighters collected at the ranch and prepared for defense…. When the Indians first appeared there were but six in the party, and their dash into the camp was the first intimation of their presence…there were sixteen seen. When they attacked the wagons, two miles down the road, the number is reported at thirty…. At Junction station the Indians drove off seven horses…. From Murray's they took ten…. From the Junction ranch, belonging to Reynolds & Ashcraft, they took sixty-eight head of horses…[316]

The attacking Indians appeared to be building up to a massive raid along the South Platte River. The raid was planned for August 21st, but two Cheyenne warriors with loyalties to Elbridge Gerry and his Cheyenne wife, warned him and he in turn warned Governor Evans:

Mr. Gerry states that two Cheyennes, Long Chin and Man-shot-by-a-bee, both chiefs and old men, came to his house about ten o'clock last night to tell him to take his stock away from the river. Mr. Gerry lives at the mouth of Crow creek, seven miles below Latham, and sixty-seven miles from Denver. They stated that there were between eight hundred and one thousand Indians of the Apache, Comanche, Kioways, Cheyenne, and Arapahoe warriors (no lodges with them) at the Point of Rocks, on Beaver creek, about one hundred and twenty-five miles from Denver; that in two nights they would make a raid on the river; they would separate in parties, one to strike the river about Fort Lupton, another about Latham, and one at the

Junction; that one party had already started for the head of Cherry creek, and still another to the mouth of the Fontaine qui Bouille pueblo. Mr. Gerry judges that they intended to keep their rendezvous at the Point of Rocks, on the Beaver, and take there their stolen stock....

These two Indians told Mr. Gerry that nearly all the old men were opposed to the war, but the young men could not be controlled; they were determined to sweep the Platte and the country as far as they could; they know that if the white men follow up the war for two or three years they would get rubbed out, but meanwhile they would kill plenty of whites[317].

Governor Evans immediately sent out the newly formed militia, the 3rd Colorado Cavalry, to warn the settlers and ready themselves for the attack[318]. However, there were no reports of Indian attacks in the coming weeks; either the Indians were deterred by the military presence or the organized plans of the attackers were exaggerated – possibly with the motive increasing militia volunteers.

Fear was increasing and the government responded by placing more troops along the trail, but the question was whether a private company, Ben Holladay's Overland Stage line, deserved federal protection. On August 10, the Overland Stage Company announced that it would no longer carry mail between Julesburg and Denver without armed protection and on August 16th the order was given to stop booking passengers on the Overland Stage until safety along the route could be improved. From mid-August to mid-September the trail was closed and no mail reached Denver[319]. The mail accumulating in Denver and Atchison, Kansas was sent to the west and east coasts respectively to be sent along an ocean route[320] and nearly a hundred passengers were delayed at Julesburg[321]. When the line re-opened, it was with military protection and using the shorter, more easily defended Cut-off route from Junction to Denver[322] and the military took control over the trail.

Troops at the Junction

On April 21st, just a week after the Battle at Fremont's Orchard, Major Downing stationed two detachments of soldiers from Companies C & H of the 1st Colorado Cavalry at ranches near Junction Station, Lieutenant Dunn commanding one and Lieutenant George H. Chase the other[323] and he based his operations at American Ranch (Downing called it Indian Ranch)[324]. In May, troops were again sent to Junction Station under the charge of Lieutenant Murrell based on reports of a war party of Cheyenne on the road to Denver[325]. The military center of the area shifted east from Camp Sanborn to the Junction[326,327] and by September, Camp Sanborn was abandoned.

Placing troops at Junction was strategic for a number of reasons. Junction was situated equidistantly between Denver and Julesburg and was located at the point at which the Cut-off road diverged from the South Platte River Road to Denver. Further, there was a telegraph office at Junction, which allowed for quick communication. The military establishment at the Junction became part of a series of military camps established approximately 100 miles apart along the trail. From Fort Kearney camps, which later became forts, were located at Fort McPherson, Fort Rankin (later Sedgwick) near Jules-

U.S. Troops guarding Overland mail. Published in The Overland Stage to California, *1901.*

burg, and Camp Wardwell (later Morgan) at the Junction[328]. During the Indian Wars, wagons were stopped at these points and collected into trains before being allowed to continue west[329].

But the 1st Colorado Cavalry could not chase Indians, man the fort, and protect the trail, so protection for the Overland Mail was placed under the control of the District of Nebraska under the command of Brigadier General Robert B. Mitchell and the 11th Ohio Cavalry.

11th Ohio Cavalry

In May of 1862, four companies of the 11th Ohio Cavalry were deployed west to Fort Laramie to protect the Oregon and Overland Trails[330]. With the escalation of Indian attacks along the South Platte River in the summer of 1864, Company C, under the command of Captain Thomas P. Clark, moved to Fremont's Orchard to protect the Overland mail and telegraph line[331,332]. Soldiers of the 11th Ohio along with the 7th Iowa Cavalry based at Julesburg, escorted trains up and down the South Platte River Road though the summer and winter of 1864 and into 1865. In December, Chivington ordered the stage line to use the cut-off instead of continuing west to Fremont's Orchard[333] and most of the troops at Fremont's Orchard marched for Fort Collins on January 6th 1865 – just a day before the allied tribes attacked Julesburg[334]. After the attack, a detachment of Company F of the 11th Ohio Cavalry under Lieutenant Hanna was immediately ordered from Fort Collins back to Fremont's Orchard[335]. Later, the 11th Ohio Cavalry was replaced by regiments of the United States Volunteer Infantry – Galvanized Yankees – stationed not at Fremont's Orchard, but at the Junction.

Tyler's Rangers

In the summer of 1864, Governor Evans petitioned Washington for permission to recruit a militia, but until the War Department authorized a militia, Tyler's Rangers, an independent company recruited from the Black Hawk mining region and named for Captain Clinton M. Tyler, patrolled up and down the South Platte[336]. After leaving Denver on August 19th, the company marched up the Cut-off to the headwaters of Bijou Creek than to the Junction, camping at Douglas Ranche (later Murray's Ranch), on to Godfrey's Ranch and along the Platte River Road past O'Fallon Bluffs before turning back west[337]. The company was relieved of service on October 14th. Though Tyler's Rangers spent little time in the Junction area, they were credited with preventing the expected August raids at the Junction[338]. During 1864, Tyler's Rangers only briefly traveled through the Fort Morgan area, but in the spring of 1865 the company would return – this time to build a fort.

3rd Colorado Cavalry

In June of 1864, the Governor of the Colorado Territory, John Evans began petitioning the government for permission to raise a militia, but it wasn't until August that he received permission and the 3rd Colorado Cavalry was formed. The unit was a volunteer organization made up of "100 day's men" so called because their enlistment in the militia lasted for 100 days. The 3rd Colorado Cavalry was officially organized on August 20, 1864 and the last men were mustered out on December 31, 1864[339].

The 3rd Colorado Cavalry was formed in direct response to the Indian raids along the South Platte and

Poster advertising for militia volunteers. August, 1864.

the murder of the Hungate family[340]. Governor Evan's request for a militia was at first denied[341], but on August 11th, permission to raise a militia was granted by the Provost-Marshal-General[342]. Governor Evans immediately began recruiting volunteers for the militia and issued a proclamation:

> Having sent special messengers to the Indians of the plains, directing the friendly to rendezvous at Fort Lyon, Fort Larned, Fort Laramie, and Camp Collins, for safety and protection, warning them that all hostile Indians would be pursued and destroyed...they have refused to do so.... [M]ost of the Indian tribes of the plains are at war and hostile to the whites....

> I, John Evans, governor of Colorado Territory, do issue this my proclamation, authorizing all citizens of Colorado, either individually or such parties as they may organize, to go in pursuit of all hostile Indians on the plains, scrupulously avoiding those [who are friendly]...also to kill and destroy as enemies of the country wherever they may be found, all such hostile Indians.... I hereby empower such citizens, or parties of citizens, to take captive, and hold to their own private use and benefit, all the property of said hostile Indians that they may capture, and to receive for all stolen property recovered from said Indians such reward as may be deemed proper and just.... [P]arties as will organize under the militia law of the Territory for the purpose, to furnish them arms and ammunition, and to present their accounts for pay, as regular soldiers, for themselves, their horses, their subsistence and transportation.... The conflict is upon us, and all good citizens are called upon to do their duty to the

defense of their homes and families[343].

The governor also ordered the friendly Indians into the various forts for their protection, a practice appears similar to that adopted in later wars with interment camps. "Friendly" Indians who came to the forts were effectively prisoners and any Indian not choosing to be confined to a fort was under a sentence of death. It appeared the Governor had found a way to rid himself of the troublesome Indians.

Both the military under the charge of Colonel Chivington and Governor Evans likely knew exactly what type of regiment they were forming – a group of frightened citizens craving blood. These men were itching for a fight and the chance to kill Indians – any Indians, with vengeance or genocide on their mind. After meeting with peaceful Indians at Camp Weld in September, Governor Evans was heard to say to his advisers, "What shall I do with the Third Colorado Regiment if I make peace? They have been raised to kill Indians, and they must kill Indians"[344].

In August 1864, the overland trail stations at Valley Station (Sterling) and Junction Station (Fort Morgan) became military outposts manned by companies of 100-days' men[345]. Company F made up of men from Denver[346] was sent to Junction Station on September 13, 1864 under the command of Captain Edward Chase[347], one of the original gold-seekers in Colorado and known as Denver's gambling king[348]. Thomas Noel described the man:

> The first "czar" of Denver's gamblers was tall, hawk-faced Edward Chase. Chase came to Denver at the age of twenty-two in 1860. For the next half century he made it his business to organize the underworld into a voting bloc

whose support could be traded for protection of his numerous sporting houses. "Big Ed" Chase had Denver's first billiard table hauled across the plains.... Tall, immaculately dressed Ed Chase perched on a high stool with a shotgun across his elbow, surveying the room. Chase prided himself on keeping an orderly house...[349]

Ed Chase and Company F would be at the Junction for only two months. In November, the unmounted Company L made up of men from Gilpin County[350] replaced the mounted Company F at the Junction. Company F marched for Sand Creek.

Company L was under the command Captain John Freeman Phillips[351] and Major Samuel M. Logan, who oversaw the military operations along the South Platte River Road from Valley Station to the Junction[352]. The young Major Logan was legendary for tearing down a Confederate flag hoisted in Denver City during one of the first civil war protests. It is said he "climbed to the roof of the store and tore the emblem down, without opposition from the crowd assembled...[and] brought the Union spirit out in force[353]." Logan, a veteran officer from the 1st Colorado Cavalry had fought at the Battle of Glorieta Pass. He was mustered out of the 1st Colorado Cavalry in April of 1864, but joined the militia in September, serving another 100 days.

While Company L and Company K at Valley were guarding the South Platte River Road, nearly all the remaining companies of the 3rd Colorado Cavalry were massing southeast of Denver. Nearly 100 days had passed since the militia was formed and few of the soldiers had seen action, lending the regiment the nickname the "Bloodless Third[354]." But almost exactly 100 days from when the first volunteers joined the militia, the "Bloodless Third" turned into the "Bloody Third."

The Sand Creek Massacre

The Sand Creek Massacre of November 29, 1864 happened near what is now Eads, Colorado on the banks of the Big Sandy Creek, approximately 130 miles southeast of Fort Morgan. The U. S. military under the command of Colonels Chivington and Shoup attacked a peaceful Cheyenne village killing hundreds of Indians. The raids along the South Platte River in the summer of 1864 along with other confrontations between the soldiers and the Indians led to this attack and the repercussions of this attack would have a tremendous impact on Fort Morgan.

As early as May 1864, the military seemed intent on punishing the Indians - any Indians for real or perceived attacks on white emigrants along the trails. After chasing Indians for a frustrating six months, the military, under Chivington were determined to teach the savages a lesson and killed not only warriors, but women and children as well. Ironically, the Indians attacked at Sand Creek were friendly and had turned themselves into the military at Fort Lyon for protection. Major Wynkoop, a military officer known for seeking peace with the Indians, had fed them, returned some of their arms, and allowed the Indians to camp on Sand Creek for the winter[355]. There were approximately 500 Indians camped at Sand Creek, the majority being women and children[356,357,358] along with an Indian trader and some soldiers.

Of the 1,000 troops that attacked the village at Sand

Creek, 240 were veterans of the 1st Colorado Cavalry[359], the rest were the volunteer "Indian Fighters" of the 3rd Colorado Cavalry. Three of the companies involved in the massacre had recently been stationed in the Fort Morgan area: Companies C and H of the 1st Colorado Cavalry had recently been stationed at Camp Sanborn and Company F under the command of Captain Edward Chase had recently been stationed at the Junction. Chase, however, resigned his commission on November 29 – the day of the massacre and seven days short of his 100[360]. There's no mention of when or why he resigned and Chase is not mentioned in any of the subsequent reports of the battle.

Battle

The battle lasted between six and eight hours. Some of the Indians were able to escape to the bluffs along the river, but most were not so lucky. Colonel Chivington reported to Major General Curtis on December 16th providing details of the attack:

> Having ascertained that the hostile Indians had proceeded south from the Platte, and were almost within striking distance of Fort Lyon, I ordered Colonel Geo. L. Shoup, 3d regiment Colorado volunteer cavalry, (100-day service,) to proceed with the mounted men of his regiment in that direction…. The command then proceeded in a northeasterly direction, travelling all night, and at daylight of the 29th November striking Sand creek about forty (40) miles from Fort Lyon. Here was discovered an Indian village of one hundred and thirty (130) lodges, composed of Black Kettle's band of Cheyennes and eight

(8) lodges of Arapahoes, with Left Hand. My line of battle was formed with Lieutenant Wilson's battalion of the 1st regiment, numbering about 125 men, on the right, Colonel Shoup's 3d regiment, numbering about 450 men, in the centre, and Major Anthony's battalion, numbering 125 men, 1st regiment, on the left.

The attack was immediately made upon the Indian's camp by Lieutenant Wilson, who dashed forward, cutting the enemy off from their herd, and driving them out of their camp, which was subsequently destroyed. The Indians, numbering from 900 to 1,000, though taken by surprise, speedily rallied and formed a line of battle across the creek, about three-fourths of a mile above the village, stubbornly contesting every inch of ground. The commands of Colonel Shoup and Major Anthony pressed rapidly forward and attacked the enemy sharply, and the engagement became general, we constantly driving the Indians, who fell back from one position to another for five miles, and finally abandoned resistance and dispersed in all directions and were pursued by my troops until nightfall.

It may, perhaps; be unnecessary for me to state that I captured no prisoners. Between five and six hundred Indians were left dead upon the field. About five hundred and fifty ponies, mules and horses were captured, and all their lodges were destroyed, the contents of which has served to supply the command with an abundance of trophies, comprising the paraphernalia of Indian warfare and life. My loss was eight (8) killed on the field and forty (40) wounded, of which two have since died. Of the conduct of the 3d regiment (100- day service) I have to say that they well sustained the reputation of our Colorado troops for bravery and effectiveness....

Of the effect of the punishment sustained by the Indians you will be the judge. Their chiefs Black Kettle, White Antelope, One Eye, Knock Knee, and Little Robe, were numbered with the killed and their bands almost annihilated. I was shown the scalp of a white man, found in one of the lodges, which could not have been taken more than two or three days previous....

The evidence is most conclusive that these Indians are the worst that have infested the routes of the Platte and Arkansas Rivers during the last spring and summer. Amongst the stock captured were the horses and mules taken by them from Lieutenant Chase, 1st Cavalry of Colorado [near the Junction], last September; several scalps of white men and women were found in the lodges; also various articles of clothing belonging to white persons. On every hand the evidence was clear that no lick was struck amiss[361].

Chivington thought the attack a success, but other officers were horrified by the massacre. Captain Silas S. Soule refused to participate in the battle and described the gruesome attack in a letter to Major Wyncoop. Two men mentioned in the letter, John S. Smith and Private David H. Louderback of Company C of the 1st Colorado Cavalry were in the Indian camp – under military authority – to trade with the Indians.

We arrived at Black Kettles and Left Hand's Camp, at day light Lieut. Wilson with Co's. "C," "E," & "G" [1st Colorado Cavalry] were ordered in advance to cut off their herd. He made a circle to the rear and formed line 200 yds from the village, and opened fire. Poor Old John Smith and [Private David] Louderbeck [sic],

Sand creek massacre. Published in Massacres of the Mountains *, 1886.*

ran out with white flags, but they paid no attention to

them, and they ran back into their tents. Anthony then rushed up with Co's "D" "K" & "G", to within one dred yards and commenced firing. I refused to fire, and swore that none but a coward would, for by this time hundreds of women and children were coming towards us, and getting on their knees for mercy. Anthony shouted, "Kill the sons of bitches." Smith and Louderbeck came to our command, although I am confident there were 200 shots fired at them, for I heard an officer say that Old Smith and any one who sympathized with Indians, ought to be killed and now was a good time to do it. The Battery then came up in our rear, and opened on them. I took my comp'y across the Creek, and by this time the whole of the 3d [Colorado Cavalry] and the Batteries were firing into them and you can form some idea of the slaughter. When the Indians found that there was no hope for them they went for the Creek, and buried themselves in the Sand and got under the banks, and some of the bucks got their Bows and a few rifles and defended themselves as well as they could. By this time there was no organization among our troops, they were a perfect mob – every man on his own hook. My Co, was the only one that kept their formation, and we did not fire a shot. The massacre lasted six or eight hours, and a good many Indians escaped...it was hard to see little children on their knees, have their brains beat out by men professing to be civilized. One Squaw was wounded, and a fellow took a hatchet to finish her, she held her arms up to defend her, and he cut one arm off, and held the other with one hand, and dashed the hatchet through her brain. One

Squaw with her two children, were on their knees, begging for their lives, of a dozen soldiers, within ten feet of them all firing – when one succeeded in hitting the Squaw in the thigh, when she took a knife and cut the throats of both children, and then killed herself. One old Squaw hung herself in the lodges – there was not enough room for her to hang and she held up her knees and choked herself to death. Some tried to escape on the Prairie, but most of them were run down by horsemen. I saw two Indians [take] hold of one anothers hands, chased until they were exhausted, when they kneeled down, and clasped each other around the neck and were both shot together, they were all scalped, and as high as half a dozen taken from one head. They were all horribly mutilated. One woman was cut open, and a child taken out of her, and scalped. White Antelope, War Bonnet, and a number of others had Ears and Privates cut off. Squaws snatches were cut out for trophies. You would think it impossible for white men to butcher and mutilate human beings as they did there, but every word I have told you is the truth, which they do not deny.... I saved little Charley Bent. Geo Bent was killed. Jack Smith was taken prisoner, and murdered the next day in his tent by one of Dunn's Co. "E." I understand the man received a horse for doing the job....

Chivington has gone to Washington to be made a General, I suppose, and get authority to raise a nine months Reg't, to hunt Indians. He and Downing will have me cashiered, if possible.... I think they will try the same for Cramer, for he has shot his mouth off a good deal, and did not shoot his pistol off in the massacre.... Chivington reports five or six hundred killed, but there were not more than two hundred: about 140 women and children and 60 bucks [warriors]. A good many were out hunting buffalo. Our best Indians were killed. Black Kettle, One Eye, Minnemic, and Left Hand. Geo Pierce of Co "F" was killed trying to save John Smith. There was one other of the 1st killed, and nine of the 3d all through their own fault. They would get up on the edge of the bank and look over, to get a shot at an Indian under them, and get an arrow put through them....[362]

Chivington and the soldiers of the Colorado Cavalry struck a blow intended to frighten the Indians into submission and for nearly three weeks, the regiments chased the fleeing Indians across the plains. Chivington expected to return a hero and a General.

Aftermath

When the sketchy news of the battle first reached Denver, there seemed to be a general rejoicing. "Bully for the Colorado Boys!" wrote the *Rocky Mountain News*[363]. The 1st and 3rd Colorado Cavalry marched into Denver as heroes:

...The active campaign of the Third [Cavalry] has been short but brilliant. They have been taunted as the "Bloodless Third" but the record shows that they have taken prominent part in the most effective expedition against the Indians ever planned and carried out....[364]

The return of the Third Regiment boys from the victorious field of Indian warfare was the grand feature of today [December 22]. Those ten companies, (the Eleventh and twelfth of the regiment being stationed at the Junction Valley Station, on the Platte, protecting that route...) were the admired of all observers, on their entry into town this morning. Headed by the First Regiment Band, and by Colonels Chivington and Shoup, Lieut. Col. Bowen and Major Sayr, the rank and file of the "bloody Thirdsters" made a most imposing procession.... As the "bold sojer boys" passed along, the sidewalks and the corner stands were thronged with citizens saluting their old friends: and the fair sex took advantage of the opportunity, wherever they could get it, of expressing their admiration for the gallant boys who donned the regimentals for the purpose of protecting the women of the country, by ridding it of red-skins....[365]

However, the details of the massacre created public outrage and before the year was out Congress undertook an investigation of the Sand Creek Massacre.

There were strong feelings on both sides. Some felt Colonel Chivington was a hero while others saw him as a butcher. One of the witnesses against Colonel Chivington, Captain Soule, was assassinated by a Chivington supporter, Private Charles W. Squire, in April of 1865[366].

Outrage arose from the witness statements. It wasn't just that the military had attacked a peaceful Indian village killing more than a hundred women and children, but it was the savagery and mutilation accompanying the attack. And it wasn't just the volunteers of the 3rd Colorado Cavalry – the 100-days' men – who committed these atrocities, but veteran soldiers of the 1st Colorado Cavalry[367]. The Congressional Committee charged with investigating the Sand Creek Massacre issued a report in July 1865 roundly condemning ernor Evans and Colonel Chivington and those who were involved in the Sand Creek massacre:

...All the testimony goes to show that the Indians under the immediate control of Black Kettle and White Antelope of the Cheyennes, and Left Hand, of the Arapahoes, were and had been friendly to the whites, and had not been guilty of any acts of hostility or depredation.... These Indians, at the suggestion of Governor Evans and Col. Chivington, repaired to Fort Lyon, and placed themselves under the protection of Maj. Wynkoop. They were led to believe that they were regarded in the light of friendly Indians, and would be treated as such so long as they conducted themselves quietly.... The Indian camp consisted of about 100 lodges of Cheyennes, under Black Kettle, and from eight to ten lodges of Arapahoes, under Left Hand. It is estimated that each lodge contained five or more persons, and that more than one-half were women and children.

THE CHEYENNE INDIAN MASSACRE.

Report of the Committee on the Conduct of the War.

EXPOSITION OF THE SANDY CREEK AFFAIR.

Scathing Condemnation of the Perpetrators.

Col. Chivington Denounced as a Barbarian and a Murderer.

Chicago Tribune headline July 25, 1865.

Upon observing the approach of the soldiers, Black Kettle, the head chief, ran up to the top of his lodge an American flag, which had been presented to him some years before by Commissioner Greenwood, with a small white flag under it, as he had been advised to do in case he met with any troops on the prairies. Mr. Smith, the interpreter, supposing they might be strange troops, unaware of the character of the Indians encamped there, advanced from his lodge to meet them, but was fired upon, and returned to his lodge. And then the scene of murder and barbarity began--men, women and children were indiscriminately slaughtered. In a few minutes all the Indians were flying over the plain in terror and confusion. A few who endeavored to hide themselves under the bank of the creek were surrounded and shot down in cold blood, offering but feeble resistance. From the sucking babe to the old warrior, all who were overtaken were deliberately murdered. Not content with killing women and children, who were incapable of offering any resistance, the soldiers indulged in acts of barbarity of the most revolting character; such, it is to be hoped, has never before disgraced the acts of men claiming to be civilized. No attempt was made by the officers to restrain the savage cruelty of the men under their command, but they stood by and witnessed these acts without one word of reproof, if they did not incite their commission. For more than two hours the work of murder and barbarity was continued, until more than one hundred dead bodies, three-fourths of them of women and children, lay on the plain as evidences of the fiendish malignity of and cruelty of the officers and men who had so sedulously and carefully plotted the massacre, and of the soldiers who had so faithfully acted out the spirit of their officers....

It is true that there seems to have existed among the people inhabiting that region of country a hostile feeling towards the Indians. Some of the Indians had committed acts of hostility towards the whites; but no effort seems to have been made by the authorities there to prevent these hostilities, other than by the commission of even worse acts. The hatred of the whites to the Indians would seem to have been inflamed and excited to the utmost; the bodies of persons killed at a great distance [presumably a reference to the Hungate family]--whether by Indians or not is not certain--were brought to the capitol of the Territory and exposed to the public gaze, for the purpose of inflaming still more the already excited feelings of the people.... [The Governor] was fully aware that the Indians massacred so brutally at Sand creek were then, and had been, actuated by the most friendly feelings toward the whites....

As to Col. Chivington, your committee can hardly find fitting terms to describe his conduct. Wearing the uniform of the United States, which should be the emblem of justice and humanity; holding the important position of a commander of a military district, and, therefore, having the honor of the Government to that extent in his keeping, he deliberately planned and executed a foul and dastardly massacre which would have disgraced the veriest [sic] savage among those who were the victims of his cruelty. Having full knowledge of their friendly character; having himself been instrumental, to some extent, in placing them in their position of fancied security, he took advantage of their inapprehension and defenceless [sic] condition to gratify the worst passions that ever cursed the heart of man. It is thought by some that desire for political preferment prompted him to this cowardly act.... Whatever may have been his motive, it is to be hoped that the authority of this Government will never again be disgraced by acts such as he and those acting with him have been guilty of committing[368].

Immediately upon publication of the Congressional report, President Andrew Johnson called for Governor Evans' resignation. He would wait nearly six weeks, but the Governor resigned in early September[369]. The last of the Third Colorado Cavalry was mustered out on December 31, 1864 and Chivington resigned in January.

Indian Reaction

The Indian tribes on the plains were shocked by the attack and quickly moved for retaliation. The Cheyenne, Arapaho, and Sioux smoked a war-pipe and 800 to 900 lodges gathered on Beaver Creek in December to plan their attack. Their first strike would be along the South Platte River Road, a major supply line to Denver now devoid of troops[370]. The plan was for the Cheyenne to attack the trail from Julesburg to Denver, the Arapaho would sack Julesburg, and the Lakota Sioux would attack the trail east of Julesburg[371]. The military anticipated attacks in the spring[372], but the allied tribes had no intention of waiting until spring - they would attack in force and they would attack immediately taking the U. S. military completely by surprise.

1865: Retaliation

Following the battle at Sand Creek, the Colorado military was in disarray: Major General Curtis called for Colonel Chivington's resignation almost immediately following the battle and received it and Colonel Thomas Moonlight of the 11th Kansas Volunteer Cavalry took command of the District of Colorado[373]; the U.S. Senate formed a committee to investigate the massacre and many officers of the 1st Colorado Cavalry were called to testify; Governor Evans was temporarily removed as governor during the investigations and Samuel H. Elbert, Secretary of the Treasury became acting-governor[374]; and the 3rd Colorado Cavalry was mustered out at Christmas after 100 days of service. In all the chaos, the South Platte River Road from Julesburg to Denver, a road vital for freight and communications with Denver and the mining regions, was left virtually unprotected. Whether the Cheyenne and allied tribes knew this or not, they chose this place to retaliate.

Overture: January 7th

The first attack on the South Platte River Road came on January 7th. From 500 to 1,500 Indians raided Julesburg and attacked overland stages along the route killing 15 soldiers and 30 Indians[375]. An additional 12 were killed at Valley Station (near Sterling)[376]. Charles Griffin Coutant described the scene in around Fort Sedgwick (near Julesburg):

> Indians under Man-Afraid-of-His-Horses and other chiefs made an attack on an incoming stage and came very near capturing it, but fortunately it escaped to the station, having one man and one horse killed. Captain O'Brien [7th Iowa Cavalry] discovered the Indians and hastily mounted thirty-seven men and leaving twelve at the fort in charge of two pieces of artillery, he dashed

down on the savages. Riding to a bluff about half a mile from the fort, they discovered that the Indians were in strong force…. The charge was sounded and the gallant heroes, with the clatter of hoofs and shouts, were soon in the midst of the savages…. The Indians in their turn, with overwhelming numbers, charged back upon the white men and for a time the carnage went on. At last Captain O'Brien, finding nearly half of his men killed, ordered the remainder to fall back…. Fourteen of the thirty-seven enlisted men lay dead on the field. The Indians, with savage shout and maddened fury, now attempted to storm the fort…two pieces of artillery…served with telling effect on the advancing savages…. [The next morning] a party was sent out to the battlefield of the day before to gather up the dead. They found them lying where they fell, but their bodies had been stripped and horribly mutilated. The dead soldiers were carried to the fort and buried with the honors of war…. It was never fully determined how many Indians were killed in this battle, but after peace had been declared they admitted their loss to have been sixty-three[377].

The Indians attacked all along the route as far west as Junction Station. Colonel Moonlight sent a frantic message for reinforcements stating, "Operators have left stations since. Unless troops are hurried out from Kearny, Lyon, or some point, people must starve. Immense excitement. I have no body to re-enforce with[378]." Companies C and H of the 1st Colorado Cavalry were dispatched to the South Platte under the commands of Lieutenants J. J. Kennedy[379] and James Olney[380]. Another order went out shortly after the attacks revoking an existing order prohibiting citizens from carrying arms noting hostile Indians now surrounded the Territory[381].

Destruction of American Ranch: January 14-15

On January 14th and 15th, the allied Indian tribes again attacked stations along the South Platte River Road including Godfrey's and the American Ranch. Watson S. Coburn, a rancher along the Platte from 1865-1867 recalled what he knew of the January attack on the American Ranch:

> ...All the men and family were in the room back of the one where all the goods were kept. Mr. Morris was playing a fiddle when suddenly Mrs. Morris heard a noise in the front part and at once called Mr. Morris' attention to it. On opening the door he saw the room was full of Indians, who immediately gave the war whoop and tried to kill him. He then opened fire with his revolver and killed three of them before they could get out of the door. After barricading the door the men were able to hold their own until the latter part of the day when the Indians set fire to the stables and a large quantity of hay adjoining the house. The smoke poured into the house in such volumes that the inmates were about to suffocate. Seeing that it would be impossible to stand it much longer, Mr. Morris took half a bottle of strychnine that he kept to poison wolves with, and divided it into two decanters of whiskey behind the counter, after shaking it up; he told his wife to take the children and go out to the front door and give herself up, while he and the men would try to escape out the back way. It was a well known fact that the Indians seldom killed a white woman, hence the plan taken. The

men, however, were all killed and scalped a short distance from the house.

Just before the attack, two men, Gus Hall and one called Big Steve...left the ranch with ox teams and started to the cedar canons, sixteen miles away, to get a load of wood. About nine o'clock in the morning, soon after the fight commenced, the Indians discovered these two men, where they had crossed the river on the ice and eleven Indians went over to get their scalps. Nine of the Indians made an attack in front while two of them took positions on the ice under the bank below and above the two men. Here they maintained a cross fire. After several hours Big Steve was killed.... Soon afterwards Gus Hall was shot in the right leg, breaking it between the knee and ankle..... When Hall peeped over the bank, an arrow shot up and passed clear through his chest and slid twenty-two feet on the ice back of him. Hall said he fell backwards and the Indian leaped up the bank with knife in his hands ready to scalp him when he raised his revolver and shot the Indian, who fell dead over on him....

Gus Hall, with one leg broken and pierced through and through, night coming on and the ranch laid in ruins and his friends killed, was left in an almost helpless condition. He thought the Wisconsin Ranch, fourteen miles down the road, might possibly be all right, and decided to try to get to it, so he commenced his journey, on his hands and knees, crawling down the ice. Arriving at the ranch, after a journey lasting seventeen hours, he found it in ruins and everybody gone.... Hall made up his mind that he would die that night, and crawled in on the warm grain where he was sheltered from the wind by the sod walls and soon became unconscious. A train of wagons with about a hundred men was making its way down to Omaha. As it passed these ranches the men would investigate the ruins to see how many had been killed and to bury the ones they found dead. While one of the party was looking around he discovered Hall curled up in a corner and holloed to the rest, "Here is a dead man." This aroused Hall and he said, "I am not dead yet, but I think I will be before long"....

Mr. Godfrey's ranch, known all over the western country as Old Fort Wicked, was the only ranch that was not either partially or totally destroyed by this raid. Godfrey had his place well fortified and as fast as Mrs. Godfrey ran the balls, he would call to his daughter, "Hurry up, Celia; more balls, Celia." As fast as Celia carried the bullets to him, he would fire at the Indians, and at every shot he would use an oath and say, "Take that, will you?" Nearly every shot took effect, and with another oath he would say, "There goes another." The Indians, getting more than they bargained for, as Godfrey would state it, soon went on to the next ranch. They succeeded in burning the hay stacks and sheds at the Beaver ranch, but the inmates saved themselves by using the sod walls as fortifications. At the next ranch the Murray brothers had six hundred head of cattle shot down and left lying on the flat; the hay and barns were burned, but the men escaped[382].

When the dust cleared, American Ranch was destroyed and 17 Indians lay dead at Godfrey's[383]. A few days later, soldiers reported finding three dead white men and two dead Indians at American Ranch[384]. William Morris's body wasn't found until April 14th; his body had been carried off by Indians and found on an island with 17 arrow wounds[385].

For Sarah Morris the attack on the American Ranch was only the start of her horrors. She and the children were captured by the Indians and would remain with them for five months before being ransomed to soldiers stationed at Fort Rice in the Dakota Territory. Her story was reported in the *Frontier Scout*, the fort's newspaper:

> I was living at American Ranche, on the Platte River in Colorado, at the time of my capture by the Cheyennes. My family consisted of my husband, William Morris, one child, my own, and an adopted one. My child's name was Charley. The adopted one we called Joseph. It was the 10th of January 1865, the Indians attacked the house where we lived. The party consisted of about one hundred…. They set the house and stables afire, and drove us into the pilgrim room. At last the doors of the pilgrim room got in flames, and we had to leave. We ran out towards the river, through the corral, hoping to make our escape…. When we got to the corral we found we could not. He told me to stop, that they would probably take me prisoner, and he possibly might get away. They surrounded, and killed him and another man as they were running to the river. The Indians stood so thickly about me, I could not see him when he was killed. He had no arms of any kind with him.
>
> My baby, fifteen months old died about a month ago. The Sioux took Joseph, and have him yet. They put me

on a pony, and went south about fifty miles. They have been traveling and I with them the most of the time since. At their first camping ground they stayed three or four days, holding their scalp dances. Since they have been moving North. About four days ago they told me they were going to bring me in to the whites, pointing this way, saying "Sioux, sugar, coffee, heap." My joy knew no bounds. I certainly know they killed my husband, for they told me there were four men killed at the Ranche....

At the time of my capture I received five wounds from arrows and six stabs from knives. They also struck me across the head with their whips. My wounds are not entirely healed. An Indian, who could talk English, told me after I arrived in camp that if I showed them the wounds in my shoulders, they would not kill me as it was their intention to do. The old chief he took me doctored me with his medicine, and my wounds partially healed up. He treated me very well, making me do scarcely anything except pack on my back a few kegs of water, and saddle my pony. He gave me plenty of meat, which was all he had. He however did not like my little boy. My baby was afraid of him, and would cry. One day he took him by the neck and threw him down, and stamped on him. The child then took sick, and died in about three weeks. They wanted to bury him before he was fairly dead. I had hard work to keep them from doing it. He sunk away, and I knew he was not entirely dead. After his death they put him in a coffee sack, and laid him in a hole in the ravine, hardly covering him over. I wanted them to dig the grave deeper, but they would not. The chief's name is White

White. He is the one that brought me in....[386]

In 1894, Sarah Morris sued the government for failing to protect the ranch and withdrawing the troops stationed at the ranch just a few days before the massacre[387]. The outcome of the case is not known, but it was clear that the military did not have sufficient troops on the South Platte River Road to protect against the Indian attacks.

Raids Continue: January 28th – February 2nd

January's destruction wasn't limited to the American Ranch, the Indians had coordinated their attacks and no settlement from Julesburg to Junction however small escaped. The downed telegraph line made communication with Denver impossible and the events of the next couple of weeks is somewhat confused.

On January 28, the Indians again raided the trail attacking and burning stations[388] and wagon trains[389]. By January 31, the entire Overland route along the South Platte River was shut down and the telegraph lines were down. All communications between Junction and Julesburg had ceased and an estimated 3,000 Indians were attacking on both sides of the South Platte River[390]. Colonel Livingston reported:

> Every ranch and stage-station from junction station to this post [Fort Sedgwick] is burned and the charred remains of every inmate who failed to escape tells of the brutality.... The troops of Colorado have been withdrawn from Valley fifty miles west of here, I surmise, to concentrate around Denver. The telegraph line to Salt Lake and the Denver branch line are destroyed for a distance of nearly ten miles on the northern route, and in different

points throughout 100 miles along the Denver road.... Be assured, general, that this is no trifling Indian war. You will hear of continued murders and robberies as long as the road is so poorly protected by troops. No stages run further west than Cottonwood. I have prevailed on agents of the stage company to move their stations close to our forts for protection.... I predict that if more troops are not sent into this district immediately this road will be stripped of every ranch and white man on it, the military posts alone excepted....[391]

Colonel Moonlight is similarly bleak in his report:

The Indians are bold in the extreme. They have burned every ranch between Julesburg and Valley Station, and nearly all the property at the latter place, driven off all the stock, both public and private, and destroyed many ranches on this side as far up as Junction. They have also destroyed about two miles of telegraph and carried off about one mile of wire. These Indians are led by white men, and have complete control of all the country outside of my district, so that I am hemmed in....[392]

One of the white men referred to in Moonlight's communication was likely George Bent, a half-breed who had reportedly been killed at Sand Creek. George had experience fighting the U. S. military. He had attended school in St. Louis and fought with Confederate troops in 1861 before being captured by the Union and sent home to Colorado[393]. Bent described the attacks from the Cheyenne perspective:

From the day we struck the South Platte, January 28 [1865], until February 2, the Indians raided up and down the road, burning every ranch and stage station between

Julesburg and Valley, capturing wagon trains loaded with goods, and running off all the cattle. Besides this, the Sioux made some raids east of Julesburg and the Cheyennes west of Valley nearly to Junction House; the raiders swept the road clean and even destroyed the telegraph line that ran from Julesburg up the South Platte to Denver. We camped there right on the road and held the line, and the soldiers could not do a thing.

In Colorado the people were nearly frantic. At that time very little food was raised in the territory and the people depended largely for food and supplies on what was brought up the Platte in the big freight wagons.... The result was a panic in Colorado. There was only enough food to last a few weeks, and prices jumped to famine rates.... Besides this, the stage line was broken up and no coaches were running; every station for a distance of nearly one hundred miles had been burned and the stock run off; the Overland telegraph had been destroyed and the government was cut off from all communication with Colorado, Utah, Nevada, and the Pacific Coast. All of this trouble was the result of Col. Chivington's "great victory" at Sand Creek....

I did not see a tenth of the things that happened along the South Platte during those stirring days, but I saw many strange things. At night the whole valley was lighted up with the flames of burning ranches and stage stations, but these places were soon all destroyed and darkness fell on the valley...when I was out with raiding parties at night, we used to halt and look for the camp-fires to tell which way the [Indian] village lay, and when

The Missing Mail. Published in Harper's Weekly, *1881.*

we could not see the fires we would listen for the drums. On a still night you could hear them for miles and miles along the valley....[394]

The Overland mail from Julesburg to Denver would remain stopped until April 1865[395]. Julesburg and Valley Stations were burned and the telegraph line destroyed. The only telegraph station left was Junction. General Dodge sent a frantic dispatch to his Colonels: "...take militia to hold the route until I can relieve them with troops on the way....repair telegraph; open communication and hold it open.... Denver must hold its part of the line[396]".

Uneasy Peace

The telegraph from Denver to Omaha was working again by February 13th and things quieted down, comparatively, along the South Platte, though there were still reports of troubles along the North Platte and near Julesburg. The military promised 2,000 troops along the line and ample protection for the mail, freight and emigrant travel[397], but it was not enough. The *Rocky Mountain News* called for troops to be moved from the Arkansas to the South Platte River:

> ...For weeks and months our mails have been interrupted and our commerce destroyed or cut off. The road is marked with the new-made graves of our citizens. Provisions are at starvation prices. Millions of dollars have been lost, directly and indirectly, to our Territory and the future is still uncertain. Yet not a hand has been raised to give us relief, beyond a few scattered detachments of soldiers usually stationed along the lower road [Arkansas]. During all this time companies and regiments are lying comparatively idle at Lyon, Larned, Zarah, Walnut Creek, Riley, Scott.... The Arkansas route is solely and directly beneficial to Kansas; hence it receives protection. The Platte route divides its benefits, hence it is left to fate.... More commerce, more money, more mails, more property and more people pass over the Platte route in a week – ordinarily – than over the other in a year. All the Territories – except New Mexico and Arizona – are dependent upon it for their mails. Three Territories, and a portion of two others, receive all their merchandise and machinery, and a great share of their provisions over it. All of the Great West is dependent upon its telegraph line... We want troops...from wherever they can be spared. We want them on the Platte route to protect it....[398]

The latest Indian attacks had shaken the citizens of Denver – and the military – badly. Soon troops from all over the country would come pouring into Colorado to be stationed along the South Platte River Road and garrisoning a new fort at the Junction.

The Indians appeared to settle back into plundering raids similar to those of the previous summer and the military, using Junction, now called Camp Wardwell, and Fort Sedgwick as bases, chased the attacking Indians. On July 28th, Indians ran off stock around Junction and were chased by Captain Kenny and a detachment of the 1st Colorado Cavalry[399] and John Murray was attacked September 28th near Fremont's Orchard. The *Rocky Mountain News* reported "[a]fter capturing the stock, [the Indians] followed Mr. Murray and man till two o'clock this morning, when they succeeded in getting into Bijou Station. They came to the Post [Junction] this morning, and Maj. Norton gave them assistance, - they are now in pursuit[400]."

In August, the Indians along the Republican River including the Kiowa, Comanche, and Apache tribes signed a peace treaty with General Sanborn and agreed to "use all our influence with the Chyenne [sic] Indians...and induce them to join us in this perpetual peace, and if they do not, we will compel them to cease all acts of violence towards the citizens of the United States...[401]" In October, General Sanborn met with Black Kettle, a Cheyenne chief and survivor of the Sand Creek Massacre who had been working for peace with the whites. Black Kettle reportedly said that the Indians must have peace, but his warriors were afraid to meet with soldiers. General Sanborn apologized for Sand Creek and offered restitution to those affected by the battle. The only request from the government was for the Cheyennes to cease hostilities and remain either south of the Arkansas River or north of the North Platte River, leaving the area around the South Platte

River free[402]. The whites and the Indians were at peace - the peace would last less than a year.

∞

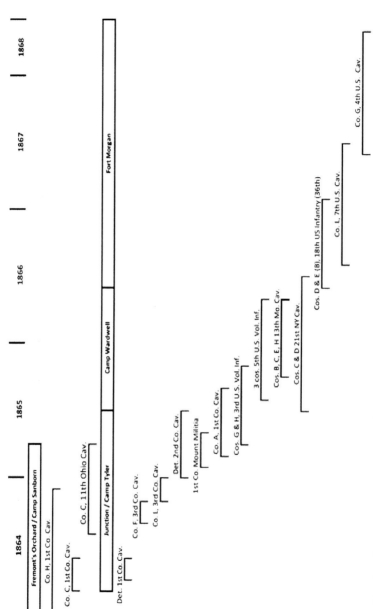

Timeline showing troops stationed in the Fort Morgan area from 1864 to 1868.

Chapter 7

Fort at the Junction

The retaliatory attacks along the South Platte River in 1865 exposed the vulnerability of the route, a vital lifeline for Denver and the mountain mining regions. They convinced the military that it was essential to have a presence along the South Platte River Road to deter the Indians and protect the Overland Mail. Troops began arriving early in 1865 and by March, plans for a permanent fort at Junction were underway. This fort would close in 1868, but in the short time the fort was active, 19 different companies from 11 regiments both cavalry and infantry, and an estimated 1,200 to 1,400 soldiers would be stationed at the fort. Fort Morgan it seems was not a place a soldier could call home.

Post Junction

Detachments of troops had camped near the Junction on-

and-off since May of 1864 first at Murray's Ranch and then near Junction Station[403]. The Junction was an obvious place to mass troops as it was almost exactly half-way between Julesburg and Denver[404], joining a line of forts along the South Platte River designed to keep the mail and emigrants safe: Fort Kearney, Fort McPherson, and Fort Sedgwick (formerly Fort Rankin) each placed approximately 100 miles apart. Further, this position fell at a cross-roads, allowing the military to protect not only the main South Platte River Road, but also the Cut-off road to Denver. Fort Morgan was referenced in military records as Junction (or Post Junction), Camp Tyler, Camp Wardwell (or Wardell), Fort Wardwell, and finally by the name Fort Morgan. Frank Root described the camp in February 1865:

> The only military post between Fort Sedgwick and Denver was Camp Wardwell...near the mouth of Bijou creek, at what was known on the upper South Platte in staging and freighting days as "the Junction." The place was about 100 miles east of Denver, by the road along the South Platte, and was in plain view of the Rockies for at least 100 miles.... Here there was a cut-off on which was a toll-road – built in the early '60's – which left the main traveled river road and passed several miles south, along which the telegraph line from old Julesburg to Denver was constructed, in the fall of 1863.... During the Indian troubles Wardwell became quite an important camp, a military officer being stationed here, who performed the duties of provost marshal.... The principal duties of the authorities were to keep people from proceeding without a minimum strength of thirty armed men, for safety

against the redskins. There was a telegraph office at the Junction, which appeared to be indispensable, especially since the Indians had possession of several hundred miles of road along the Platte[405].

Fort Morgan was established about ½ mile south of the South Platte River near Sam Ashcraft's ranch[406]. The fort was built on a natural plateau known as Morgan Flats and allowed for a clear view of the surrounding area[407].

In June of 1866, a traveler through the area, James F. Meline, described his approach to the camp highlighted against the awesome Rocky Mountains:

> Camp Wardwell is distinctly seen across the tableland by which you approach it, a distance of ten miles. Beyond it I perceived piles of remarkable clouds on the western horizon, and on reaching the camp, discovered that they had a fixed outline of cones and peaks and that I beheld, not clouds, but – the Rocky Mountains! I had not expected to see them so soon, and all my anticipants were so entirely surpassed that my gaze was as much of surprise as of admiration…. A line of infinite green prairie, apparently terminating half way up a misty wall of black granite, over and above which, in billowy confusion, are massed, higher and still higher, cloudy worlds of nebulous snow, their outline espousing the canopy of heaven, is all I can say as an apology for the attempt[408].

Colorado Cavalry

When the 3rd Colorado Cavalry was mustered out of service at the end of 1864, the troops stationed at Junction Station were replaced with 75 new recruits of the 2nd Colorado Cavalry under the command of Lieutenant Albert Walter a veteran officer of the 1st Colorado Cavalry[409,410]. This detachment had been formed to escort "The Big Train," a collection of 300 wagons starting from Denver on January 14th, just as the allied Indian tribes were preparing for a second full-scale attack on the South Platte River Road. The train was attacked three times between Junction and Valley stations, but the Indians were repelled[411]. At Julesburg, with the train safely out of the Colorado Territory, the detachment returned west along the South Platte River Road heading for the Junction and escorting two mail coaches - arriving just in time for a rescue at Valley Station on January 29th.

...I [Lt. Walter] arrived at Valley Station, finding that the fight had ceased, the Indians having taken 500 to 600 head of cattle with them. I detailed twenty of my men and Lieutenant Kennedy with the same number of his command. Started at 3 p. m. in pursuit of the Indians in direct northerly direction. At 10 o'clock at night we came in sight of some stock. We concluded to remain at that place during the night. At daybreak we continued our march. At sunrise we discovered the Indians moving out of their camp, over 100 in number. The Indians having noticed our approach, after a few minutes' interval the fight commenced. The skirmish was kept up two hours, my command killing 9 Indians, and the Indians injured 3 of my men slightly. None of my horses killed or wounded. I recaptured with my command 200 head of cattle. The men strictly obeyed my orders and commands during the fight. The most of the fighting was done on foot. After I reached the level ground the Indians retired back to their bluffs, looking very distressfully after us....The 30th I started for Godfrey's ranch, twenty miles from Valley Station. The Indians were more numerous in sight that day than ever before, moving up the river. Arriving at Godfrey's ranch, I noticed that evening the smoke of the ranches set on fire beyond Valley Station, and between Valley Station and Godfrey's ranch. The 31st of January I marched for the Junction, escorting three families in my wagons, including Godfrey's, to this place. The Indians during that day followed my command close in my rear, and scattered, ten miles from the Junction, into the bluffs. At 4 p.m. I arrived at the Junction; my horses are in very bad condition.... The detachment stationed at the Junction before I relieved them, according to the statement of Citizen Ashcraft, had no guard out during two nights in succession. Upon my arrival at this place the detachment did not act soldier-like. I am scouting the country....[412]

Lieutenant Walter reported relieving troops stationed at the Junction on January 31, 1865, but there is no mention of which company this might be. Company L of the 3rd Colorado Cavalry, previously stationed at the Junction, would have been mustered out with the rest of the volunteers just after Christmas and there is no mention in the history of the regiment of a company being held over. In any case, Lieutenant Walter was not impressed with their service. A month later, Lieutenant George W. Hawkins, commanding Company A of the 1st Colorado Cavalry, joined Lieutenant Walter at the Junction[413].

1*st* Colorado Mounted Militia (Tyler's Rangers)

The United States military at this time were scrambling to get enough troops onto the trail to protect Denver and the settlers on the plains and open the Overland mail routes. To add to the confusion, the South Platte River Road from Julesburg to Denver fell between the District of Nebraska under the command of Brigadier General Robert B. Mitchell and Colonel Robert R. Livingston and the Department of Missouri under Major General Grenville M. Dodge and Colonel Thomas Moonlight. There seemed much confusion in the communications of the time and neither colonel seemed to know who was responsible for protecting the route. On February 13, 1865, both Colonels Livingston and Moonlight stated unequivocally that the South Platte River road was not in their district:

> Livingston: "No portion of my district includes any portion of Colorado, as I understand it. I will put a part of a squadron at or near Harlow's ranch. Do you expect me to take charge as far as Junction?[414]"
>
> Moonlight: "The entire line from Julesburg to this side Junction is not in my district.... Expect help and cooperation from you as far as Valley Station at least[415]."

In the end, it fell to Moonlight to protect the road, but the Colonel was simply overwhelmed. He did not have enough troops to fight the attacking Indians and protect the route. Moonlight wrote to Major General Dodge airing his frustration: "...I am expected to protect these points on Overland route with no troops.... No depredations committed in my district; all in General Mitchell's[416]." He also wrote

to the Speaker of the House of Representatives trying to spur
the territorial government to action:

> I have been looking eagerly and waiting patiently for
> the passage of the bill which was designed to relieve the
> people of this Territory from the ravages of the Indians....
> I cannot longer await the action of your honorable body,
> for this night's despatches [sic] from Junction inform me

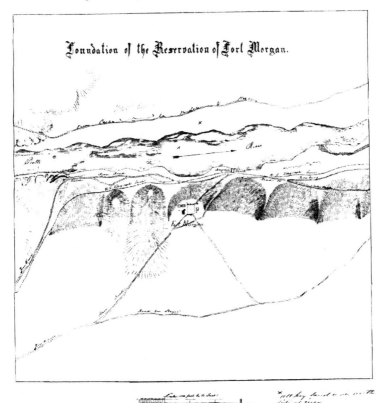

Position of Fort Morgan likely included with Rusling's 1866 report.
Document has been digitally cleaned. Courtesy of the Fort Morgan
Museum.

that about three thousand (3,000) Indians are marching up the Platte on both sides. Unless the legislature, within forty-eight hours, does something to relieve suffering humanity, and save this country from ruin and devastation, I will be compelled, much against my will, to proclaim martial law, shut up all houses of business, and force every man able to bear arms into the ranks, and send them out to protect their brethren, kill off the Indians, and establish permanent communication with the east. I cannot quietly look on and perform my duty *to this people, my country, and my God....*[417]

Moonlight was desperate. The Indians were attacking, threatening the U. S. mail and endangering emigrants. He was new in his position having taken over from Chivington only days before the first Indian attack at Julesburg and most of the soldiers under his command had been mustered out. In the end, Colonel Moonlight declared martial law and with the acting-Governor of the Colorado Territory, Samuel H. Elbert, raised a volunteer militia[418]. The 1st Regiment of the Colorado Mounted Militia consisting of six companies of 60 men each was called into service on February 6, 1865 by proclamation of the acting-governor. It would be the job of this militia to open the Overland Mail route and protect the trail.

Colonel Samuel E. Browne took command of the militia from his base at the Junction, now designated a permanent military station. Colonel Moonlight wrote Colonel Browne on March 2, 1865:

In sending out the companies of your regiment I have so far assigned them to stations, but I desire you to give this matter your personal supervision and attention. There will be six companies stationed from Julesburg to the Junction, not including the former, which would make the stations on an average about sixteen miles apart. With a view to facilitate operations of stage company, &c., Junction and Valley Stations will be permanently regarded as military stations, throwing two companies east of Valley and two west of Valley, making six. Hereafter I will order the companies as I send them out to report to you at Junction for assignment to station. The object of stationing these companies along the line in the manner above is for the protection of all travelers going to or from Colorado. Such escorts as may from time to time be needed by the stage company will be furnished by your station commanders…. The property of all civilians must be carefully respected, as well as the interests of the Government watched…. Your mission is to protect the whites and kill the redskins….[419]

One company of the 1st Colorado Mounted Militia in particular was central to the efforts to open and protect the trail. Company D was stationed at militia headquarters at Junction. This company was the reprise of the volunteer company, Tyler's Rangers, who had protected the trail a year earlier. Edward W. Hayes was elected Captain and Edward B. Stillings and A. L. Perkins, lieutenants. During their time at Junction, March and April 1965, Junction would be known – at least informally – as Camp Tyler[420].

On March 29th 1865, Captain Hayes issued an order for Chief Engineer Lieutenant Stillings to erect a fort at this station[421]. The militia was only in residence for a couple of months and it is unknown how far their plans progressed, but the idea of the fort was settled. "Camp Tyler" became "Fort Tyler"[422].

The Congressional investigation into the Sand Creek Massacre began in March and possibly with this in mind, Colonel Browne added a cautionary note to orders sent to the 1st Colorado Mounted Militia at Camp Tyler:

> Your mission is to kill, but not mutulate [sic].... [A solider] who mutilates any dead body, (in any way) will at once be arrested and most severely punished. The Cruelties of savage warfare can never the same Enormaties [sic] in the Soldiers of a great magnanimous and civilized people....[423]

But, the military of the time was distrustful of Colorado's volunteer militia. A large part of the 3rd Colorado Cavalry, "The Bloody Third," had participated in Chivington's massacre and it was possible that some (or most) of the same men who participated were members of the 1865 militia. On April 29, 1865, Brigadier General P. Edward Connor disbanded the 1st Colorado Mounted Militia[424,425] noting that United States troops had arrived and implying that Colonel Moonlight and the acting Governor had overstepped their authority. The military did not want a repeat of Chivington's Massacre, but the South Platte River Road needed protection so the troops sent to the Junction to replace the militia had no history with the Indians.

Camp Wardwell

The South Comes West: Galvanized Yankees

By April 30, 1865, the regular army, approximately 275

men, had arrived at Junction with detachments positioned along the road 55 miles to the east and 45 miles to the west of the camp[426]. Joining the 1st Colorado Cavalry were three companies of the U. S. Volunteer Infantry[427] otherwise known as "Galvanized Yankees".

The Civil War was in full swing during the Indian troubles of 1864 and 1865 leaving few troops to man the posts out west. Major General Dodge of the Department of Missouri was aware of the desperate situation in Colorado, and as his command was in St. Louis, Missouri – just across the river from a prisoner of war camp in Alton, Illinois – he had an idea:

> There are some 250 men in confinement at Alton, Ill., known as the "galvanized Yankees," i.e., men who were taken prisoners by the enemy during the last year, and who, to avoid starvation and death, enlisted in Burke's battalion, of the Confederate Army, and who in the recent raid deserted on the approach of our forces to us. These men have already applied to be sent back to their regiments, but it is not considered safe to send them where they will be in danger of capture by the enemy. There are also 1,000 prisoners of war and conscripts who refuse to be exchanged – claim to be deserters, unwilling conscripts, &c. These men have applied to enlist in our army. I respectfully submit if we had not better organize a regiment of these men and put them on the plains, where they can be made of use to our Government, relieve our prisons, and I have no doubt in most cases make better men and good soldiers. They are now a burden and expense to us. We cannot exchange them, and if I am

authorized I am confident I can form an effective regiment from them by placing old reliable officers over them. I have 3,000 miles of overland mail and telegraph route to guard, and every regiment of infantry that I can put along it will relieve that number of cavalry to use in offensive operations against the Indians, who I am satisfied, are determined to make aggressive war upon all our overland routes this spring and summer...[428]

Nearly 6,000 ex-confederate soldiers, "Galvanized Yankees" as they called themselves or "Whitewashed Rebs" as they were called by Union soldiers[429], deserted from the Confederate army and volunteered for the Union army; deciding the west was better than prison. From September 1864 until November 1866[430], six regiments of "Galvanized Yankees," officially called the United States Volunteer Infantry, were deployed to western military forts. Companies of the 3rd, 5th, and 6th U. S. Volunteers were sent to the Colorado Territory to protect the mail and emigrant routes from Indian attacks. The 3rd U. S. Volunteer Infantry had been recruited from a military prison in Rock Island, Illinois, southwest of Chicago[431] and the 5th was recruited from military prisons at Alton, Illinois and Camp Douglas[432].

An online genealogy project includes a biography of one Galvanized Yankees stationed at the Junction. Private James D. Rowland of Company G, 3rd U.S. Volunteer Infantry was born in Bedford, Tennessee in 1843 and enlisted in the Confederate army in February of 1862 and was placed in Company G of the 37th Mississippi Infantry (later the 34th Mississippi Infantry). He was captured on November 24, 1863 at the Battle of Lookout Mountain near Chattanooga,

Tennessee and from November 1863 until October 1864, Rowland was imprisoned at the Rock Island Barracks in Illinois[433]. Of the 5,000 prisoners taken along with Rowland to Rock Island, 700 died within the first three months[434]. The conditions in the prisons were terrible with little to eat and little in the way of clothing. The military denied most of the negative press reports about the prisons, but thousands of the prisoners elected to pledge allegiance to the union and take posts in the western frontier[435] with rations, clothing, $100, and some semblance of freedom.

James Rowland joined the Rock Island Rebels and along with Company G of the 3rd U. S. Volunteer Infantry left Illinois in February 1865 travelling to Fort Leavenworth, Kansas and then on to Fort Kearney, Nebraska. Two companies of the 3rd U. S. Volunteers Infantry were sent to Junction in May of 1865: Company G under Captain S. W. Matthews and Company H arrived under Captain Thomas Kenny to protect the Overland mail route leaving twelve to fifteen sol-

Galvanized Yankees protecting a wagon train. Drawing by Frederic Remington.

diers at each station[436]. They arrived at the Junction at the end of their rations in need of shoes and supplies and found neither. Captain Kenny reported that "[s]curvy has broken out among the men and I have neither medical supplies nor a surgeon attached to my command[437]."

Desertion was a major problem with the Galvanized Yankees. Once free from their prisons, many held no loyalty to the Union military and were likely not interested in the Indian troubles so far from their own homes. Mores H. Coffin wrote of deserters specifically from Fort Morgan:

> They were anxious to exchange Uncle Sam's uniforms for citizen's clothes, being deserters from Ft. Morgan. Most, if not all of them, were "galvanized" rebels... They were to be seen a little away from the road and half-naked, afraid to show the army blue. They were to be pitied, surely, as they knew not whom to trust, and were mere boys, homesick as it was possible to be. Most of them needed to be with their mothers. We were as kind to them as we dared to be, trading all the cheap clothes to be spared, and buying some things of them, as they were anxious for a little money. I imagine the officers were not especially zealous in searching for the missing ones[438].

Though it is noted in Rowland's online biography that only five men had deserted from his company of the 3rd U. S. Volunteers which was lower than for the regular army.

In June, Company B of the 6th U. S. Volunteers under Lieutenant Colonel W. Willard Smith arrived at the Junction. Smith was from Dubuque, Iowa and had served as aide-de-camp under General Halleck during the Battle of Gettysburg[439]. Under Colonel Smith's command, the fort grew and became known as Camp or Fort Wardwell:

[June 29, 1865] I have the honor to report that two hundred and twenty feet of sod walls about six feet high and three wide at base, with stone loopholes, is now built, also, a foundation two hundred and twenty feet long and same width is laid. One well dug and started up another in progress...and are now pushing the work as rapidly as possible. The lack of timber, boards and tools will cause some delay but as soon as the walls for one building are completed another will be commenced.... [A]ll government stores have been removed to the site selected. Commissary stores, are under cover and will [be] secured in tents...[440]

[July 19, 1865] I have the honor to report that the sod walls 440 feet by 3 feet wide and 8 high mentioned in letter of June 29th 65 is completed, the walls and foundations for ovens to bake house 17 by 40 is completed, the walls for store house 28 by 100 will be finished to-day, the frame building 24 by 100 sent from Denver is up but there was not boards and scantling enough sent to roof it. All the above buildings are awaiting boards, scanting, windows doors &c. The bakery also lacks bricks and two iron doors for ovens. Ten loads of long poles have been brought from...80 miles distant eleven loads more sent for and twelve loads cottonwood now here. Much delay has been caused for want of material long since called for....[441]

The fort constructed both of sod and lumber was underway.

With the building of permanent structures, Post Junction became Post Wardwell, or Fort Wardwell (in some sources spelled Wardell)[442]. The reason for the name Wardwell is unclear. At the time, camps could bear the name of the commanding officer, but there is no record of an officer by that name at the fort. Other camps were named in honor of an individual and it is possible that the fort was named for Burnham Wardwell, a Union loyalist living in Richmond who refused to swear allegiance to the Confederate government and was imprisoned for most of the war[443], but there is no obvious connection between the union activist in Richmond and the troops stationed at the fort in Colorado.

The 3rd U. S. Volunteer Infantry was mustered out on November 29, 1965[444] to be replaced by more Galvanized Yankees; three companies of the 5th U. S. Volunteer Infantry under the command of Captain John S. Cochrane. The troops wintered at Camp Wardwell and then marched for Fort Lyon on April 1, 1866. The 5th U. S. Volunteers was the last regiment of Galvanized Yankees mustered out of service[445]. The Civil War was at its end and the ex-Confederate soldiers could now return to their southern roots leaving the dust of the west behind.

The 13th Missouri Cavalry

The main reason for the military presence along the route was for the protection of the emigrants. Fort Wardwell and to a lesser extent Valley Station (Sterling) along with Fort Sedgwick at Julesburg formed the military backbone of the South Platte River Road. Soldiers from these points escorted mail and travelers along the route and were ready for confrontations with the Indians. In May of 1865, the military began organizing civilian wagons into trains of not less than 100 at

Forts Kearney and at the Junction[446]. Sometimes, wagons waited at the fort for days until a sufficient number of wagons could be organized, though during the height of the gold rush, an estimated 140 wagons rolled through Fort Wardwell each day[447]. In 1866, the traffic had slowed to an average of 50 wagons per day[448] and by 1867, only an average of 12 to 13 wagons trickled through[449].

In August of 1865, General Pope, commander of the Department of the Missouri outlined plans to consolidate military forces on the plains. The plan was to concentrate forces at Camp Fillmore, Fort Garland, and Camp Wardwell[450]. Accordingly, the regular army troops, the 11th Ohio Cavalry stationed at Fremont's Orchard, were replaced first with companies from the U. S. Volunteers and then with companies B, C, E, and H from the 13th Missouri Cavalry. The commanding officers were Captain Austin A. King and Colonel John E. Mayo.

Confessions of Stone and Foster, the Murderers of Isaac H. Augustus and Mr. Sluman, Sentenced to be Executed, Thursday, May 24, 1866.

Stone Denies his complicity in the Murders, but Confesses the Commission of Four Murders in the States.

Foster Confesses his Guilt and Implicates Stone.

Murder confession headline
Rocky Mountain News, *1866.*

There were frequent attacks by Indians at this time, but emigrants and settlers encountered other dangers as a member of Powell's Scientific Expedition noted:

My observations lead to the conclusion that some Indians are trying to obtain fine horses to sell to their warriors, and under the cover of Indian troubles many whites, half-breeds and traders are doing a general highway business, wholesale and retail, and the Indians get the credit of it all. To commit all the depredations claimed, would require an organized force of a hundred men at least....[451]

White savages were doing some of the stealing and murdering. During this time, Fort Wardwell earned some unwelcome notoriety. On January 8, 1866, two soldiers from the 13th Missouri Cavalry stationed at Camp Wardwell were arrested for the murders of Isaac H. Augustus and F. H. Sluman, freighters working for Carney & Stevens out of Leavenworth, Kansas[452,453]. Privates Frank Foster and Henry Stone of Company E, 13th Missouri Cavalry were arrested for the murders and brought to Denver for trial[454]. The soldiers were found guilty and sentenced to be hanged[455]. The details of the murders were reported as part of Franklin Foster's confession:

> ...On the 5th day of January last, about two o'clock in the evening, myself and Henry Stone started to Central City on horseback, we intended to desert.... We bore in to the Platte river road, struck the Platte at Bijou creek. We went up the road about one mile. Stone and I talked a few minutes to Augustus, and Sluman, then we went up the road about one mile, then we turned back. I said to Mr. Stone, "I bet them men has got plenty of money." Mr. Stone said "lets go for them." I seconded the motion. We came on down to where they was camped, we hitched our horses to their wagon, (Augustus and Sluman's wagon). I asked Mr. Augustus if anything was broke, he said he had some horses broke loose the night before, he was

hunting them that day. Henry Stone on my right in front of Sluman, Stone drew his revolver and was looking at Sluman and revolving the cylender [sic] in his hand. I knew what he aimed to do. I would have called the shots if I could. I drew my revolver I don't know what delayed him in his shots that he could not shoot quicker, whether he was frightened of his revolver would not go off. I fired six shots while he was firing two. I shot Augustus...Mr. Stone shot Sluman.... We searched the bodies; I myself got one hundred dollars in greenbacks out of the shirt pocket of Augustus; whether Stone got anything I don't know....[456]

The confession of Henry Stone was also recorded, though his story was markedly different. He denied his part in the Augustus and Sluman murders, though he confessed to three others:

I was born on the 30th day of January 1843, in the town of Perryville, Perry County, Missouri.... I left home at the age of sixteen – went to Illinois – left home on account of getting in a fight with my brother. I thought I had killed him. I took to gambling and horse racing – got in a fuss with a man named Johnson over a game of cards. I followed him about a mile from town and killed him, by shooting him with a revolver.... I took from this man's person seven hundred dollars...[and] joined the Thirteenth Missouri cavalry; staid [sic] at Rolla Missouri, about five months, I killed a man whose name I do not know, near the town of Dillon. I killed for his money.... We then received marching orders and went onto the Platte road. We were stationed at Camp Wardwell, myself and Franklin Foster on the fifth day of January, 1866, left Camp Wardwell to hunt for antelope. When from five to eight miles above camp, on the cut-off road, we parted company; I went about due south, Foster going west or north of west. We were separated about two hours. I started back towards Foster, met him about a mile from some wagons…. Foster said to me, "let us desert from the army." I told him I would'nt [sic] do it. While I was away from Foster I heard nine or ten shots fired in the direction of the wagons. Foster was coming from the wagons when I came up to him…. On the next morning I was informed for the first time that two men had been murdered up the Platte river. This was the first that I knew of the murder….[457]

Both Foster and Stone were hung publically on May 24, 1866 outside of Denver along Cherry Creek in front of about 3,000 spectators[458]. The execution was one of the last public hangings in Denver and it was reported in graphic detail:

At the Gallows. They [Foster and Stone] up the steps without a quivering muscle, and indeed preserved the same stoical indifference until the final trap dropped from under them. They were accompanied to the platform by Sheriff Sopris and officers, Revs. McClure, Potter and Clark. Rev. Mr. McClure read some passages of scripture, the hymn commencing "Rock of ages"….

Stone had nothing further to say in relation to his confession. In 4 minutes after the drop fell, the pulsations of Stone were yet distinct, while those of Foster were a trifle stronger than natural. In 6 minutes the heart of Stone had nearly ceased beating. In 7 minutes they were both perfectly unconscious and dying fast. In 10 minutes the straps were removed from their arms and at 9 minutes to 2 after they had hung 17 minutes they were both pronounced dead and were cut down. There was probably not less than 3000 spectators present, who were very quiet a more orderly and well behaved crowd was never seen together in any country. Not a loud remark or an action calculated to mar the solemnity of the occasion from any one. Lieut. Williams was on the ground with his company, "B" of the 5th U. S. which surrounded a small space around the gallows and the space enclosing the coffins. After the bodies were cut down the vast crowd dispersed in the same orderly manner that they had witnessed the soldiers vindication of the laws....[459]

The hanging of Foster and Stone came only weeks after the hanging of stage driver Frank Williams by vigilantes from Montana. Williams and 11 confederates robbed and killed two gold prospectors traveling from Montana to Missouri. A posse followed Williams and captured him at Godfrey's Ranch and hanged him[460]. Travelers across the American West not only had reason to fear the Indians, but the soldiers and stage drivers who were supposed to protect them.

The New York 21st

Stationed with the 13th Missouri were Companies C, D and E of the New York 21st Cavalry, a veteran regiment organized in Troy, New York in 1863[461]. The regiment was active during the Civil War and for their final deployment were sent to Colorado under the command of Colonel Charles Fitzsimmons based at Fort Collins[462]. Major Charles G. Otis and

Captain W. G. McNulty were in command at Fort Wardwell[463,464,465]. Life in camp could be difficult and sometimes
boring, especially during the winter months, but occasionally
there was cause to celebrate:

This usually dull post is the scene, to-day, of a very
interesting and exciting ceremony. A handsome pole
which has been in process of formation for some weeks
has been elevated to the perpendicular, and for the first
time the Stars and Stripes wave o'er our adobe barracks.
The pole was raised by ropes and shears, both manned by
the sturdy muscle of the Empire State, and the whole undertaking was ably engineered by the post carpenters, Mr.
Samuel Allen and Mr. Holbrook assisted by our mutual
and beloved friend Dr. Yates, late of the 1st Colorado Cavalry. As the gigantic stick was gradually elevated, the
beauty of its proportions was made apparent, and we feel
content in saying that it is the finest pole in the Territory.
Rigged like the mizzen mast of a clipper ship, with cros-
strees and stays, it seems emblematic of the progress of
civilization, which will ere many years cause the ships of
commerce to float through this sandy desert upon the bo-
som of broad canals, bearing the rich fruits of this
productive State to the east and west. Major Chas. G.
Otis of the 21st N. Y. Cavalry designed this pole, and it
does great credit to his taste. The pole being raised the
command was paraded and the cannons manned at 2
p.m., and our glorious flag slowly ascended to its proud
position with all due honors – presented arms and the
thunder of artillery. Thirty seven guns were fired, one for
each State, not forgetting the one we are stationed in. The

parade was dismissed after the salute, and a barrel of ale broached under the shadow of the National banner was the principal attraction for their thirsty patriots. The scene was picturesque. An enthusiastic crowd of soldiers, pledging their flag under the clear sky of heaven, with the roar of artillery momentarily adding emphasis to the carless toast. The 37th gun for Colorado was carefully loaded with a charge of uncommon powder, and as its thunder echoed over the surrounding bluffs, three cheers for the new State was proposed and given with a will…. All the officers participated in trying to make the thing pass off pleasantly, and we noticed frequently, the heavy moustache and smiling countenance of our esteemed commanding officer, Capt. W. G. McNulty, who enjoyed the whole thing immensely, and rendered himself beloved by all beholders by his urbanity and kindness….[466]

During this time, Fort Morgan was truly a military post, filled with soldiers, horses, guns, and the adrenaline that comes from confrontations with the Indians. With more than 500 troops, the fort must have been exceedingly crowded. A traveler through the area in March of 1866, Nathanial P. Hill, reported the fort (called Bijou in his letter) was "…so destitute of all comfort and so crowded with a drunken rabble of soldiers, that we bribed the driver by paying him $15 to go on[467]."

On June 30, 1866, just before the troops were to be mustered out, a memorial to the 21st New York Cavalry was published in the *Rocky Mountain News* penned by their anonymous correspondent "Snoggs":

We are forced to chronicle the death, not of an individual, but of an organization. One that has for nearly a year lived, moved and had its being in this western country. In short – the 21st New York Cavalry, is no more. They – the men of this regiment, are being mustered out of service by companies, and are changing their official titles for those of a less fiery, but more quiet and civil nature. Notwithstanding the pleasure we all feel, in becoming once more free men, there is a certain regret that will mingle with our happiness, a feeling that we are parting from each other for an indefinite period. Men who have ridden side by side into the face of danger, who have at Piedmont, New Market, Purcellville, Darkville, Solomon's Gap, Snicker's Gap, Ashby's Gap, Winchester, Charlestown, and numerous other smaller skirmishes, proved to each other their willingness to protect our free Government…. Now will Colorado, in view of our quiet decrease, pass all our improper actions by, and give precedence to our few virtues in their retrospect of the old 21st N. Y. Cavalry…[468]

The 21st New York were the last of the civil war volunteers to be mustered out of service and sent home.

Fort Morgan

18th (36th) U. S. Infantry

In 1865 and early 1866, between five and eight companies were stationed at the fort. Adding to the cavalry, were companies from the 18th (reformed as the 36th[469]) United States Infantry. The 18th U. S. Infantry was charged with protecting the building of the railway across the vast plains. In 1866, most of the surveyed routes for the transcontinental railroad included Denver, with the railroad following the South Platte River. Companies B and D were sent to Fort Wardwell – soon to change names to Fort Morgan – and other companies were dispatched along the route in Kansas, Nebraska, Wyoming and Utah[470].

Brevet Major Lyman M. Kellogg assumed command of Fort Wardwell on June 13, 1866[471]. Kellogg was accompanied by his wife and son Harry[472]. Kellogg was a career military man who graduated from West Point in 1852[473]. He had enlisted with the 24th Ohio Infantry and in 1861 was promoted to Captain in the 18th U. S. Infantry[474], but his rise in rank was not without problems. In August 1862, Kellogg was dismissed from the service on the charges of "drunkenness on duty, disobedience of orders, and conduct prejudicial to good order and military discipline"[475]. Kellogg was reinstated in 1864 as a Captain of the 18th Infantry[476] and fought at the battle of Jonesboro, which allowed Union forces to capture Atlanta, but was severely wounded and sent to recuperate at Jefferson Barracks near St. Louis. For his service during the battle, he was promoted to Major[477] and sent west.

By the time Kellogg arrived, the fort consisted of four wooden storehouses, three barracks with kitchens, and a stable. There were also a number of adobe buildings with wooden roofs housing headquarters, a hospital, a blacksmith, carpenter and a sutlers shop, and another unroofed stable which contained about 80 horses. The buildings were generally in good repair except for the roofs over the adobe buildings which leaked and there was not yet quarters for the officers[478]. Kellogg set about building officer's quarters and making improvements to the fort, possibly with a view to making the posting permanent. However, orders soon came through for his transfer and he appealed directly to General Ulysses S. Grant for his transfer to be canceled, "My present Co. "D" 36th Infantry, is one, I have taken particular pains with, and I am confident it will run down should I leave it, My family being with me this transfer will cause much distress to my Wife and great pecuniary loss to myself[479]." Grant cancelled the transfer, allowing Kellogg to remain in command of Fort Morgan for a few months longer[480].

If Kellogg viewed Fort Morgan as a favorable command, a place he could settle with his family, he would not have been alone. Albert Barnitz, a Captain in the 7th U. S. Cavalry, wrote to his wife of a conversation with Generals Custer, Smith and Gibbs planning peaceful days after a treaty could be reached with the Kiowa and Cheyenne:

> ...we will go back to [Fort] Harker or close to Hayes (45 miles N. of here) where we will remain until about the middle of May, or later, and all the officers who are named and wish to take their wives west with them will be allowed to go to Fort Riley for them.... [T]he regiment will then go west...into a beautiful country, and part to Fort Morgan about 70 miles N. of Denver City, where permanent buildings (of stone) will be erected by the soldiers, aided by employees of the Q. M. Dept. and we will be allowed to remain there and do about as we please, fishing, hunting and cultivating gardens indefinitely! [sic] (A brilliant prospect, truly!) Genl. Custer seems very much pleased with the idea – expects to take his wife. If however, the Indians will not accept the terms offered them, then we are to commence hostilities, and make

them do so – and finally, if they break the treaty...then *of course* we will have to ride about and "expend" a few thousand of them![481]

This utopia, however did not come to pass. The peace treaty with the Kiowa and Cheyenne was not signed and the soldiers and Indians continued to fight.

Kellogg and Custer may have had plans for Fort Morgan, but the fort was not always described with such high praise:

Fort Morgan at the junction of the Platte valley and cut off roads from Denver and Golden cities, is a small dirty insignificant post of two companies, situated on top of the high sandy ridge which here crowns the valley of the south side of Platte; three miles east of Bijou; it is built of crumbling sods, or rough dressed pine timber. As a post for protection or for protecting the road, it is of no value, but as a stand point of vexation for the trade of the great Platte Valley and Colorado, it answers its purpose admirably. On mere pretense of enforcing orders requiring trains to consolidate until 20 or more men are gathered together; vexatious delay in winter, when forage and fuel are both extremely scarce and dear, has been the cause of large losses to traders and freighters. Rumor has it that some one at that post is in "cahoots" with nameless ranches, etc. etc., in that immediate vicinity....[482]

In the summer of 1866, peace talks between the United States government and the Indians in the area broke down and the tribes were again on the war path[483]. There was not much Kellogg's infantry could do. Their charge was to organize trains and ride along the trail adding extra protection to the emigrants and freighters. The unmounted company wasn't very useful on the vast plains. Further, it was the job if the 18th Infantry to protect the building of the railway, which was now planned through Wyoming rather than Denver[484]. In January 1867, Kellogg and his company marched for Casper, Wyoming leaving Fort Morgan in the hands of the 7th United States Cavalry.

Colonel Christopher A. Morgan

On June 23rd 1866, soon after the arrival of the 18th U. S. Infantry, Fort Wardwell was renamed, Fort Morgan[485] by order of General John Pope commander of the District of Missouri[486]. The fort was named to honor the late Colonel Christopher A. Morgan, an aide-de-camp for General Pope. (Note: A number of sources mistakenly attribute the fort's name to Major Christopher A Morgan of the 1st Illinois Cavalry and some state that Morgan was the first commander of the fort – this is incorrect.). Morgan had no direct connection with the fort[487], but as the fort – and later the town – was named for him, a slight digression is warranted.

Morgan was born in Cincinnati, Ohio on December 7, 1821 to Ephraim and Charlotte Morgan[488]. He joined the Ohio 39th Infantry as a Captain at the age of 39[489]. Morgan was soon appointed aide-de-camp to General Pope[490] and by March 1862, Morgan was in the field with the General who was then commanding the Army of the Mississippi. Morgan was with the General during his most famous battle, the capture of New Madrid, Missouri and Island No. 10 in the Mississippi River which freed the river from a Confederate blockade[491]. Morgan was also with General Pope during the Campaign in Virginia and at the 2nd Battle of Bull Run at the end of August 1862. In 1865, Pope took command of the Military Division of the Missouri (Department of Missouri) based in St. Louis, Missouri. Morgan followed General Pope and it was here, at 206 Chouteau Avenue[492], that he would die in a domestic accident.

Morgan's death would top the local news in the St. Louis. The *Missouri Republican* described the death and the full military funeral under the headline "Terrible and Unexpected Death of a Prominent Staff Officer – The Ceremonies To-Day":

Death in any shape is terrible enough to blanch the cheek of even those who stand ready to meet it at the call of duty, but when it suddenly summons in the full enjoyment of perfect health through unfamiliar agencies, the shock is intensified. Our own community, particularly the military circles was yesterday thrilled by the news of the death of Col. C. A. Morgan, widely known as the inspector General of Gen. Pope's Department of the Missouri, a gentleman whose personal worth, accomplishments and virtues were most keenly appreciated by those who knew him best, but who has made himself a host of friends among the civilians of our city who have had the pleasure of his acquaintance. In the enjoyment of perfect health he retired to his room, in Gen. Pope's residence, on Chouteau avenue, on Friday night, and no one in the household even suspected that any thing had gone wrong with him until in the morning, when his unusual absence from the breakfast table was remarked, and Gen. Pope went to his room, and, getting no response, on opening the door, found, to his utter astonishment and dismay, that the Colonel was dead, asphyxiated by the escape of gas from a stove in his room constructed to burn coal gas. A physician was immediately sent for, and, on his arrival, pronounced that death must have ensued at least two hours previously....

[T]he body of Col. Morgan will be sent to-day to Cincinnati where his relatives reside...Four companies of the 3d U. S. Infantry, under the command of Lieut. Col. Grover, with the regimental band, will accompany the remains to the Levee....[493]

Morgan's body was sent back to his home state and is buried in the Spring Grove Cemetery in Cincinnati, Ohio[494].

Later that year, General Pope set off on a tour of the Plains, the Rocky Mountains and

DEATH OF COL. MORGAN

Terrible Effect of Inhaling Gas.

Col. Morgan, Inspector General on General Pope's staff, was found dead in his bed yesterday morning, by Gen. Pope. He died from inhaling gas, the pipe of which had bursted. Gen. Pope went to call him to breakfast, and found him dead. Physicians who were called said he had been dead two hours. Col. M. was a perfect gentleman, lived in Cincinnati, and will be universally lamented by a large circle of military as well as civil friends.

An inquest was held upon the body of the Colonel by Coroner O'Reilly, yesterday morning shortly after the discovery of his death. A post mortem examination was also made by Dr. A. S. Barnes. The verdict of the jury was that the deceased came to his death from congestion of the lungs, superinduced by the inhaling of gas.

Announcement of Col. Morgan's death. St. Louis Press. *1866.*

New Mexico. During his trip he would stay at Fort Wardwell (June 22-24) commanded at the time by Major Kellogg. General Pope's impressions of the fort are not recorded, but Colonel James Meline was in General Pope's party and wrote poetically about his first view of Fort Wardwell with the mountains behind in the book *Two Thousand Miles on Horse-*

back:

> Jefferson spoke of the scenery at the point where the Potomac and Shenandoah mingle their waters as worth a voyage across the ocean. If he be right, the spectacle I now have before me is worth a journey across both oceans and more continents than exist. I am inclined to believe, though, that Jefferson had not seen much grand American scenery.... The point from which my first view of the mountains was obtained, is one hundred and thirty-five miles east of Long's Peak, which looms up, the grand centre and pinnacle of the Rocky Mountain range in this latitude. The distance is less to the outside eastern boundary of the chain, which rises like a Titanic wall straight up from the body of the plain, but the Peak with its bodyguard of grand snowy elevations, is plainly visible to the naked eye.... The first satisfactory view the European traveler obtains of the Bernese Alps...is at sixty miles. The view of these American mountains, at more than twice the distance, impresses me as incomparably finer; and I solemnly abandon the last of my cherished illusions on the subject of European scenery.... The English have made such a noise, in prose and verse...about Italian sunsets, that I could hardly trust the evidence of my senses when I saw their inferiority to those I had been looking at all my life in my native land...I have before me now a stretch of one hundred and twenty miles of snow-capped and snow-clad mountains, and these by no means the most elevated, nor the grandest...and pronounce it sublime.[495]

Also accompanying General Pope was the landscape painter Thomas Worthington Whittredge. He was as enthralled as Meline with the plains and a number of his landscapes are set along the Platte River (see front and back covers of this book). He specifically recalled the trip through Colorado and New Mexico with General Pope in his autobiography:

I had never seen the plains or anything like them. They impressed me deeply. I cared more for them than for the mountains, and very few of my western pictures have been produced from sketches made in the mountains, but rather from those made on the plains with the mountains in the distance. Whoever crossed the plains at that period, notwithstanding its herds of buffalo and flocks of antelope, its wild horses, deer and fleet rabbits, could hardly fail to be impressed with its vastness and silence and the appearance everywhere of an innocent, primitive existence. There was the nomad and the rattlesnake to be taken into consideration, and they both occasionally made some noise. We usually made a march of thirty-three miles a day, which was performed between daybreak and one o'clock in the afternoon. On arriving in camp I gave my horse to an orderly and went at once to the wagon for my sketch box which was usually covered deep with camp furniture, but I always got it out, and while the officers were lounging in their tents and awaiting their dinners, I went to make a sketch, seldom returning before sundown...[496]

Major Kellogg, a native of Ohio, had assumed command of the fort just a fortnight earlier and it is possible that during the General's visit, he talked of his former aide-de-camp, also a native of Ohio for during his stay at Fort Wardwell, General

Pope ordered the name of the fort changed to Fort Morgan. The words of General Pope's co-travelers suggest that the fort wasn't chosen randomly to honor a fallen friend.

The Fort

On March 23, 1865, soon after the 1865 attacks along the South Platte, Colonel Thomas Moonlight ordered Colonel Samuel Browne, then commanding the 1st Colorado Mounted Militia, to begin erecting forts in the Fort Morgan area[497]. The plan was to build a fort around a parade ground containing an company quarters, a hospital and the adjutant's office on the north side, officer's quarters on the east, additional company quarters, the quartermaster's office and a sutlers store on the south and storehouses and shops on the west. Additionally there was a coral west of the fort where travelers' wagons were parked around which stood an eight foot sod wall. Around the coral were stables, equipment rooms, quarters for teamsters and wagon masters, a blacksmith shop, a harness shop, and a wagon shop. The 1st Colorado Mounted Militia began building, but were mustered out of service only a month later. The companies of Galvanized Yankees who were next stationed at the post were likely built the majority of the fort.

In 1866, the fort had three completed barracks (one used as a stable), a hospital, several storehouses, a shop, a corral, a stable, a sutler store, and a variety of sod buildings[498]. The buildings faced the parade ground and were surrounded by a five foot high earthen embankment with cannons mounted on the northeast and southwest corners of the enclosure[499]. The officers were still quartered in tents, but there were plans for the building of officers' quarters.

Given the rarity of wood in the area, many of the structures were made mostly of sod and adobe though lumber for some structures was imported from Denver. The fort, like most forts on the western plains was crudely built by the soldiers garrisoned there and of local materials. General Pope requested materials be sent from other posts, but his requests were denied[500]. However, the fort did have one distinctive quality – the adobe made from alkali water dried white[501].

The fort was burned and fell into ruins after the soldiers

Wagon Train on the Plains, Platte River c. 1866. By Thomas Worthington Whittredge.

left in 1868, though some of the structures were still evident twenty years later when the town was built. However, by 1911, there was nothing left of the fort.

Life in Camp

Life at Camp Wardwell was not easy and the troops complained bitterly, especially during the winter months. Colonel John E. Mayo stationed at Camp Wardwell reported in December of 1865:

...Justice to the men serving at the posts demands a

statement of the neglect from which they have suffered to such a degree as to task the utmost endurance of human nature. Being located in a bleak desert, accessible at all points to the rough winds in the season of frost and snow, they have up to the present time, been unprovided with quarters of any description, being compelled by the necessities of the climate, to shelter themselves in the low and moist banks of the Platte. Being removed near a hundred miles from the woodlands, no provision has been made up to the present time for fuel, the men being left to battle with the rigors of the season without firs, frequently not even the amount requisite for the preparation of their food. The repeated efforts of Colonel King to correct these evils have this far failed to produce the necessary remedies. It cannot be surprising that the men should be turning longing eyes towards their homes and being anxious to be relieved from a service in which their labors appear to be so little appreciated, and their claims to meet with no attention[502].

The fort was inspected by Brevet Brigadier General James F. Rusling the next autumn. General Rusling was an Inspector with the Quartermaster Department[503] and sent out to inspect the military posts west to San Francisco, especially with a view to suggest economies. He inspected forts Leavenworth, Riley, Kearney, McPherson, Sedgwick, Morgan, and Denver. He seemed to enjoy the trip along the Platte River and even this seasoned traveler was not immune to the sight of the Rocky Mountains at Fort Morgan:

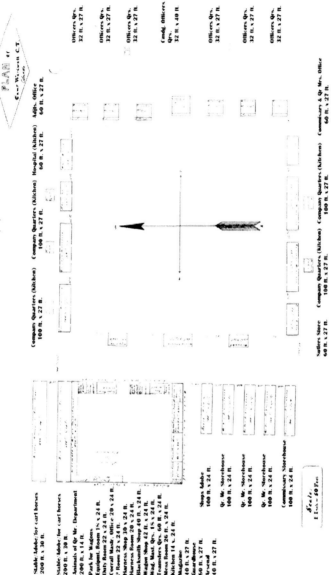

Plan of Camp Wardwell. Image has been digitally cleaned and script transcribed into margins.
Courtesy of the Fort Morgan Museum.

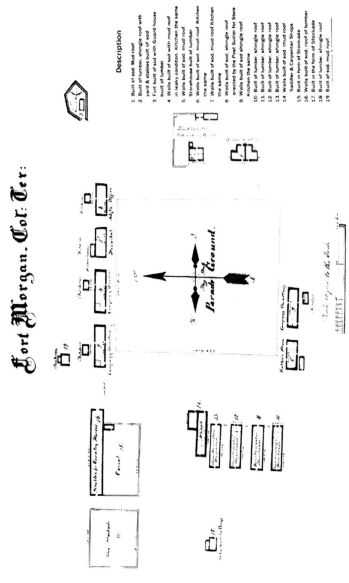

Description

1. Built of sod. Mud roof
2. Built of lumber, shingle roof with yard & stables built of sod
3. Fort built of sod with Guard house built of lumber
4. Walls built of sod with mud roof in leaky condition. Kitchen the same
5. Walls built of sod. mud roof
6. Storehouse built of lumber
7. Walls built of sod. mud roof Kitchen the same
8. Walls built of sod. mud roof Kitchen the same
9. Walls built of sod, shingle roof erected by the Post Sutler for Store
10. Walls built of sod shingle roof. Kitchen the same
11. Built of lumber. shingle roof
12. Built of lumber. shingle roof
13. Built of lumber. shingle roof
14. Walls built of sod. mud roof
15. Saddler & Carpenter Shops
16. Built in form of Stockade
17. Walls built of sod. roof of lumber
18. Built in the form of Stockade
19. Built of lumber. shingle roof

Plan of Fort Morgan c. 1866. Image has been digitally cleaned and script transcribed. Courtesy of the Fort Morgan Museum.

Every hundred miles or so we stopped over a day or two to inspect some Military Post, and so got rested. The scenery from day to day was ever fresh and changing.... I have few pleasanter recollections than in thus staging it outside, across the Plains, and up the Platte to Denver. One night, however, a wind-storm from the summit of the Rocky Mountains struck us, and for hours raged furiously – raw and gusty, piercing to the bone. But at midnight we rolled into Fort Morgan, and halting in its hospitable quarters, waited until the wind blew itself out....

Down in the valley proper, the field of vision is limited by the side bluffs, and you see but comparatively little of the country generally. But ascend the bluffs on either side, and the vast ocean of the Plains stretches boundlessly before you – not flat, but billowy with swells and ridges, an illimitable plateau, with only here and there a solitary "butte," sharply defined against the clear sky. In the sprint this whole vast extent is a wilderness of verdure and flowers; but the summer skies, untempered by rain...scorch and burn the ground to cinders...[but the] short and sweet buffalo-grass is indigenous through all this region, and is said to be nutritious, even when dried up, the year round. What a magnificent range for stock these great Plains will yet afford, when the country becomes more thickly settled up! Much of this region is marked on the old maps as the "Great American Desert;" but from all we saw and heard I doubt not, as a whole, it will yet become the great stock-raising and dairy region of the Republic, whence we shall export beef and mutton, leather and wool....

We had several fine rides with brother-officers among the cañon and bluffs while stopping to inspect our military posts *en route,* and a grand gallop one bright September morning over the Plains and far away after antelope..... The ride itself, however, was a great satisfaction, full of excitement, exhilaration, enjoyment. The sky was a perfect sapphire, without cloud or haze. The clear atmosphere braced one's nerves like wine, and revealed distant objects with a pre-Raphaelite distinctness. A pyramid-like "butte," off to the southwest, seemed near at hand, though more than twenty miles away..... There was just a spice of danger in the ride, too, as Indians were reported prowling about, but none appeared. We left the Platte with its bluffs and cañons behind us, and out into the boundless Plains we rode, on and on, and only drew rein when we discovered that we had lost our reckoning, and were without a compass...and suddenly we found ourselves at sea, without guide or headland. Fortunately we had the well-worn buffalo-trails, that there run almost due north and south – the old paths over which they formerly went to and from the Platte for water – and following up one of these, after an hour or two, we found ourselves in sight of the river again....

The Plains after awhile became somewhat of a bore, they are so vast and outstretched, and you long for a change, something to break the monotony. To us this came one evening, just beyond Fort Morgan, when a hundred and fifty miles away, just peeping above the horizon, we descried the cone-like summit of Long's Peak, all pink and rosy in the sunset. "Driver, isn't that the Mountains?"… "You bet…Tisn't often you can see the Peak this fur; but it is mighty clar to-day!"[504]

Rusling seemed to enjoy his time on the plains, but was less than complimentary about the running of the fort (not an uncommon criticism in his reports of western forts), the quartermaster and the commanding officer – Captain Kellogg. Though Rusling suggested closure of the fort (along with that of Fort Kearney), his report provides great detail about the day-to-day running and construction of the fort and it is reproduced here[505]:

> OFFICE INSPECTOR QUARTERMASTER'S DEPARTMENT,
> *Fort Morgan, C. T., September 4, 1866.*
> GENERAL: I have the honor to announce my arrival here yesterday, and beg leave to submit the following report related to the affairs of quartermaster's department at Fort Morgan, Colorado Territory: This post is situated on the south bank of the South Platte, 105 miles west of Fort Sedgwick and 85 miles east of Denver. At this point the mail road branches off southwest to Denver. Near here is an old Indian crossing of the Platte for tribes moving north or south, formerly much used, but now quite abandoned. The country around is barren and desolate, with no timber growing within fifty miles or more. The garrison consists of two companies 18th infantry, Brevet Major Kellogg commanding; in all, 118 men present. The post does not seem to be of the slightest use at present as Major Kellogg says, and in this I concur. It supplies no other points, and there are no Indians adjacent to overawe.

Denver and its mining regions exerting a salutary influence thus far east and further. It is a costly point to maintain for a variety of reasons, with no adequate return, so far as I can see; so, too the situation is so desolate that it is the next thing to imprisonment to send officers and troops here. I don't wonder at their general discontent and dissatisfaction, of which the natural fruits are more desertions than at any point I have inspected. In view of all the facts, I recommend its abandonment early next season, the troops and supplies to be sent elsewhere.

I. – OFFICERS.

The quartermaster on duty here is Second Lieutenant W. M. Harshberger, 5th United States volunteers and acting assistant quartermaster. He is inexperienced and unfit for his duties, and I recommend his immediate relief, if orders have not already been given for the muster out of his regiment. His chief clerk is actually quartermaster and a tolerably good one, Lieutenant Harshberger contenting himself with signing papers that he knows little or nothing about, nor will he ever learn, as he is of a heavy, sluggish nature, that cares only to drift along. He has not yet learned the first duty of an officer, *implicit obedience*, but quibbles and complaints where he should act promptly. Like most volunteer officers I have met recently, especially those of the 5th and 6th United States volunteers, he has lost all interest in the service, and seems particularly worthless for all army purposes.

II. – PUBLIC ANIMALS.

These consist of fifty horses and eighty-five mules; of these fourteen six-mule teams, one four-horse team, and two four-horse ambulances are in daily use at the post. In addition, thirty-eight horses are held here in pursuance of General Orders No. 33, headquarters department of Missouri, current series, for use of mounted infantry. This order was issued some months ago, but no men have ever been detailed to mount them and the horses have been much neglected, if not improperly used. Their condition now is very bad, though grazed and fed pretty regularly, and the quartermaster alleges that the commanding officer allows the enlisted men to ride them about on pleasure excursions to the neighboring ranches, and off on hunting parties, to their serious detriment. I transmit herewith a copy of a letter, marked A, on this and other subjects, recently addressed to General Easton by Lieutenant Harshberger, and think there is probably some truth in his statements. As the horses have not been used and probably will not be required for the purposes they were sent here for, I respectfully recommend, as the best solution of the difficulties here, that they be ordered elsewhere to mount cavalry, or sent to Denver for sale, where horses are now rating high. As to the balance of animals here, I recommend that they be reduced to ten six-mule teams with sufficient for contingencies, and that all the rest be ordered to Omaha for sale or transfer, according to the necessities of the department. Forage is too costly an article at Morgan to feed more animals here than are absolutely required. The thirty-eight horses above referred to, I should say, are not on the return of the quartermaster, but of a Lieutenant Wilcox, now at Salt Lake and not expected back. But they are at the post and should be disposed of in some way.

III. – CLOTHING, CAMP, AND GARRISON EQUIPAGE

The amount [of clothing, camp and garrison equipage] on hand foots up about four hundred suits, with excess of many articles. The quality is good, and it is all well stored. I recommend its retention here for the present.

IV. – RAIL AND RIVER TRANSPORTATION

The pacific railroad passes west some distance north of here, going up Lodge Pole creek, as stated in my report on Fort Sedgwick at length. It will not avail much for this post, even when completed. Now all supplies are delivered here by wagon transportation from the Missouri and Denver, and the system is working excellently well. I passed a train of thirty wagons, of subsistence principally, twenty miles east of here, *en route* to Fort Morgan, and its marching condition was admirable. I have seen no better nor more ship-shape trains in the army or elsewhere. All officers concur in awarding Mr. Caldwell, the contractor on this route, the highest praise, and I deem it but justice to record the fact here....

V. – REGULAR SUPPLIES.

(a) Fuel. - A year's supply of wood is on hand – about 1,100 cords. This was delivered here from Denver at a cost of $24.95 per cord – a very reasonable price when the cost of freight is considered. It was delivered here chiefly by return freight trains going east. No peat has been discovered in this vicinity, though the Platte bottom undoubtedly contains it. Of coal, however, there is a bet-

ter prospect. Mr. Yates, chief clerk quartermaster's partment, thinks coal can be found within ten or twelve miles, and is positive that it exists sixty miles southeast on the Bijou, a dry stream here. He says both bituminous and cannel coal have been found there, and that the country between contains sufficient water to supply trains *en route.* I directed Lieutenant Harshberger, verbally, to look well into this coal question; and also requested Major Kellogg to see that due attention was given it. Should this post be maintained, this coal supply is a very important matter here, and the quartermaster on duty ought to press it with vigor.

(b) Forage. - There are no oats; but of corn there is on hand 6,705 bushels – about a year's supply for animals on hand; it is in good condition, and well housed in a substantial frame forage house.... The amount on hand had better be retained for the present, for current use and issue. The hay on hand consists of about one hundred and thirty tons; this was received last year, at from five to twenty miles away and cost delivered there $29.50 per ton – a most egregious and costly folly as much of it was north of the Platte, and still stands in stack there, the Platte not being fordable now, and has not been for several weeks; moreover, the bulk of it is believed spoiled now, and I think it safe to report the whole one hundred and thirty tons as unserviceable and worthless, as a further supply of five hundred tons has recently been contracted for, sufficient for twelve months, to be delivered at the post at a cost of $12 per ton, which does not seem a living price for the contractor – so at least citizens and others say

here; and their only explanation is, that the contractor has many other contracts, and hopes to make off of them sufficient to play for his loss on this. He is a Mr. John H. Martin, of Denver; and Colonel Howard deserves much credit for getting the hay supplied at this low figure; it is certainly very reasonable. This hay will all be delivered at the post, and a forage-yard is being constructed to protect it. The hay itself is cut on the islands and Platte bottoms adjacent to the post embraced in the reservation, and the mowing machines belonging to the post are loaned to the contractor.

VI. – RESERVATION, PUBLIC AND PRIVATE BUILDINGS.

The reservation here is an area of land four miles square, embracing both sides of the Platte. I cannot learn anything of its origin, there being no records on file here. The post itself was established in 1864. A map has just been completed for General Easton, and I have directed a copy to be sent to you. The public buildings consist of several good frame storehouses, sufficient for a year's supply of all stores needed at the post, and a variety of sod buildings, all practically worthless. A report is herewith showing buildings more particularly. The barracks are intended for three companies; only two are occupied, the third being now used as a cow stable and guard-house. There are no floors in any of these. The roofs are dirt and sods, and all leak badly. The hospital is about the same as the barracks; it has a capacity of a dozen patients, but there are no sick at the post. There are no quarters for officers of any kind. The commanding officer lives in a hospital tent, and the other officers quarter in the store-house and hospital. Two sod buildings are now going up – one for post commandant, and the other for officers' quarters; but both are badly planned, and will probably tumble down before completion; the walls are too high, and are already cracking and bulging out, though the roofs are not yet on. No attempt has been made at abodes proper. Some lumber sent here from Denver, for floors, &c., for these buildings, cost, delivered here, $45 per thousand feet for boards, and $4.50 per thousand for shingles. I am persuaded that this will put up buildings at Fort Morgan cheaper than either sod or adobe, besides being infinitely more comfortable and suitable for troops in all respects. I am the more convinced of this from observing the practice of settlers here – a safe rule ordinarily to go by. All or very nearly all their buildings going up about here are frame; and they tell me the same is the case from here to Denver. The overland stage company especially knows what it is about, and its sod-buildings all ceased some stations back. It finds it cheaper and better to import lumber from Denver, and I think the quartermaster's department would find it the same, so far as Fort Morgan is concerned. The post seems to have been established without much regard to system, and, as a whole, reflects little credit on the service. The storehouses, shops, corral, stable, and sutler store, all face on the parade ground as the post now stands; and, as I have before said, one of the barracks is used as a post cow-stable. It is but just to say that the plan of the post, when completed, excludes part of these. Still its present appearance is anything but inviting, and I know of nothing better than to repeat my former recommendation, namely to break it up and abandon it early next season. Indeed, this might be done this year, I think, without loss to the service. Should the post, however be maintained, I recommend the use of lumber in preference to all other building materials here. There is no stone. Drawings of the buildings at the post are just about being completed in accordance with existing orders, and they will be forwarded to you without delay. There are no quarters for employees except tents, and no chapel or reading-room. All of these will have to be provided should the post be maintained.

VII. - EMPLOYÉS

The roll of employés foots up 28 men, at a total cost per month of $2,075, exclusive of quarters and rations. In addition to these the bulk of the troops at the post are constantly employed in putting up sod buildings and doing other necessary work, so that the actual working force at the post is considerable. None of these, however, have been hitherto reported. I direct this to be done hereafter. The force of clerks I think unduly large. I recommend them to be reduced to one. This, with such detailed men as the garrison would readily afford, I judge sufficient, and in this Major Kellogg concurs. The rest of the employés will be necessary until the post is housed; but by December 1 the force ought to be reduced still further.

VIII. – CEMETERY.

There is no cemetery proper here. A sort of a post burying-ground exists half a mile or so east, in which there are eight graves, supposed to be civilians, and three soldiers are buried a quarter of a mile away in another place by the roadside. No headboards worth mentioning are at any of these. I directed Lieutenant Harshberger to remove the soldier graves to the place occupied by the eight others, as they are on an isolated bluff, and to enclose not exceeding half an acre there with a substantial sod wall. A report of these graves, I was told, had been duly rendered to your office.

IX. – FIRE DEPARTMENT.

No provision whatever against fires exists at this post. Water is supplied from the Platte by a water wagon.... Of course I found inflammable oils in the main warehouses; so, too, the post wood-pile was just up against the principal storehouse. I directed the removal of these, and the placing of barrels and buckets of water in all the storehouses, and a well to be dug without delay; also a requisition to be made for a pump, which I recommend to be sent to Fort Morgan from Denver....

XI. – MISCELLANEOUS.

1. I regret to say that the general arrangement of this post seems bad. The quartermaster neither knows his duties nor wants to, and should never have been assigned to such a duty. The larger part of his duties are actually performed by Colonel Howard, at Denver, who makes all his contracts, and the balance are done by his chief clerk.

2. I think the post commander, Major Kellogg, interferes too much with the quartermaster's department, and is not sufficiently courteous to the quartermaster. He is in the bad habit of sending orders direct to Lieutenant

Harshberger's employés instead of to or through him, and these usually only verbal ones by soldiers indiscriminately. Because some of these have not been promptly obeyed, the employés insisting that their orders should come from the quartermaster, Major Kellogg has peremptorily ordered their discharge. This is wrong, for obvious reasons, and I recommend that Major Kellogg be instructed accordingly.

RECAPITULATION.

1. I recommend that Lieutenant Harshberger be relieved from duty as post quartermaster....

2. I recommend that the public animals at the post be reduced to 10 six-mule teams, with sufficient contingencies, and that the surplus be sent to Omaha for sale or transfer, according to the necessities of the department....

3. I recommend lumber as the proper and cheapest material for building purposes at Fort Morgan....

4. I recommend that Lieutenant Harshbberger's clerks be reduced to one, and that the force of employés be still further reduced by December 1....

5. I recommend that a pump be sent to Fort Morgan, from Denver, for use of a well to be dug there immediately....

6. I recommend the post to be broken up and abandoned as no longer necessary....

7. I recommend that the post commander, Major Kellogg, be instructed in his duties as to the quartermaster's department....

Copies of orders issued while here are herewith enclosed.

I am, general, very respectfully, your obedient servant,

JAMES F. RUSLING,
Brevet Brigadier General, Inspector Q. M. D.

Rusling recommended the closure of the fort, but the military was making plans to control the Indians on the plains and these plans included Fort Morgan.

The 7th Cavalry: A Tale of Desertion

The 7th U. S. Cavalry was formed July 28, 1866 to fight Indians on the plains and to protect the overland mail and work crews building the railroad. In the spring of 1867, Major General Winfield Scott Hancock and Lieutenant Colonel George A. Custer set off on what became known as the Hancock Expedition. The purpose was to meet with the various tribes and discuss peace, but if necessary fight the Indians roaming in western Kansas and Nebraska and eastern Colorado[506]. In support of the Hancock Expedition, companies of the newly formed 7th U. S. Cavalry were stationed at key forts including Fort Morgan. Company L of the 7th U. S. Cavalry was stationed at Fort Morgan under the command of Captain Michael V. Sheridan[507]. Rusling's report does not mention the cavalry company suggesting that the company was still *en route* to Fort Morgan at the time his report was written.

Captain Michael Sheridan was the brother of General Philip H. Sheridan, but he did not seem to be the leader that his brother was. On January 14, 1867, almost immediately after Major Kellogg and the 18th U. S. Infantry marched for Casper, Wyoming and Captain Sheridan took over command of Fort Morgan, all hell broke loose. Thirty-one soldiers under Sheridan's command deserted *en masse* stealing horses and heading south along the Cut-off, robbing a stagecoach along the way. Captain Sheridan reported the incident to General Chauncey McKeever:

> I regret to inform you that on the morning of the 14th inst. At half past one o'clock, twenty-nine men of Co. "L" 7th U. S. Cavalry deserted from this post taking with them their horses and equipments. I became aware of their intention to desert on the 9th instant and succeeded in foiling their first attempt by visiting the stables at an unexpected hour on the night of the 10th and catching their horses saddled. On account of the darkness I could catch none of the men. On the morning of the 14th they succeeded in getting off after having "backed" my farrier whom I had ordered to sleep in the stables to prevent his giving information. All the members of the guard went with the party except two. I am satisfied they intend going to Mexico and from information received while pursuing them I think their route will be Fort Union. They are a desperate band of men and have already commenced depredations in the country by robbing passengers in the Overland coach and stealing horses from citizens[508].

This renegade detachment, consisting of three sergeants, five corporals and 21 privates[509], was rumored to be heading to Denver to attack and pillage the city[510] "well mounted and very heavily armed, each one having two revolvers and about two hundred rounds of ammunition[511]." Denver had feared an attack, but their fears were directed at the Indian tribes in the area; the threat of attack from the very soldiers sent to protect them was unthinkable. The *Rocky Mountain News* reported on the panic following news of the desertion:

A considerable excitement existed in the city, last night, over…the desertion of thirty-one men from Fort Morgan, who were bound for Denver, with burglarious intent…. Our citizens, generally, got their shooting irons in readiness, the police force was increased, and a squad of mounted men, some twenty in number, patrolled the approaches to the city. The excitement lulled as the small hours drew on, although there was no time in the night, when a few pistol shots would not have alarmed the city, and insured the promised visitants from Fort Morgan, a warm reception. There was good cause for this preparation on the part of our citizens, as the information that led to it came from Captain John [sic] Sheridan, commanding at the post where the men deserted…. Many of the more timorous were sadly frightened…. Many others indulged in pouring libations to Bacchus until they forgot their fears and become oblivious of danger. The most improbable part of the story is, that old experienced soldiers should start on a desperate venture of this kind, and leave the telegraph intact, so that knowledge of their movements could be sent in advance of them. No soldier, who fought or served in the late war, would be so forgetful as to neglect breaking the line of communication – a thing that all have so frequently witnessed or performed in the war[512].

Denver waited and watched, but the marauders never arrived. Majors DoMary and Logan went from Denver in pursuit but with no success. Over a week later, four of the deserters stumbled into Denver with a tale to tell:

> ...The desertion was planned by a sergeant of the company, and the party escaping comprised the guard on duty the night they left. Among them were seven men who opposed the movement, but the sargeant [sic] and his followers compelled them to go along to secure their own safety. From Kiowa they followed the Smoky Hill road, and at a point twenty miles beyond the junction, the deserting party robbed the seven men referred to, of horses, guns, pistols, &c., and left them upon the prairie. They tried to find settlements, and after undergoing incredible hardships from hunger and cold, at length succeeded; or at least the four who came in here did. They are of the opinion that the three are also safe....[513]

There are various contradictory stories about the desertion. In the above version, the soldiers were taken unwillingly from the fort, in another version the soldiers had no intention of deserting[514]:

> ...The first sergeant, after tattoo roll call, went into the barrack room and designated thirty men to saddle their horses for detached service, armed and equipped, and had the cooks issue each man rations for a period of days. The sergeant mounted the detachment, marched it quietly out of the post, and when some distance away, moved rapidly until about thirty miles from the post. Then he halted the detachment and informed the men that they were all deserters and it was then every man for himself, said good-bye, and started south for the mining region. Two or three at once turned back, returned to the

fort and gave themselves up, and told the story of their deception[515].

However, Colonel Powell, the commanding officer of the company that relieved the 7th U. S. Cavalry at Fort Morgan, told yet a different story:

> …The men had grown weary of the isolation, and a plan was formed for a wholesale exit from the post. It is also claimed that the leaders contemplated an attack on Denver, then a flourishing frontier village, and the looting of the place. The plans were well laid and were carried out without a hindrance in any particular. Each man was given a special duty to perform. It was so arranged that none but conspirators were on guard at the time of the departure. Orders were given that if any officer attempted to leave the quarters on the evening the plot was to be put into effect he was to be shot down without mercy. The evening was very cold, and fortunately for the officers not one of them left his room. The men were to ride away from the post. The horses were fully equipped and the party carried abundant supplies of food and ammunition. The deserters carried the guard with them, and the surprise of the troops remaining at the garrison the next morning may be imagined….
>
> One of the strangest features about the affair, however, is the mysterious disappearance of the men. Not a single person in the deserting party was ever afterward heard from. It is not known whether the men were massacred by the Indians, lost on the plains, or whether they reached the seashore and started for some distant country….[516]

Colonel Powell noted that none of the 31 deserters were found, but the newspaper story of January 23 was based on the account of 4 of the deserters. A frozen deserter was also found abandoned near Kiowa stage station the night after the desertion[517] and six additional deserters were reportedly found at Sand Creek by Sergeant Kelley and a group of Denver volunteers[518]. The remaining 20 were still at large in April 1867 possibly moving south as rumored to make a new life in one of the southern states or Mexico else succumbing to Indians or the bitter winter of the plains.

Even though the desertions from Fort Morgan were notable because of the sheer number of soldiers who deserted, desertion was a major problem in the military of the time, especially for the 7th U. S. Cavalry. Soldiers found the winter months on the plains harsh and became bored when not chasing Indians or escorting trains. Other finding themselves close to the gold mining camps, deserted in order to pursue their fortune[519]. Between April and July of 1867, 120 men reportedly deserted from the regiment[520]. Even General Sherman's command was not immune. In June of 1867, Generals Sherman and Augur commenced a tour of the forts along the South Platte River. After the soldier charged with guarding General Sherman's tent deserted with an officer's horse, he placed a Pawnee guard on the tent – and the horses[521,522]. When an additional 13 soldiers deserted from General Custer's command near Fort Morgan in broad daylight, seven taking horses, Custer ordered the men found and brought back – by what ever means necessary[523]. During the chase, six of the deserters were shot and Custer famously ordered that the wounded not be given medical treatment[524]. For this,

General Custer was court martialed[525].

Custer excused his actions arguing that "...the desertions from his command were so frequent, and had at last become so numerous as to threaten the safety of the command.[526]" Referring to the deserters from Fort Morgan, Custer argued in his own defense:

...I answer orders from superior authority and the customs of war. The orders to which I refer, and which afford ample authority for my acts, emanated from Major General Hancock, at that time commanding the Department in which I was serving, and under whose orders I had set out upon the expedition in which I was then engaged. These orders had been sent by General Hancock to almost every post in his Department, including the remote ones of New Mexico, and had reference to a party of forty deserters that had left my regiment, or a portion of it at that time commanded by Colonel Sheridan, a brother of the General's. This party had deserted from Colonel Sheridan's command in time of peace, and under much less aggravating circumstances than those attending the desertions which took place at the time of which I write. General Hancock, upon receiving the intelligence of this desertion, telegraphed an order to Colonel Sheridan, commanding at Fort Morgan, and to almost every subordinate commander in his Department to be on the alert for this party of deserters, as, in making their escape to the settlements, they would probably pass in the vicinity of some military post. General Hancock further ordered that the entire party should be "killed or captured," adding that it would have a decidedly good effect upon the army if his order could be carried out[527].

Custer's defence did not work and he was found guilty and suspended for one year.

As for the remaining troops at Fort Morgan, Captain Sheridan was quietly removed from command and became an aide to his brother[528,529] and as soon as the weather permitted, the company of the 7th U. S. Cavalry left Fort Morgan now under the command of Lieutenant Gillette[530] with orders to build a military post at Reed's Springs[531]. Before arriving, the plans for the military post were abandoned and Company L was sent to Fort Reynolds near Pueblo.

The Hancock expedition had not been a success. In April of 1967, General Hancock met with Cheyenne and Sioux chiefs camped near Fort Larned, Kansas on the Smoky Hill Route. When the chiefs delayed the meeting and then secretly abandoned the village, possibly fearing a reprise of the Sand Creek Massacre, General Hancock ordered the village destroyed and over the next months, Custer and the 7th U. S. Cavalry chased the Indians across the plains[532], but while Custer's troops were at the Republican River, the Indians attacked the Platte route. By the time Custer's troops arrived at the Platte, the Indians were back attacking the southern routes[533,534]. By the middle of 1867, the people of Colorado were frustrated with the military's inability to control the Indians and feelings ran high. General Sherman refused to allow a militia of local men either because he did not trust the men of Colorado or in his pride thought that the military could handle the situation.

Final Salute: 4th U. S. Infantry

The days of Fort Morgan as a military post were coming to an end. The worst of the Indian attacks had moved away from the South Platte River and the overland mail was quickly being replaced by the railroad. The South Platte River Road was no longer the center of Indian troubles, but that did not mean the road was safe and quiet. In many ways, the summer of 1867 was much like the summer of 1864 with Indians attacking stage stations and trains and running off stock despite the presence of soldiers along the route:

From Junction – or the cut-off – 100 miles east of Denver to Bishop's Ranche, a distance of 180 miles, the road is lined with burned ranches. Some of them have been burned within the last week. The reign of terror is on the plains. Pilgrims go cautiously and well armed. Bushwackers walk the river side keep their heavily-loaded wagons between the and bluffs and themselves, proceeding step by step with the greatest caution, examining every ravine, dubiously peering into every bush, their carbines on their half-cock, their wagons in close column, and thus the trader's goods are being conveyed the weary road across the plains to the gold regions, literally groping their way. All indications on the Plains point to a determination on the part of the Indians to avenge the conflagration at Pawnee Fork. The insufficiency of soldiers along the great highway to the West is one great cause which prompts the Indians to muster in force on the Platte…[535]

The desertions of the 7th Cavalry left the fort's manpower severely depleted, but relief was on the way in the form of

Company G of the 4th U. S. Infantry under the command of Captain William H. Powell. Company G consisted of 102 men including four commissioned officers[536]. This company of the 4th U. S. Infantry would be the last to man the fort.

Captain Powell was an active military man serving in the Civil War battles of Malvern Hill, the 2nd Battle of Bull Run, Antietam, Fredericksburg, and Gettysburg. He was made Brevet Captain for his service at Antietam and Brevet Major for suppressing the Fenian raid in 1866[537]. Captain Powell and his company started from Madison Barracks, New York in March of 1867, marching west to Omaha and then in May moving onto Fort Morgan arriving on June 3[rd538]. On their way to Fort Morgan, they watched Indians attack an emigrant train across the river, but were powerless to intercede.

…Within view of the soldiers a large wagon train was attacked by Indians and the entire force in charge of the train was wiped out of existence. The white men made a gallant resistance, but the redskins outnumbered them ten to one. After killing the escort the Indians seized such property as they liked and set fire to the wagons. A great

Attack on an Overland stage. Published in Harper's Weekly, *1866.*

smoke rising toward the sky gave notice for many miles in all directions of the awful deed.... [W]e could do absolutely nothing [said Powell]. The river was a raging torrent and the quicksands made it wholly impossible for us to cross to the opposite side, where the battle was in progress. The road which the train was following was quite a distance on the north side. We were on foot on the south bank of the stream. From our position we saw the Indians sweep down upon the train, saw the hasty gathering of the wagons in a circle and the last desperate struggle. We never learned from what point the wagons came or whither they were going. There were perhaps fifty wagons in the train....[539].

In August 1867, a treaty was signed with the Arapaho and Cheyenne in which the tribes agreed to withdraw from the Platte River area[540]. The military, with the new agility afforded them by the railroads, centralized operations at larger forts, closing smaller outposts[541]. In September of 1967, the Overland Mail was discontinued[542], the mail service being taken over by the less vulnerable railroad and most of the telegraph offices were closed, though the one at Junction remained open to relay messages to Denver. Troops would still ride the South Platte for years to come, but Fort Morgan was abandoned as a base of operations and the equipment and provisions at the fort were sold at auction. On May 18, 1868, the flag was lowered for the last time and the cannon fired a last salute. Captain Powell and the 4th U. S. Infantry marched to Fort Laramie[543]. The fort lay amongst buffalo and buffalo grass and waited; the sod fort melting back into the plains.

∞

Chapter 8

Of Cattle and Crops

A quarter of a century elapsed between the closing of the fort and the rise of the town of Fort Morgan. The prospectors of the 1860s were, on the whole, transient, looking for riches rather than a new home, but it wouldn't be long before another venture brought westward travelers – this time with their eye set on the land under their feet rather than the mountains on the horizon.

Few early travelers saw the potential in the arid sand. The Platte Valley was "comparatively worthless for agricultural purposes, there are some bottom lands and islands it is true, which will yield good crops, but these bear a very small proportion to the whole, there is no soil at all much of the way, and then *alkali* whitens and poisons thousands of acres in other places[544]." The plains were described as a "howling wilderness...sparsely grasssed [sic]...destitute of timber, and fitted for pastoral purposes only, from the scarcity of water[545]." The lands were dry, yet four rivers wandered across the plains of northeast Colorado. The grass was sparse, yet enormous herds of buffalo favored the area. The land was a howling wilderness, yet many Cheyenne fought and died to retain it. Hardy emigrants saw the contradictions and looked for the potential in the land. Cattle came first and then, when the engineers came to harness the water, crops.

The Great American Pasture

Buffalo during the 19th century wandered in great herds across northeastern Colorado living off of the sweet buffalo grass growing on the plains. It was the buffalo that brought trappers into the area in the early part of the century and Fremont, upon entering the Fort Morgan area for the first time in 1842 noted that "buffalo absolutely covered the plain on both sides the river, and whenever we ascended the hills, scattered herds gave life to the view in every direction[546]." In 1873, there were still herds of buffalo along the South Platte River. A. R. Ross wrote of a hunting trip with his brother-in-law Johnny Frazier near the ruins of Fort Morgan:

Buffalo herd on the plains. From A Dangerous Crossing and what Happened on the Other Side.

...When we arrived at Fort Morgan Flats, we didn't need to hunt buffalo any farther, the whole face of the country was covered with them. I will not attempt to describe the scene before me. Thousands of them were moving to and fro regardless of our presence. We drove through this vast herd of peaceable buffalo until we could find room and a suitable place to camp, and get ready for the hunt.

We started out the next day.... [M]et up with a band of Indians chasing a bunch of buffalo. The twang of the bow and swish of the arrow as it sped on its mission sounded distinctly in our ears above the confusion and noise of pounding hoofs. Johnny leaped on the back of our saddle horse with a Navy 6 revolver in his hand and took part in the chase. When we counted the crippled buffalo lying along the line of chase, five were shot in the "coupling," or the small of the back, and had no arrows in them. Therefore, our claim to them could not be disputed. Johnny had shot six times and had downed five buffaloes....

...the whole country was still alive with buffalo grazing along the roadside and not interested in our outfit in the least. They were coming in to the flats from all directions. We became interested as we watched them browsing leisurely over this vast tract of land. Nothing but the crumbling wall of the Old Fort was visible on the entire flat.... [The buffalo] had been closing in on us from all directions and were pawing and hooking the bloody hide. We were being surrounded by the furious animals and were fortunate to get to the wagon...[547]

By the end of the century, the large herds of buffalo would be gone, hunted to near extinction for their meat and hides and for sport, but it was clear the land could support mammoth herds of bovine – a fact not lost on ranchers. The potential for raising cattle on the eastern plains was discovered as early as 1859 when weak animals left by prospectors in the winter were found alive and well the next spring[548]. The lands in the Fort Morgan area, especially the grasslands north of the South Platte River, were prime grazing lands and many ranchers began herds in the area.

In the 1871, Lyman H. Cole, one of the members of the Southwestern Colony, established a ranch at Fremont's Orchard[549] and Bruce F. Johnson established the 22 Ranch near Merino, Colorado[550]. At "the old Junction" Mark Boughton had about 2,500 cattle with "as fine a cattle-range as there is in the world, not excluding the pampas of South America and the tablelands of Australia[551]." By 1887, dozens of ranches had spread across the plains.

Stock were left to wander freely, fattening naturally on the rich grass on the plains surrounding the South Platte River. Each spring, the ranchers separated out their stock for sale or to drive them back to their home ranges and the calves were branded. This was known as the spring round-up. Eugene Williams, a cow puncher from 1871 until 1886 described the process:

> Each of the ranchers along the river had from a few hundred to many thousand head of cattle on the range and during the winter months many of the cattle would drift many miles away from the home range. The event of most interest to the stockman every year was the spring

roundup, when the stray cattle were gathered and driven back to the home range.... As soon as the new grass got high enough to keep the saddle horses in good condition, the roundup would start. Each of the larger outfits would send a wagon with as many men and horses as were needed to handle their cattle. The smaller outfits would be represented by from one to three men, all going with one wagon. There were from five to ten men with each wagon and each man would have from six to ten saddle horses. With each wagon there was one man called the horse wrangler, whose duty it was to take charge of the horses during the day. Another man stayed with the horses at night.

From fifteen to twenty wagons, with the men and horses, would meet at Julesburg where a round-up boss would be appointed. On the morning when work was to start, all the riders would go to the outfit the boss was with and there get their orders for the day's work. There would be from one hundred to one hundred and fifty men and they were sent out (on horseback) in the shape of a fan, with the base at the point where the roundup was to be held. All cattle within that radius and from five to ten miles out from the river were to be driven in to the roundup grounds. As many as ten thousand were driven in sometimes, but if there were more than twenty-five hundred or three thousand they were cut into bunches of about two thousand head, as larger bunches were unwieldy and hard to handle.

After the cattle were brought in everybody would go to camp and get dinner and change horses, leaving just enough men to keep the cattle together…. Men would be stationed at short intervals around the herd to keep them closely bunched, while a few men rode into the herd and cut out any cattle with the brand they were representing.

The reading of brands is a business in itself and it requires years of experience to become expert in it. The cutting out was always done by older men. When the men who were in the herd found an animal with their brand it was cut out from the herd and driven outside and held until all the cattle of that brand were taken out…. These small bunches, cut from the larger herd, were called cavys…. After all the outfits had worked all the herds and taken out all the cattle claimed by them, the rest of the herd was turned loose to back to the hills….[552]

Each year, the time and place for the round up was announced to all the ranchers in the area and cattle by the thousand were gathered in[553]. The 1875 Arapaho and Weld round-up was held at the mouth of Beaver Creek[554] and in 1884, the new town of Brush was the chosen site. Denver sightseers went by the thousands to see the cowboys at work. On July 4, 1884, a correspondent from the *Chicago Daily Tribune* traveled by rail to witness the scene first hand and romanticize on the life of a cowboy:

…[A] picturesque scene lay under the broiling sun and blue Colorado skies. There was the line of teams winding over the plains, horsemen dashing hither and thither; here a red-shirted rider – a bright bit of color – there three or four racing cowboys; in one direction a herd of horses, here and there white tents, before the great mass of cattle with restless movement, lowing and bleating, above them a cloud of dust rising from their constant tread, away beyond, a second group of cattle, a pond sparkling in the sunlight, and away, far as the eye could reach, green, green meadows off to the distant, hazy horizon. The teams made a stand on a small hillock where a good view of the cattle was obtained and where there was safety from the peregrinations of the frenzied steers separated from the herd by the drivers – and, by the way, those cattle were good runners, needing a quick horse to herd them, and tearing across the plain in a 2:40 gait....

The first bunch of cattle seen contained perhaps 1,000 head, the grand round-up having taken place Saturday, and yesterday's program being a final culling and separating of the different brands. The cowboy enters the herd, picks out a particular brand, and drives the animal some distance from the herd; other boys do likewise; in some cases the animals went peaceably; in others they rushed madly in any but the desired direction, leading to a grand chase. One or two cows...openly rebelled and had to be dragged. The cowboy lassoes such an animal by the horns, then by some dexterous movement entangles its foot in the rope, and down falls the cow to come to terms. Some steers invaded the hillock crowd, but created no alarm.... A couple of sightseers attempted to cross the prairie beyond the cattle, but were prevented in time, for the sight of people on foot at such a time often causes a herd to stampede from fright....

The cowboys life is an exciting one, hardy, and adventurous. He eats in a tent, lives on his steed, and sleeps under the stars, seldom with blanket or fire.... He must be quick, of ring eye and aim, nervy to try new horses, to venture into wild herds of excited, angry cattle.... The round-up lasts ten or twelve days longer and will take in the Platte to Ogalalla and Bijou and Muddy Creeks and Weld County entire....[555]

Brush, ten miles east of Fort Morgan, was to become a major shipping point for cattle once the Burlington Railroad was completed in 1882, but there were a number of cattle trails running north and south from Texas and Oklahoma through to Wyoming and Montana that traversed the

COLORADO BRAND BOOK.

Name	Brand
A. Anderson, Fort Morgan.	N
Argo & Archibald, Pinneo.	K/ KY
F. E. Baker, Fort Morgan.	FEB
E. A. Boyle, Brush.	B,
M. R. Clark, Snyder.	
Larry H. Conner, Fort Morgan.	ZHZ
J. A. Conyers, Fort Morgan.	
J. B. Courtney, Ft. Morgan.	
A. M. Crawford, Port Morgan.	L>
C. E. Dorsey, Merino.	L+ u. b. l. e.
Downs & Simpson, Brush.	4B
Levi A. Farwell, Orchard.	JF l. sh. & s., o. b. r. e. h. b. same l. sh.
William Fick, Brush.	6F l. s. o. b. r., u. b. l. e, h. b. same l. h.
The Fort Morgan Live Stock and Land Co., Ft. Morgan.	
W. H. & M. B. Gill, Brush.	22 h. b. r. th.
Wm. T. Gilley, Brush.	JU
Cuba Godfrey, Brush.	6+ h. l. th.
Hippolyte Girardet, Orchard.	l. s., c. b. e. l. s., c. b. e. h. b. l. sh.
Fred B. Girardot, Orchard.	X l. s., r. b. e.
Gaume & Shumate, Deuell.	l. s., c. b. e. h. b. same l. sh.
Gaume & Saunier, Duell.	l. s. h. b. same l. sh.
Wm. Hallock, Deuel.	UH
H. C. Hatch, Merino.	Y8
H. C. Heaven, Orchard.	
Frank'n B. Hotchkiss, Ft. Morgan.	r. & l. s., ho. b. e. h. b. same r. & l. sh.
L. A. Jackson, Orchard.	l. s., or h., c. & s. r., s. l. e. h, b. same l. sh. or th.
J. H. Johnston, Brush.	
Jas. H. Jones, Orchard.	
Mich. Kleckner, Fort Morgan.	R
W. J. Kram, Brush.	l. s. & h. h. b. same l. sh.
C. I. Lawton, Brush.	l. s. (line round l. fore leg cattle) h. b. same l. sh.
Christ Liehe, Brush.	OIO r. & l. s., s. b. e. h. b. same l. sh.
J. H. McGinnis, Brush.	Z+
H. B. Marvin, Corona.	l. s. h. b. same l. sh.
A. Miller, Merino.	M l. s., ho. r. e. h. b. same l. h.
Robert J. Minter, Orchard.	UP
Nelson & Kinkel, Fort Morgan.	HH
Bennet N. Nelson, Fort Morgan.	ZL l. h. h. b. same l. th.
Rasmus Nelson, Brush.	l. h., s. f. l. e. h. b. same l. sh.
A. D. Preston, Orchard.	8P l. s. h. b. same l. sh.
Samuel Raugh, Brush.	H l. b. h. b. same l. sh.
Geo. B. Redfield, Fort Morgan.	
Edward Richter, Brush.	R
D. E. Rissdorph, Snyder.	l. s. & h., or a. p. s., o. s. l. e. h. b. same l. th. or. a. p. a.
Gerrard Rough, Brush.	
H. N. Rouse, Fort Morgan.	HR l. s., or h., j u, h, l, e., w. r. n, h. b. same l. sh.
A. A. Smith, Snyder.	ho. r. e.
Frank O. Thompson, Corona.	l. s. & h., g. r. e. h. b. same l. sh.
Thomson & Nelson, Orchard.	8-0
John T. Wylie, Brush.	+iY l. sh. h. b. same l. sh. h. b. l. th.

Brands in the Fort Morgan area from the Colorado Brand Book for 1887. Abbreviations refer to where the brand was located (e.g., l.sh. = left shoulder.)

Fort Morgan area including the Potter and Bacon Trail and a fork of the Goodnight and Loving Trail. The Potter and Bacon Trail named for Colonel Jack Potter and Alfred T. Bacon of the New England Cattle Company[556] was a variant of the Western Trail, branching off at Albany, Texas before heading north to Cheyenne, Wyoming. This trail was also known as the Potter and Blocker Trail (or the XIT trail[557]), after Abner P. Blocker of the XIT (Ten In Texas) Ranch who used a similar route after 1885 to move herds from Texas to Montana. Jack Potter described the blazing of the trail:

In the spring of '83 we received a bunch of cattle at Pena station on the Texas and Mexican

Swimming the Platte. From The Log of a Cowboy

railroad...[and] came into the Western trail at San Antonio. I drove this herd seven hundred miles before it rained on us.... Alfred T. Bacon, who headquartered at Greeley, Colorado, manager of the New England Cattle Company, the company for which I was working, sent me instructions for the rest of the drive, which included a map with a trail outlined on it, telling me that if I could follow the route designated I would save about twenty days' time. On the way-bill of this map was Goodnight ranch, Tascosa, Buffalo Springs, the OX ranch on the Cimarron, Fort Lyons on the Arkansas, and South Platt [sic] at the mouth of the Bijou. I got through all right by having a fuss with the Goodnight people and having to detour around their range because their cattle, having been driven from the north, were not immune from tick fever. Leih Duyer, Goodnight's brother-in-law, told me this was the first through herd that had ventured out from the Western trail, and since I had opened the way he thought others would follow and cause them a good deal of trouble. I have seen this trail marked on different maps and called by different names. I am sure I blazed this trail and it should be named the Potter and Bacon trail. Bacon mapped it and Potter drove it.[558]

The Potter and Bacon trail was short-lived. Ranchers in Oklahoma such as Charles Goodnight moved to block the influx of Texas cattle along the trail near his ranch for fear of disease. But while it lasted, this trail linked two "cattle kings", Charles Goodnight and John W. Iliff.

Iliff

John Wesley Iliff, one of the early emigrants to Denver, started with a ranch near Elbridge Gerry's (near Greeley) and then when drought hit the area, moved east to Fremont's Orchard at the source of Kiowa Creek[559]. From there Iliff would build a cattle empire that became a western legend.

Iliff began by buying sick or injured stock from passing emigrants, which he fattened on the lush grasslands[560]. In 1866, Iliff bought 750[561] head from Oklahoma cattle king Charles Goodnight, 6,000 more in 1868 and three years later, Goodnight delivered another 25,000-30,000 cattle to Iliff[562]. Goodnight and Oliver Loving drove the stock to Iliff's then pressed on to Cheyenne with the rest of the herd along the trail that became known as the Loving or the Goodnight and Loving Trail[563]. The cattle crossed the South Platte River near Crow Creek (just west of Fremont's Orchard) and Goodnight described the Texas longhorn swimming across the river with only their heads and horns above the water "looked like a million floating rocking chairs[564]."

Iliff's ranch – if it could be described as just one ranch – expanded to include much of northeastern Colorado and included the land north of the Fort Morgan area. Ranch houses were located all along the South Platte River including one near Iliff, Colorado (northeast of Sterling) and on the Wildcat Creek near Fort Morgan[565,566]. In 1875, the *New York Times* published a piece entitled "The Cattle King of the West" describing Iliff's empire[567].

Iliff had amassed a huge herd, but he also controlled much of the grazing lands in northeastern Colorado in a triangle from Julesburg to Denver to Cheyenne. But it wasn't just the amount of land or the size of his stock that made him successful, Iliff controlled the land by controling the water on the range. Iliff purchased only 15,558 acres of land, but he monopolized the water rights along the South Platte[568]. Other ranchers could operate only if he granted them access to streams and ponds. By owning the best of the scarcest, Iliff became the effective proprietor of far, far more[569]. He was also a very good businessman and stock trader. He sold to builders of the Union Pacific, government depots and agents in charge of Indian reservations[570]. His stock also found its way to prime eastern markets, selling for top-dollar.

Most of the ranchers did not permanently reside on their ranches in northeast Colorado, instead basing their operations out of Greeley, Denver, or Cheyenne Wyoming, but Iliff was a hands-on rancher, living with his men and cattle. :

> Iliff preferred to ride the range with his cowboys and to help in the everyday work of caring for the cattle. He was with his men on the roundups, he ate with them at the chuck-wagon, and he slept with them under the heavens of the western skies. His wages were good, but along with the good wages, he expected good service and work from his men. Therefore he insisted that they did not drink for he said, "Cows and whiskey do not mix."… He was against carrying any weapon of any kind but had an iron nerve and ruled his cattle domain with a stern hand[571].

Likely, this lifestyle prematurely ended his life. In 1877, Iliff became ill with a gall bladder obstruction caused by drinking the alkali water so prevalent on the Colorado plains. When Iliff died in 1878, his wife Elizabeth continued the business and became the richest woman in Colorado and a "Cattle Queen."

Snyder Brothers

After John Iliff's death, Elizabeth Iliff entrusted her husband's ranches to the Snyder brothers, John W. and Dudley

H., Texas ranchers who had a large ranch near Brush[572,573].

> ...In 1877 Col. Snyder made what proved to be the greatest deal of his experience and began huge operations that led to the making and losing of hundreds of thousands of dollars. A contract was made with J. W. Iliff, then noted banker and ranchman of Denver, who proposed to furnish ninety per cent of the money for the operation, Snyder Bros. to furnish ten per cent and handle all the details of the transaction. Iliff was to receive forty-five per cent of the profits and Snyder Bros. the remaining fifty-five per cent. The contract called for the delivery in Colorado of 17,500 head of two and three-year-old steers, and not only was this contract fulfilled, but a total of 28,000 head were handled by these wizards of the cattle industry before the season closed. Before the contract was completed Mr. Iliff died and upon request of Mrs. Iliff, Col. Snyder closed up the business of his deceased friend and business associate. The estate owned one of the greatest ranches in the Northwest, and Captain J. W. Snyder was placed in charge of this vast property and handled same in a most successful manner for nine years [until 1887], the business growing into a great syndicate with thousands of head of the finest cattle and horses in the world...[574]

The Snyder brothers moved back to Texas after losing most of their stock in the harsh winter of 1886[575], but the town of Snyder, Colorado commemorates these Texas ranchers.

Brush Brothers

Like Iliff, Jared L. Brush was among the early prospectors coming to Colorado from Ohio in 1859. In 1862, he abandoned prospecting for cattle raising[576] with a herd estimated at between 3,000 and 4,000 head. Brush lived primarily in Greeley, but had agricultural interests in the Fort Morgan area near the town of Brush (named for him) and served as sheriff for Weld County. Later, from 1895-1899, Brush served as Lieutenant Governor of the state of Colorado.

John M. Brush, Jared's brother, also had a herd located west of the Fort Morgan area near the Eagle's Nest stage station (the next station west of Fremont's Orchard). Just months after Fort Morgan was abandoned, Indians attacked Brush's ranch, killing his brother William, cousin Jared Conroy and a hired man Halstead Olson Dunning[577] and stampeding his stock. The military was now based at Fort Laramie, so the men of the region formed their own militia and took off after the Indians. The militia consisted of about forty men and included Holon Godfrey, Sam Ashcraft, and Elbridge Gerry. They caught up with the Indians near Latham. Five of the Indians were reportedly killed and fifteen wounded[578].

With the fort deserted, the ranchers were on their own just as they had been in the early 1860s at the start of the Indian War. Indian attacks continued and on January 2, 1869 the abandoned fort was burned[579] as was Iliff's ranch at Fremont's Orchard[580]. Though hostilities with the Cheyenne in northeastern Colorado mostly ended with their defeat at Summit Springs July 11, 1869, sporadic attacks would continue until the various Indian tribes were moved onto reservations. As late as 1876, just weeks before the Battle of Little Bighorn, Sioux attacked ranchers during a round-up at Fremont's Orchard killing fifteen men employed by Lyman Cole and John Iliff[581].

With the encroaching railroads, cattle drives became a thing of the past. Cattle could now be herded to the nearest railroad and shipped anywhere in the country, removing the need to drive the cattle across the plains. But the land had proved itself useful – the Great American Desert was now – as it had always been – profitable pastureland. The next challenge was to turn a desert into an oasis.

Canals & Crops

The South Platte River ran through a barren plain, watering only its immediate banks. Holon Godfrey brought water inland by digging a mile-long irrigation ditch to his land, which in 1872 was expanded into the first irrigation ditch in the area, the Fort Wicked Ditch, and later expanded again into the South Platte Ditch[582]. Ditches such as this would change the Great American Desert into prime agricultural land. A short history of the canals was provided in the August 30, 1889 issue of the *Fort Morgan Times* starting with the efforts of the Green and Union colonists:

In 1873-4 Dr. Green of Philadelphia, with a colony of southern gentlemen of means attempted the construction of a ditch and the building of a town at what has since been known as the "Green City Flats..." [T]he ditch proved a failure...[and] the colonists abandoned the enterprise...[but] the Putnam brothers came from the west down the Platte Valley, and built a large canal to water the fine bottom known as Weldon Valley, and made a decided success of the enterprise…. Their ditch watered "second" bottom lands and followed the valley line, the failure of the Green City venture onto the plateau warning them to avoid the table lands. The idea of the old-timers was that only the bottom lands were adapted to irrigation, and consequently farming.

The Union colonists were laughed at for attempting to farm the sandy uplands…. In the summer following the construction of the Weldon Valley ditch, B. H. Eaton, Bruch Johnson, Jud Brush, J. C. Scott, J. Max Clark and other Union colony pioneers, enlisted other capital with them and built the Platte and Beaver canal, to water the lower or eastern end of the Fort Morgan flat…. This line of ditch had been planned a year before, by A. S. Baker, one of the Union Colony pioneers, who had been doing considerable contracting on ditch work further up the river. By his indomitable will power and pluck, Mr. Baker secured the interest of Lord Airlie of Scotland… After the company name had been organized, he relinquished his intention to put the line through himself, and joined with the others in the enterprise. The ditch was built between June 1882, and January 1883. Mr. Baker and Hon. Lyulph Ogilvy, son of Lord Airlie who died before the ditch was completed, taking the contract for its construction.

Having seen this enterprise to a successful termination, Mr. Baker at once entered into a plan to build a second canal which would water the heart of the magnificent flat, the future of which he could best foresee, and the construction of this ditch and the opening of the lands under it to cultivation, became his ambition and his desire.

In May, 1883 work commenced on the Fort Morgan canal which was completed in 1884 and the same season water was furnished to the farmers who had joined Mr. Baker in the work. Connected with the success of the canal, Mr. Baker had looked forward to the location of the town to be called after the old fort situated one-half mile away.... The men who assisted Mr. Baker in the construction of the canal are found here to-day, playing the role of farmer. Broad, green acres, huge granaries, handsome homes attest the success they strove for....

Having finished this canal, it was Mr. Baker's intention to at once commence the construction of the third large system of irrigating ditches, which should complete the redemption of the Fort Morgan flat. A series of unfortunate reverses both delayed Mr. Baker and taught lessons in finance to all interested in the success of the new enterprise, to the effect that the proper builders and promoters of canal enterprises were the farmers and land owners whom the construction would benefit. With such thoughts in view, it was not until the fall of last year, 1888, that it was thought advisable for the farmers to burden themselves with the construction of this system. Then the work commenced, and with such vigor that before the season of 1890 rolls around, the whole of the magnificent Fort Morgan flat will be under irrigation and a territory of the richest farming land in Colorado, thirty by twelve miles in extent, will be tributary to the trading point and mercantile center which has been the outcome of all these vast enterprises – Fort Morgan[583].

Baker's financial backer was the Earl of Airlie who seemed to have formed a fascination with northeastern Colorado, touring the area on a number of occasions and purchasing a 30,000 acre sheep ranch near Greeley for his son Lord Ogilvy[584].

Getting water onto the plains was no easy feat. A lengthy description of the process was included in the first issue of the *Fort Morgan Times:*

The bottom of the river is rocky, making it impossible for sandbars to form at the mouth of the canal. This advantage alone is worth thousands of dollars to the enterprise. Like the Missouri, the Platte river is a treacherous stream, and in a very few places can one find rocky bottom between the mountains and Omaha. Having built a substantial head-gate…Mr. Baker proceeded to extend the canal toward the table land, taking advantage of the grade to reach the higher levels in the shortest possible distance…. Beginning at the head of what is known as the Hubschle Bottom…the canal skirts the bluff, crossing the grass lands between the second "bench" and the river. Ten miles from the head-gate the canal reaches Bijou Creek having banks seventy feet high and a bottom half a mile wide. The flume or aqueduct over this stream exceeds any similar structure in the State. To appreciate it, one must consider the size of the ditch and the amount of water it carries. Its capacity for twenty miles from the head-gate will warrant its being extended forty or fifty miles further, if necessary; for the present its length will be only thirty-one miles. With a depth of from four and a half to six feet, a width of thirty feet on the bottom, and a descending grade of eighteen inches to the mile, it will carry enough water to float a western steamboat. cutting down the high bluff bank on the side toward the mountains, its height above the bed of the creek has been reduced to only twenty-two and a half feet. Its carrying capacity is a solid body of water four feet deep by twenty feet wide, with a down grade of three feet to the mile, or eighteen inches in the flume, being double the grade the canal. To bear the immense weight of water passing over it, the structure has been built upon 733 piles of the toughest mountain timber.

Length of aqueduct with approaches, 2,212 feet; width of water-way in the clear, 20 feet; height above the bed of the creek, 22 ½ feet; number of stringers, (each 3x12 feet, 16 feet long), 297 feet; number of bents (16 feet apart), 134; number of piles, 733; number of feet of lumber, 360,000 feet; number of planks in the flume, 8,848, (each 14 feet long); number of nails used, 265,440; total cost of the structure, $18,000; weight of water resting on each bent of piles, 80,000 lbs; total weight of water in the flume when full, 11,060,009 lbs; amount of water passing a given point per second, 380 cubic feet.

Having given this brief outline of the aqueduct, we shall return to the canal. Work was begun on it last year on the 1st of May, with twenty-five teams and thirty men. The force was soon increased to fifty teams, and notwithstanding Mr. Baker's heavy contracts on other ditches, in the San Luis park and elsewhere, good progress was made, considering the protracted delays caused by bad weather, lack of timber, etc. East of Little Beaver Creek, the canal is only twelve feet wide, but will be enlarged when necessary. After crossing the Bijou Creek on the half-mile aqueduct the ditch enters the table lands of what is known as the "third bench." The landscape, magnificent and vast, stretches away like a sea toward the swelling divide of the Republican river. Four miles east of the aqueduct, and about three-quarters of a mile from the Platte, the canal crosses the Burlington & Missouri railway, just north of the town of Fort Morgan[585].

By 1889, there were 200 miles of canal lines representing an investment of $750,000 including the Bijou Canal, Putnam Ditch, Weldon Valley Ditch, Fort Morgan Canal, Platte and Beaver Canal, Deuel and Snyder Canal (More & Tracy ditch), and the Brown & Pyott Canal[586].

The irrigation canals winding their way across Colorado's northeastern plains brought water to the arid soil producing a wide variety of crops. Lyman Baker described the agricultural scene in Morgan County in 1895:

The county has a fine system of irrigation. There are over two hundred and fifty miles of main ditches in operation, which secure their water supply from the South Platte River and the Beaver and Bijou creeks, and furnish water for the irrigation of 250,000 acres of as fine agricultural lands as there are in the world, 50,000 acres of this land being now in actual cultivation. These lands are very level and can be easily irrigated. There are no cradle knolls or hummocks, and there is an average fall toward the east of ten feet, and toward the north of eight feet per mile, which causes the water to spread evenly and entirely over the surface, and to be conducted over the land without the building of dykes or cuts in the small lateral ditches, and with less labor than almost any other locality in the State. The soil is a dark sandy loam of good depth, with clay subsoil, and is especially free from those qualities that cause hardening or baking after being irrigated. This locality has an altitude of 4,000 feet above sea level, and is adapted to the raising of all crops embraced in what is called common or general farming, and including fruits of various kinds; and to this date there has not been a single failure, attributable to the soil or locality, of any variety or class of crops that have been tried. Statistics show that the average yield of small grain in this locality for the last three years has excelled that of any in the State. The average yield in Morgan County of grain for the season of 1893, was wheat 28, oats 37, barley 32, rye 26 and corn 44 bushels per acre, and the records for the preceding eight years show the figures given as a fair average during that time. Many individual cases show, under thorough and proper cultivation, yields of wheat 45, oats 80, barley 79, rye 38 and corn 60 bushels per acre, and there is no reason why these yields should not be obtained every year by farmers who know how to farm and are willing to work....[587]

As the prospectors did in the mountains, farmers and ranchers staked a claim to land on the plains, building a cabin and tilling fields. The land belonged to no one, so the land belonged to everyone. Claims clubs formed as early as 1860 to protect the interests of squatters on public lands. When the Arapahoe County Claims Club, which encompassed the land bordered in the north by the South Platte River, formed in 1860, their constitution stated that:

> ...each and every claim holder, who holds claim for farming purposes, shall make, or cause to be made, improvements on his or their claim, by breaking one acre of land; or building a house sufficiently good to live in....any person taking a claim for farming purposes shall be entitled to one hundred and sixty acres in one body...with the courses plainly marked by stakes, trees, or mounds, and have the claimant's name written plainly thereon...within sixty days after [claim] being filed on, have the following improvements made...must be occupied by the owner or claimant...fencing or enclosing in a good and substantial manner five acres of land or its equivalent in fencing or ditching, and by plowing one acre of land for agricultural purposes[588].

In November 1861, Colorado recognized the rights of claim holders. Any person could claim public land (except land with mines) and:

> ...maintain trespass, ejectment [sic], and other actions for the protection of his possessory rights extending to the boundaries of his "claim". It was provided in the law that the claim should not exceed 160 acres in extent; that the boundaries should be so marked as to be easily traced; and that the claim should be improved and occupied, with at least five acres enclosed by a reasonable fence....land within the boundary of Colorado Territory on the bank or margin of a stream "shall be entitled to the use of the

water of said stream," for the purpose of irrigation[589]. In many respects, this act foreshadowed the 1862 *Homestead Act*.

In 1862, Congress passed *The Homestead Act* offering up to 160 acres of public land to settlers for a small fee ($1.25 or less per acre) and a promise to live on and work the land for five years. The goal was to reduce crowding in the east and open up the western frontier[590]. Public lands were sectioned into townships, six miles square, and then divided again into 36, square mile sections, each consisting of 640 acres. Each homesteader was allowed up to a ¼ of a section or 160 acres of land. The townships were designated by where they lay relative to the Base Line and Principal Meridian. The town of Fort Morgan, for instance, is located in Township 3 North, Range 57 of the 6th Principal Meridian in Section 6. The homesteaders worked the land, either raising cattle or later as irrigation watered the arid land, raising crops. The *Homestead Act* would bring thousands to Colorado over the next few decades.

Starting in 1871, hundreds of homesteads were granted in the Fort Morgan area. The earliest homesteads were along the South Platte River often near established ranches or stations used by the Overland Mail in the 1860s. One of the earliest homesteads in the area, granted on December 15, 1871, was to Martin A. Boughton who took over the Ashcraft ranch near the old fort (4N 57W S31) and in 1871 to John Cole who based his cattle ranch on a near Fremont's Orchard (4N 60W S1, 2, 3). John C. Sumner, a member of Powell's expedition up the Colorado River, was granted a homestead in June of 1872 on the site of the old Beaver Creek Station (4N

55W S8) and Holon Godfrey was granted a homestead on May 20, 1875 (6N 54W S35) at the site of his ranch[591]. The immediate area around the town of Fort Morgan was first settled on the north side of the river in the 1870s and then on the south side once the town plat was filed in 1884 and the railroads came through.

Homesteads were limited to 160 acres and this was sufficient land for farmers and sheep ranchers, but cattle needed vast amounts of acreage to maintain a herd – ten to thirty acres of grassland was needed to feed one steer necessitating

TOWNSHIP 4 NORTH RANGE 57 WEST OF THE 6th PRINCIPAL MERIDIAN, COLORADO

TOWNSHIP 3 NORTH RANGE 57 WEST OF THE 6th PRINCIPAL MERIDIAN, COLORADO

1870-1879 Homestead   1880-1889 Homestead

Early homesteads in immediate the Fort Morgan area (Townships 3 and 4 N, 57 W) granted pre-1890. Note: The northern railroad track shown follows roughly along the north bank of the South Platte River.

ranches of thousands of acres. Ranchers appealed for more land, but it was difficult to convince Congress of the need[592] so ranchers claimed homesteads near water and then unofficially appropriated adjoining public land. They also took advantage of the Timber Culture Act of 1873 and the Desert Land Act of 1877, which allowed claim to more land if the claimant planted trees or if the land was to be irrigated[593] though the ranchers did not always plant the promised trees or dig the promised ditches[594,595].

With the expansion of the cattle industry on the plains, the grasslands became overused and the forage quickly exhausted. Fences were constructed to protect the best forage and water sources; to keep herds in and other herds out. These fences quickly spread across public land breaking up the open range[596]. But fences prohibited cattle from finding better forage and the harsh winter of 1886-1887 decimated herds[597]. In 1885, President Grover Cleveland ordered that all fences erected on public land be removed, though it was impossible to enforce the order[598]. Fortunately, the farmers in the area found the perfect substitute for the natural grasses on the plains – alfalfa[599].

The area surrounding the abandoned fort was now a center for ranchers and agriculture, but the town would need one thing more before it could grow from the prairie.

∞

Chapter 9

Railroads & Railroad Towns

In the 1860s, the military fort called Fort Morgan was built at what was known as the "Junction," a place where the South Platte River Road split with one road

Railroad Building on the Great Plains. Published in Harper's Weekly. *1875.*

leading directly west towards the mountains and another southwest to Denver. Two decades later, it would be at this place that another junction would be established – this time a sort of railroad junction. The town of Fort Morgan became the point where two rival railroads, each heading west on independent lines came within one mile of each other. The Union Pacific passed to the north and the Chicago, Burlington & Quincy passed to the south of the town "…giving it the best train service with the outside world; [with] eight passenger trains daily each way…"[600]. A wagon bridge was built spanning the river between the two lines; this bridge was replaced in 1922 with now famous Rainbow (Arch) Bridge built by Charles G. Shelly.

But laying the rails across the Colorado plains proved more difficult than originally thought. The enterprise was tied up in the era of railroad expansion complete with corporate take-overs, bankruptcies, court battles, politics, and the financial collapse of the country. Nine years would elapse before Denver, then the fourth most populated city in the west[601], and the mining districts of the Rockies could link directly with the eastern markets. Again, Fort Morgan was to be part of the link.

Union Pacific: Julesburg Branch

In the mid-1860s, with the passing of the Pacific Railway Act of 1862, the Union Pacific Railroad began building westward from Omaha, Nebraska intending to link with the Central Pacific Railroad building eastwards from San Francisco, California[602]. By 1866, it seemed as if the railroad would be completed in record time:

The rapidity with which the Platte River Railroad and the Kansas River Railroad are being constructed surpasses all precedent in American railroad construction. Last spring the first section of forty miles of the Platte road, west of Omaha, was completed. Since then two hundred miles of track have been graded, and the rail laid down. The road is now completed fifty miles west of Fort Kearney.... The track is moving up the Platte at the rate of *ten miles per week!*... It is hard to realize that a railway which was commenced last spring is already stretched across nearly half of the distance between Omaha and Denver City....[603]

The track laid however was not destined for Fort Morgan – or even Denver. In 1866, surveys were made of ten possible

1864 U.S. Map Colorado [Excerpt] Note: Proposed Central Pacific Railroad follows South Platte. Fort Morgan lies on the map's crease.

routes west from Omaha. Seven of those considered included Denver, with the favored along the South Platte River through Fort Morgan and Greeley before turning northwest to Cheyenne. But the topography of the mountains in Colorado made these routes less desirable and instead, the line went along the North Platte River and the Oregon Trail to Cheyenne and over South Pass[604,605], bypassing Denver completely. On May 10, 1869, the Union Pacific Railroad and the Central Pacific Railroad of California met at Promontory

Summit, Utah linking the east and west coasts by rail for the first time[606].

Denver desperately needed to establish a rail connection with the east. Rival railroad projects began in the early 1970s linking Denver with Cheyenne (via Greeley) and Kansas City (via Strasburg). The Denver Pacific and the Kansas Pacific railroads became the local rivals to the Union Pacific[607] and the rivalry ran deep. The *Chicago Tribune* reported that "…the Union Pacific has discriminated against passengers going over the Kansas Pacific when they were bound through either east or west. Much ingenuity has been shown by each corporation in manipulating its schedule-time as against the other….[608]" The newspaper went on to predict the construction of another independent branch connecting Denver to the Union Pacific at Julesburg and plans for this branch were already underway.

The Colorado Central Railroad Company, with the backing of the Union Pacific, had multiple projects in various stages of construction in the early 1870s and one of them was the Julesburg Branch along the north bank of the South Platte River through Fort Morgan[609]. Funding was obtained and work commenced on the Julesburg Branch on May 22, 1872[610] and it appeared the line would be pushed to completion in record time:

> Golden and Julesburg. Upon this line – better known as the "Golden and Pine bluffs" – an engineering party, in charge of Mr. W. Clayborne, is now engaged in locating the line from Julesburg westward, along the South Platte. Preliminary surveys of this line were made some years since, which enabled the corps now at work to progress

rapidly with the location, which at last advices was being made and definitely staked at the rate of four miles per day. This should bring them to Golden by the first or middle of May. As soon as the whole is located, the line will be divided into five-mile sections, ready for proposals from contractors by the 1st of June. The object of the company in dividing the work into such small sections, is to push it to completion in the shortest time

UNION PACIFIC RAILWAY

OMAHA & DENVER SHORT LINE.
Nebraska Division.

This is the famous Omaha and Denver Short Line. Omaha to Denver in 20 hours. The Omaha and Denver Short Line Leads all Competitors in Time, Distance and Equipment.

Exp	Exp	Tk't fare	May 30, 1886. Lve. Arr.	Exp	Exp
A.M.	P.M.			A.M.	P.M.
10 35	7 50	....	C'NC'L B'F8 21557	†8 15	5 45
10 55	8 20	0	OMAHA.....61895	7 50	5 20
11 35	....	15	Papillion 553	7 09	4 45
11 51	....	21	Millard 340	6 54	4 32
12 18	....	31	Waterloo 298	6 30	4 10
12 37	9 52	36	Valley 100	6 20	4 02
12 53	10 19	47	Fremont....4014	5 53	3 40
1 30	10 54	62	North Bend 1106	5 19	3 10
2 07	11 27	76	Schuyler....1588	4 15	2 42
2 44	12 19	92	Columbus...2573	4 08	2 05
3 22	12 52	109	Silver Creek 186	3 25	1 35
3 45	1 25	121	Clarks.......385	2 59	1 16
4 09	1 45	132	Central City 1232	2 33	12 58
4 15	2 55	154	G'ND ISLAND 5040	1 40	12 20
5 50	3 37	170	Wood River..422	12 46	11 32
6 06	3 55	177	Shelton.....538	12 29	11 18
6 18	4 19	183	Gibbon.......582	12 15	11 08
6 44	4 43	195	Kearney Cy.3601	11 43	10 45
8 00	6 15	231	Plum Creek .825	10 12	9 40
8 29	6 52	246	Cozad 267	9 58	9 14
8 40	7 04	250	Willow Isl'd.961	9 26	9 04
8 58	8 10	291	NO. PLATTE.2540	7 45	7 45
10 03	8 59	315	Dexter.......+	5 42	5 37
10 38	9 33	332	Roscoe.......+	5 12	5 07
11 01	9 56	342	Ogallala.....349	4 56	4 50
11 57	10 50	369	Barton.......+	3 57	3 59
12 08	11 05	...	{ DENVER JC. }	3 45	3 45
12 15	11 10	371	{ ....100 }	3 35	3 50
12 43	11 37	396	Sedgewick ..+	3 04	3 23
1 17	12 05	400	Crook........+	2 52	2 57
1 47	12 35	417	Illff.........+	2 02	2 31
2 15	1 20	429	Sterling 125	1 40	2 08
2 39	1 44	441	Merino......+	12 53	1 37
3 12	2 15	458	Snyder......+	12 21	1 09
4 13	3 05	489	Orchard .....+	11 21	12 17
4 47	3 88	506	Hardin.......+	10 45	11 45
5 21	4 17	522	La Salle.....+	10 13	11 20
5 53	4 40	553	Platteville...+	9 40	8 40
6 10	4 57	541	Lupton......+	9 25	8 25
6 24	5 10	549	Brighton.....+	9 13	8 12
....	5 22	554	Henderson...+	....	....
7 00	5 50	566	Jersey.......+	8 40	7 40
7 10	6 00	569	DENVER...55630	*8 30	7 30
Arr.	Lve.			A.M.	P.M.

Standard Time.—Between Omaha and North Platte trains run on Central time; between North Platte and Denver on Mountain time.

Rand-McNally Official Railway Guide. 1886 timetable.

possible. And it will be a bright day for the mountains when this is accomplished, giving us, as it will, a direct through connection with the Union Pacific on the short-est possible line[611].

The Julesburg branch was sometimes known as the Gol-den-Julesburg or as in the previous news story Golden-Pine Bluffs [Nebraska] branch as the termination points were not yet fixed. The line was also known as the Julesburg-La Salle branch as the goal was to reach La Salle (near Greeley) where passengers could connect to either Denver or Cheyenne. There was much debate about the route and the people of Denver were not pleased that the line by-passed the city for Golden or La Salle. The Denver and Platte Valley Railway Company was formed in 1872 to build a branch line from Denver to connect with the Julesburg branch at Fort Morgan though this line was never built[612].

The plan entailed building 151 miles of rail – and build it quickly. The company directors decided "…that work on the Julesburg road be pushed vigorously forward. Nothing of im-portance will be done for twenty or thirty days, save to clean up and put in better shape that part of the road now in opera-tion…[613]". The plan was to have the railroad operational by the fall of 1873. Hundreds of men were employed grading the land and laying track and by April of 1873, the workers had reached Fort Morgan[614]. Here, the workers encountered a problem at the Narrows, just west of Fort Morgan, but the news was confident that the work would progress quickly:

> The Golden and Julesburg which suffered temporary paralysis after its completion to Longmont, is now in the full vigor of active progress and will be pushed forward to Julesburg with all possible expedition. Less than forty miles…remain to be graded. Of this distance, but five or

six miles present any obstacles. This section, called "the narrows," will require deep cutting, but work will be commenced at both sides, and hastened as rapidly as men and capital can do it. This done, the road will be practically opened for the iron. It is hoped that before winter sets in, the Golden and Julesburg railroad will be an accomplished fact, and a new outlet to the East placed at the disposal of the growing commerce of our Territory[615].

The plan was to complete the track by September[616], but other projects needed attention and there were delays bringing in the iron for the rails[617]. The company was also fighting court cases seeking injunction to the issuance of bonds passed in early 1873 by the voters of Jefferson County[618,619]. Then in September 1873 the bankruptcy of Jay Cooke & Associates, financiers of the Northern Pacific Railroad, incited a financial crash that spiraled the country into a depression[620]. Work on the railroad ceased[621] and the Colorado Central Railroad Company teetered on the brink of bankruptcy[622]; the Julesburg Branch was abandoned[623].

By 1880, the country had recovered from the depression and the Union Pacific took up the Central Colorado charter[624]. The Julesburg branch, also called the Denver branch or the "short line," was completed and the first passenger train along the Union Pacific Denver branch was November 6, 1881[625]. The stations were Julesburg (or Denver Junction), Sedgwick, Crook, Iliff, Sterling, Buffalo (Merino), Snyder, Deuel (the town directly north of Fort Morgan), Orchard, Hardin, La Salle at which point, passengers changed to trains running between Cheyenne and Denver on the Denver Pacific[626]. The Union Pacific now controlled a direct line to

Denver.

The Julesburg branch of the Union Pacific railroad would have a turbulent history. After nine years, the line was finally open, but it would be abandoned in 1894 when the Union Pacific went into receivership[627]. The line would then be taken over by Union Pacific, Denver & Gulf Railway only to be returned to the Union Pacific in 1899[628]. The line was used for nearly a century before finally being abandoned in the early 1990s.

Chicago, Burlington & Quincy

Before the Julesburg Branch of the Union Pacific was completed in 1881, came the first rumors of another line extending to Denver:

> Again it is whispered in railroad circles that the Burlington & Missouri, or rather its parent and legal guardian, the Chicago, Burlington & Quincy Railroad, will sound the slogan, "On to Denver," in a few days it is rumored in Denver that a combination has been made by the corporation and the Denver & Rio Grande, which is rapidly pushing its branches across every mountain range and into every valley in Colorado, New Mexico, and Utah, and that by virtue of this combination the Chicago, Burlington, & Quincy will reach out to the Rockies and eventually have a standing upon the Pacific coast. One of the results of the completion of the Lincoln line to Denver will be the extension of the Denver & Rio Grande combination to Ogden giving direct communication with the Central Pacific, and competing everywhere with the Union Pacific lines...[629]

In other words, the Chicago, Burlington, and Quincy Railroad (CB&Q) was pushing to complete their own transcontinental line in order to compete with the Union Pacific and they planned to take their line directly through Denver. Their plans for a line along the South Platte River from Omaha through Lincoln Nebraska to Denver, sent the railroads into a building competition. Already competitive in Nebraska, the two companies were now eyeing the Colorado market. After the announcement that the Burlington was planning a route to Denver, the Union Pacific announced they would take over and complete the unfinished Golden and Julesburg line started by the Colorado Central Railroad[630]. The railroads were effectively at war.

"BURLINGTON ROUTE."

238   CHICAGO, BURLINGTON & QUINCY R. R.—Continued.

THIS LINE, MORE POPULARLY KNOWN AS THE

Great "Burlington Route,"

Rand-McNally Official Railway Guide. 1886 timetable excerpt.

The Union Pacific line had a six year head start with the Julesburg Branch partially completed, and they were the first to send passenger trains to Denver in November 1881, but the Burlington Railroad wasn't far behind. The Chicago, Burlington & Colorado railroad filed articles of incorporation in September 1881 and began building from the eastern edge of Weld County towards Denver[631]. The route came across the plains of Colorado to Akron and then veered northwest to Brush and Fort Morgan before turning again, southwest, into Denver. The stations in the area of Fort Morgan from east to west were: Wray, Robb, Eckley, Yuma, Hyde, Otis, Akron, Pinnero, Brush, Fort Morgan, Corona, Dixon, and Roggen[632]. It took the company only six months to complete the line, reaching Brush on April 7, 1882 and Fort Morgan on April 17th[633]. The first trains ran to Denver on May 29, 1882[634]. Both companies now had independent lines to Denver.

In 1900, the CB&Q added a 150-mile long spur line between Brush, Colorado and Alliance, opening up a direct route from the northern states to Denver[635]. The Burlington Railroad is still in use today.

Railroad Towns & Colonies

Towns on the eastern plains grew with the westward expansion. Some towns were centered on long-abandoned stations on the Overland Trail, others based around new railroad stations. The Overland Trail and sections of the Chicago, Burlington & Quincy Railroad followed the south bank of the South Platte River while the Union Pacific Railroad followed the north bank. Because of this configuration, many towns in the Fort Morgan area were roughly platted in pairs, one on the north bank of the South Platte River and the other on the south bank.

Colonies were also being forming on the Colorado plains. Men and women moving west bonded together into communities with the hopes of forming a better life for their families. In the plains, they saw a fresh start where they could build a community with their own hands away from problems of the urban centers in the east. Colonies were often formed based on shared ideals and by-laws were written for the community to enforce these ideals. Union Colony, the center of which was Greeley, for instance, forbid the manufacture and sale of intoxicating drinks, writing temperance clauses into leases. Only members of the colony could obtain land in the area and the payment for land was scaled based on the affluence of the member[636]. Union Colony was one of the more successful colonies, spinning off other communities such as Fort Morgan.

South Platte & Buffalo (Merino)

The earliest towns in the Fort Morgan area were South Platte and Buffalo (known today as Merino), platted in the early 1870s between Fort Morgan and Sterling. A post office was opened in 1873 at South Platte near the site of American Ranch, a stage station on the Overland Trail[637], and became an important hub in the area being one of the most populated communities in the Platte Valley[638]. Initially, a railroad station for the Colorado Central was planned at South Platte, but when the Union Pacific built the road[639], the station was placed on the north side of the river. The town could not sur-

vive without a railroad station and faded from existence
fore the turn of the century.

Across the river from South Platte was the town of Buffalo, platted just as the Union Pacific railroad was being built
along the river. Buffalo would become a stop on the Union
Pacific and was on the site of the Beaver Colony:

A new town has been started away down on the South
Platte, which promises to become a large place in course
of time, as it will be the commercial center of one of the
finest bodies of land within the borders of the Territory.
This place is named Buffalo, and is the property of an enterprising colony, of which Dr. G. W. Boteler is
President; J. S. Flory, Secretary; and J. R. Holland, Superintendent. The plateau of alluvial land on which Beaver
Colony, of which Buffalo is the town site, is located, includes the splendid bottom at the confluence of Beaver
creek and the Platte, and is described by Capt. Berthoud
as "extending for many miles up and down the Platte Valley on both sides of the river the largest continuous body
of irrigable land in Colorado." The town is located just
below Godfrey's Bluffs and opposite the old American
Ranch. It is directly on the line of the Julesburg branch of
the C. C. R. R. [Colorado Central Railroad], and will
probably be an eating station on that road. It is distant
from Julesburg 67 ½ miles; from Buffalo to Greeley is 78
miles and to Golden 152 miles. The entire town is watered by a ditch of large size – being ten feet wide on the
bottom – taken from the Platte a short distance above,
and this ditch will be extended for thirty miles down the
river. A canal on the opposite side of the river supplies

water to the Colony land on that side. The town already contains a number of houses, and will grow very fast[640].

A post office was opened in Buffalo in 1874[641]. In 1881, the town was renamed Merino, after the type of sheep pastured in the area[642,643]. But the town did not see the growth forecast by the newspaper article above. In 1900, the population of Merino with outlying areas was 224[644] and in 2000, 246 people resided in Merino[645].

Brush & Snyder

Ten to fifteen miles east of Fort Morgan lay Snyder and Brush, both named for important ranchers in the area. As mentioned earlier, Brush was named for Jared L. (Jud) Brush, rancher and later Lieutenant Governor of Colorado[646] and Snyder was named for John W. Snyder and Dudley H. Snyder, Texas ranchers[647] who managed John Iliff's ranch after his death. Both towns were established in 1882 with the opening of post offices and rail stations: Brush, a station on the Burlington line[648] and Snyder on the Union Pacific[649]. Brush was also located near the old Overland stage station of Beaver Creek at the confluence of Beaver Creek and the South Platte River and was on the Texas-Montana cattle trail[650]. Brush was platted in June 1882 for the Lincoln Land Company (part of the Burlington railroad)[651] and incorporated in November 1884 making it the first platted town in Morgan County[652].

In 1900, the town of Brush had a population of 391[653] and 5,117 in 2000, making it the second largest town in Morgan County[654]. Snyder was not listed separately on either census so the population was presumably counted as part of Brush.

Fort Morgan & Deuel (Weldon, Weldona)

The town of Fort Morgan was platted just south of the fort's ruins on May 1, 1884[655]. Fort Morgan was a direct extension of the Union Colony at Greeley with the founders, including the Baker brothers, Lyman and Abner, being original members of the Union Colony[656]. Fort Morgan was formed based on the Union Colony's ideals, which included temperance. A short description of the town and the Baker brothers was included in the history of the Union Colony:

The Fort Morgan enterprise owes its inception to Abner S. Baker, brother-in-law of J. Max. Clark. If the name only sounded as well the town ought to have been called Bakerville. Mr. George R. Baker, father of the "Baker Boys," came from Wisconsin soon after the undertaking was commenced and has put his wealth and effort into it. Lyman Baker, long employed upon *The Greeley Tribune*, is and has been since its start, the editor of *The Fort Morgan Times*. Ed. Baker, long the successful manager of our Number Two canal, has also an interest there, although his family still lives in Greeley. Mr. Kimball, one of the most extensive cultivators under the Fort Morgan ditches, is a brother-in-law of Abner S. Baker. There are also other more or less remote connections of the "Baker Family" to be found there, but it is not to be inferred that none others are admitted. The projector, Abner S. Baker, has had his ups and downs since coming in the summer of 1870 to Colorado. First we see him managing our "Co-operative Stock and Dairy Association," neither for our nor his profit. Then he and Ed. farm together for some three years and fail on account of grasshoppers and rusty,

low-priced wheat. Then Abner conceives the idea of taking an irrigating ditch out the Poudre to gather up the
seepage water which, from the irrigation above on its
banks, is returning yearly in larger quantities to the bed of
the stream below the heads of all existing ditches. L.
Ogilvy, the son of the Earl of Airlie, of Scotland, sees the
point, too, and goes into the undertaking with Baker.
When all is completed, Baker sells out to Ogilvy and has
now several thousands of dollars in his pocket, and is
ready to undertake new adventures. He is one of the
"Platte and Beaver" projectors, and upon the completion
of this
enter-
prise
forms a
company
to build
the Fort
Morgan
ditches
and
found

1894 relief map excerpt of Morgan County.
Note both Fort Morgan and North Fort Morgan.

the town. This latter is named after a United States Fort
of that name, that was near the site of the town. The
ditch had to be built largely from borowed [sic] capital,
and pay-day came before the water-rights could be sold to
meet maturing obligations. Lawsuits and general embar-
rassment followed, but it appears that the way is being
won to the open country, and the parties are all solvent
and are building up a fine town and country. Abner is a

genuine Yankee, of whom Emerson says: "He is like a cat. Toss him up as you like, he is sure to light on his feet[657].

The original railroad station on the Burlington line was at Ensign, a couple of miles west of the town of Fort Morgan. Baker knew that for his town to survive, it had to have a railroad station. According to Lute Johnson, one of Fort Morgan's early residents, Baker persuaded the Lincoln Land Company to move the station to Fort Morgan by deeding alternate plots of the newly platted town to the company[658]. In 1884, the section house at Ensign was moved two miles and placed in Fort Morgan at the head of Ensign Street[659]. The train ran through town five times per day and the fare to Denver was $3.90[660].

Fort Morgan was located on the south side of the river on the Burlington railroad, but on the north side of the river was another station called Morgan or North Fort Morgan on the Union Pacific railroad. In 1868, when the fort and post office closed, Lafayette More ran an informal post office bringing mail from Greeley by stage[661]. In 1880, an official post office was established in Fort Morgan - on the North side of the river - with Lafayette More as postmaster[662]. The post office was renamed Deuel in February 1883[663] and the town of Deuel was surveyed in 1885 and laid off by Lafayette More in April 1886[664]. Crofutt's guide noted Harry P. Deuel, a ticket agent at Omaha, as the namesake of the town, but William A. Deuel was an Assistant Superintendant in the Nebraska Division of the Union Pacific and later became Superintendent of the Colorado Division, so it is possible the station was named for William rather than Harry[665,666]. At this time, the two new towns were true rivals. An 1894 relief map of Morgan County shows the towns of Fort Morgan and Deuel (on the map called North Fort Morgan) as towns similar in size.

The two towns were connected by a wagon bridge built over the South Platte River in 1875[667]. In 1889, the bridge was moved to its current position, approximately two miles east, at the head of Main Street (Highway 52). In 1923, the wagon bridge was replaced by the famous Rainbow Arch Bridge, the world's longest rainbow arch bridge[668], but by this time, the town of Deuel had faded from existence. The Rainbow Bridge remains a reminder of a time when twin towns stationed rival railroads.

The towns shared an economic interest, but differed in at least one respect: Fort Morgan was dry, a reflection of the Union Colony roots, and Deuel was not[669]. Like Greeley, Fort Morgan land deeds included forfeiture clauses prohibiting the sale of alcohol on the premises or the land would revert back to Baker. The clause was enforced for ten years, up until 1894[670]. But for those wanting a drink, it was just a quick trip over the river to S. D. Karns' Cash Store in Deuel

Rainbow Bridge across the South Platte River in Fort Morgan. Photo by author.

and pharmacy[671]. A pointed reminder of the temperate nature of Fort Morgan was published in the *Fort Morgan Times* in 1889 referencing recent conflicts with drunk individuals making their way from Deuel to Morgan:

> We also wish to call the attention of the Town Boad [sic] to ordinance No. 13. Sec.1. *** "all persons are hereby prohibited from giving away any intoxicating malt, vinous, mixed, or fermented liquors, or proprietary medicines containing alcohol, in any street, alley, public park, hotel, boarding house, eating house, restaurant, place of traffic or public resort, or upon any vacant lot within the town of Fort Morgan," and describes the penalty for so doing. In this connection, and referring to the late outrages on decency, would like to know why the hotel management did not arrest the parties for a violation of the ordinance, having ample testimony at hand to convict the parties.... Wednesday night another of those disgraceful sprees occurred in town, by the same parties who were previously implicated, carrying on their drunken revels during the day and night. The people of the town have exhausted their patience, and say that it [sic] the law will uphold the selling of liquor adjoining a town where its sale is prohibited, that they will take matters in hand in such a manner that neither one of the dives now in blast will have cause to complain because the clean-up was not complete.... Many have asked us where the town marshal was that he did not arrest this drunken mob.... The editor of the Times has heard of threats made against his person, because of his denunciation of the low whisky shops located near us, and of the insults and degrading in-

fluences traceable to them, but the person is yet unborn who can frighten us from exposing a curse so ruinous to our prosperity and happiness. That we are backed in this sentiment by nine-tenths of the property owners here, goes without saying, and we rely on them in our crusade against all lawless proceedings[672].

Until 1899, Deuel appears on maps of Colorado almost directly opposite Fort Morgan, but Deuel station, followed by the post office, moved northwest to Weldon (later Weldona) and the Union Pacific station north of Fort Morgan was relabeled North Ft. Morgan[673]. The Deuel post office was renamed Weldona in 1907[674] and the town of Deuel disappeared.

Orchard, Corona (Wiggins), & Green City

Orchard, is located on the north bank of the South Platte River as a station on the Union Pacific, but it was named for Fremont's Orchard, a station on the Overland Trail located across the river about five miles east of the town[675]. The Orchard post office was established in 1882[676] and George H. West, a co-founder of Golden, and P. W. Putnam[677], a member of the Union Colony in Greeley, filed a town plat on July 21, 1890[678]. Nearly a century later, Orchard would become the site for the television mini-series "Centennial" based on a book by James A. Michener.

Across the river, approximately ten miles south of Orchard, lies the town of Wiggins on the Burlington line. The town originally began as Green City (or Greensboro), part of the Southwestern Colony[679]. The Southwestern Colony, also known as the Tennessee Colony or the Memphis Colony, was organized in 1871 by David S. Green and was expected to have the same success as other colonies in the area[680]. The organizers of the colony had grand plans and persuasive advertising and for a time, the colony seemed to be thriving. A post office was established in Green City in 1871 to serve a budding town of about 60 with 12 additional families in the surrounding area[681], but it was not long before there were problems in their paradise. An exposé of the colony was printed in the *Chicago Tribune*. The article begins with the claims of the colony and then an interview with the brother of David S. Green, the colony's founder, who admitted there were problems including many desertions and finally ends with a statement from one of the deserting colonists, Robert Abernathy:

HOMES AND WORK FOR ALL! Are you any better off than you were one, ten, or twenty years ago? Do you feel contented living under another man's roof? Is the rented home one that you want to leave your wife and children when you die? When you are sick have you an income; or is your hands your support?.... This circular is not intended for those who are satisfied and contented in their homes, but those who are seeking after homes.... A colony is formed for the purpose of combining the strength of the people financially as well as physically, and that we may be able to build up society, churches, and schools.... The Southwestern Colony of Colorado is located on the great Platte Valley, along which a railroad is now building, and which will carry our produce into the gold and silver mines.... The Platte Valley produces the most abundant crops and the finest quality raised on this

Continent.... The building of the hundreds of miles of railroad in that new country, as well as the thousands of people that go to Colorado every year and are contented, testify to and prove these four things: *First* – That it is the healthiest part of America. *Second* – That it is the richest mineral country on the face of the globe.... *Third* – That its soil produces the most abundant crops.... *Fourth* – Texas men say it is a much better grazing field than their famous land....

The Southwestern Colony is fully established in this rich and beautiful Valley; having already built more than thirty houses, dug one irrigating canal 16 miles long and opened up several farms.... We charge you for membership to this colony $50. You pay before starting $10 of that money, and we give you a certificate which virtually constitutes you a member, and gives you the benefit of our cheap *first-class* railroad transportation for yourself and family.... When you arrive in the colony, if you like it, you then locate one town lot, and pay the remaining $40 on your membership – which you have the privilege of paying either in work or money.... As a member of the colony you will have the right to locate 160 acres of land inside of the irrigating canals; this gives a value to your land of at least $10 per acre.... This land costs you $12 when you go on to it, and you live on it five years and pay $10 more and get a title to it.... Over 400 have already gone out, and we have about one hundred more ready to go.... We want blacksmiths, shoemakers, dry-goods merchants, grocerymen, druggists.... No employment or any of these benefits will be given to any one who is not a member of the colony.... Unless you are good, honest, industrious men and women, we would rather you would not go with us, for we are building up a nice town and a nice colony. That none may be disappointed, we want to say that *whisky* is not allowed in the colony....

TALKING WITH GREEN.... "Now," said Mr. Green, in a paternal way, "I'll be plain and tell you that a man has no business near the Green River Colony unless he carries a lot of sand in his craw!"...

"But, Mr. Green, your circular would seem to indicate that the colony for which you are agent is another Arcadia?"

"Some people are satisfied with it," said he; "some have come back and, like all those who return, they growl and raise a fuss.... Some of the parties who have returned have accused my brother of deserting the colonists when he got them out. That is a falsehood. He has been suffering from catarrh for many years, and is, I fear consumptive. He has been sick in Denver for several weeks.... He has been at war with a Capt. Pace, from Tennessee, who is President of the Colony, for some time. Pace wants to ignore my brother altogether, and has been pre-empting lands for his own friends...and does all he can to discourage Eastern colonists..."

ROBERT ABERNETHY....*To the Editor of the Chicago Tribune:*

Sir: Basil Green...a few weeks ago represented to me that they were agents of the "Southwestern Colony of Colorado," at Green City, on the South Platte River; that Government land could be had which could be preempted under the Homestead law upon the river bottom on the south side of the Platte River, within a mile of Green City; that the Colony had built more than thirty houses there; that there was an irrigating canal sixteen miles long; that blacksmiths, merchants, shoemakers, etc., and a stone and hardware man were wanted…. Relying upon his representations…went to Green City, and found his representations nearly all absolutely false. There is no Government land in the river-bottom such as named…within 15 miles. There are but eleven houses at Green City, instead of thirty, and but twenty all told within a territory 10 miles long; some of them are shanties with mud roofs. The statement of the circular is absolutely false with regard to the lands inside of the canal. There is none whatever…. There are but nineteen men of whom we could obtain any knowledge in the sixteen miles of Colony. The President of the Corporation, Capt. Pace, told us at Green City, that the Green Brothers were not agents of the Colony and every certificate of membership issued by them was a fraud…. The "irrigating canal"…was perfectly dry…and perhaps a foot deep, the citizens told us water was never in it nearer than two miles of Green City…. Last winter the Greens sent out from Chicago about twenty families; only one of them now remains in Green City, and they are unable to get away, but are fed by a citizen, to keep them from starving…the victims of D. S. Green, who abandoned them…. Nearly all who go are poor, and many unable to get back. Basil Green yesterday admitted to me in his own office that some of the most important representations in his circular are not true, but he continues to circulate them....[682]

Southwestern colony did not succeed[683] and the remaining settlers changed the name of Green City to Corona in 1874[684] though there remains on modern maps a reference to Green City Flats as a reminder of the original settlement located northwest of Wiggins. In 1882, a new Corona post office was established nearer to present day Wiggins and on the Burlington railroad line near Cotsworth station[685]. The town of Corona was described in glowing terms with no mention of its past history but with claims no less grand than those of the Green brothers:

THE CORONA COLONY is located in Weld county, on both sides of the South Platte river, and only the line of the Colorado Central railroad, about 75 miles below Denver. The town of Corona, the nucleus of this promising enterprise, embraces one section (640 acres) of land, on a remarkably level and beautiful plateau on the south side of the river, commanding a fine view of the Rocky mountains for more than 200 miles, including Long's and Pike's peaks, with a sketch of snowy peaks to the north. For a nearer vista, the wide valley of the Platte with its dark green meadows, and scattered groves of cottonwood, with a background of green, rolling bluffs, forms a pleasant picture. Nature has certainly done her share in supplying so favorable a location; and the wisely liberal policy adopted by the present officers will operate strongly in favor of the future prosperity of the town. The prospective growth and success of Corona is based on its position, and the many side issues flowing from it. Its location is at the focal point of a vast and wonderfully fertile agricultural and pastoral region, including the wide slopes bordering the Platte, and the valleys of the Kiowa and Lost creeks. The immediate river bottom produces an abundance of excellent hay, and the uplands furnish unlimited pasturage. The colony irrigating canal, already seventeen and one-half miles long, will soon be extended so as to cover about 5,000 acres more of very desirable land. All this will be tributary to Corona, and will be sufficient to sustain a thriving town. These resources, in themselves, only avail the developing power of an industrious population, a power already enlisted, and speedily to be exerted. At and in the vicinity of Corona, the pleasure-seeker, the invalid, and the tourist, will, alike, find an

1883 map [Excerpt] showing Tennessee Colony, Corona & Corona Sta..H.H. Hardesty & Company.

interesting field. The plains and the streams abound in game of every description. The distance from the mountains, about fifty miles, makes it peculiarly inviting to invalids desiring a dry and invigorating atmosphere, while the surrounding landscape scenery is rarely equaled. The inhabitants themselves are high-minded, cultivated and hospitable, and make up a delightful social circle, in which the most refined and intelligent may find pleasurable companionship. Agricultural and pastoral pursuits furnish for the present the principal occupations, but upon the completion of the Colorado Central railroad, merchandising, manufact-uring, and appertinent enterprises, will meet with dear attention, and doubtless lead to satisfactory results. A weekly line of stages will, until the completion of the railroad, take visitors and colonists from Evans, on the Denver Pacific, about twenty-five miles to Corona, at a moderate fair....[686]

The post office name was changed to Wiggins in 1896[687] and a town plat was filed in 1908[688]. The name Wiggins was chosen for frontiersman Oliver Perry Wiggins ("Old Scout"), a local resident and famed for being a scout and trapper with "Kit" Carson. The writer Edwin L. Sabin interviewed Wiggins and used him as a character and source for in his books *Kit Carson Days* and *Adventuring with Carson and Frémont.* The books are based on Fremont's exploration of the midwest with Wiggins as a boy tagging along. Wiggins' stories were the stuff of legend – and so they proved to be as many of his stories have proven completely fictional[689].

In 1870, northeastern Colorado was open pasture land with no towns or population centers. The towns that grew from the land centered on historical places such as stations on the Overland Trail, or the promise of future commerce that came with the railroads. Towns such as Brush and Fort Morgan had both. Some towns survived and some towns died, but one town would grow to become the predominant center of commerce and government in the area.

∞

Chapter 10

Birth of a Town

The town of Fort Morgan was platted not on a random piece of land in the Great American Desert, but along a trail used for hundreds of years, near the banks of a river that provided irrigating water across the land, at a junction where once a military fort stood, and between two major railroads. The placement of the town was serendipitous and would influence the town's survival.

The town of Fort Morgan was platted just south of the old military fort's ruins on May 1, 1884. It was not the first platted town in the area; South Platte, Buffalo/Merino, Brush and Green City/Corona all pre-date Fort Morgan. The idea for the town was Abner Baker's and his family were among the first residents. As original members of Greeley's Union Colony, they built the new town on the principals of the colony.

Advertisement for Fort Morgan as the new county seat. Published in
the Fort Morgan Times *March 1, 1889.*

The newspaper was one of the first businesses to be established, announcing the town. An introduction to the town of Fort Morgan was published in the first issue of the *Fort Morgan Times* on September 4, 1884. The article is a reprint of one written by Ralph Meeker and published in May in the *Greeley Tribune* with the note that the hotel and depot have already been built:

Fort Morgan is situated southeast of the Narrows of the Platte river, fifty miles below Greeley and about seventy miles from Denver, The town proper is directly on the line of the Burlington & Missouri railway, and a short walk from Deuel the nearest Union Pacific station. With two great railways at its door and the Platte river flowing along its boundary, it is destined to become one of the important towns of Northern Colorado. Irrigation appears on a magnificent scale here, where one finds the most extensive canals in the State. Before going into details, a brief sketch of the country will be pertinent.

Fort Morgan in early days. Years ago – in 1859, when the Pike's Peak gold fever was at its height, thousands of miners with their outfits followed up the Platte river to the mountains. The site of Fort Morgan was a favorite camping place. An immense sod corral on the bands of the river, under the bluff, protected the stores of the ranchero who had charge of the station. Another corral was used for stable purposes. Concord stages, freight wagons, emigrant trains, stopped there for refreshments and good water. With the exception of the adobe and sod stations, twenty or thirty miles apart along the river, the country was a wilderness. Indians and buffalo roamed the plains and at night the silence was only broken by the howl of the gray coyote. Fremont, the path-finder, journeyed up this river on his way to the Pacific, and every important point is invested with historic interest. The great north and south trails of the Cheyennes and Sioux crossed the Platte near the Narrows. In those days the dangers of travel were many, and at any hour the emigrant might be shot down in cold blood. Indians followed every train; to straggle away or fall behind was death to a white man. To protect emigrants and the United States mail service, the government, in 1864, established a military post on the Morgan Flats, which commanded wide views of the country up and down the river for a long distance. Captain McNitt, the present surveyor of Weld county, who came to Colorado from the army about that time, says that Fort Morgan was the largest post on the river. Nearly a regiment of men were quartered there, supported by a battery of guns of a caliber calculated to keep the red skins at a distance.

When the Greeley colony came to Colorado in 1870, the country around Fort Morgan was still the haunt of Indians and buffalo, and it was not until the South Platte branch of the Union Pacific railway was built to Denver that settlers began to make permanent improvements. The possibilities of the Beaver Creek country and its superiority for agricultural purposes, attracted Mr. Baker's attention while hunting buffalo in 1874, and his scheme for taking out ditches in that section was the problem of many years' thought; but as immense capital was required for building the canals, the enterprise did not seem feasible until Earl Airlie and his son appeared on the scene....They not only encouraged the construction of the canal, but promised financial co-operation. Soon after the first survey of the Platte and Beaver canal was made, the deal of the Earl rendered it necessary to organize what is now known as the Platte and Beaver Company.... The Fort Morgan plateau is an immense tract laying above the bed of the river. To get water on the land, it was necessary to begin the canal about fourteen miles above Fort Morgan....

Heath and Fine Scenery. As the delighted visitor expands his lungs in the free bracing air, he experiences the sensations peculiar to the plateaus of the Andes, as described by Humboldt. The landscape is as level as a floor, and yet it seems far above the world. The stranger instinctively looks around as to gaze upon the plains below him. This feeling of altitude exalts the senses, and with the sight of the Rocky Mountains unrolling their snowy chain, only a stupid man complains of "monotony." The view from Fort Morgan is very fine. It is just ninety miles to Long's Peak, where the great range lifts its mighty crest far into the sky.

On the quarter sections of the outlying lands, houses have been built, and in many instances land plowed for a considerable distance from the town. To appreciate the magnitude of the work already done, it should be considered that the settlement was only begun this spring. The canal with its present capacity will water about 25,000 acres. In this magnificent domain, Mr. A. S. Baker owns a large share of the land and the water. Notwithstanding the exceptional advantages possessed by the town in the way of railway facilities, water, good health, and unlimited agricultural resources, the founders do not seem very anxious to force its expansion; and instead of rushing into speculation and the sale of town lots, they are sowing alfalfa, increasing their herds of blooded stock, and developing the farming lands with remarkable energy. Miles of laterals, sub-ditches and wire fences have been made, and already the cactus is giving way to the verdure of civilization. Still, in spite of the attention bestowed on outside improvements, the town is making a healthful growth. A side track has been put in, a storehouse built and stocked with goods, a newspaper projected, and a handsome depot promised by the railway company....

The capital stock of Mr. Baker's Fort Morgan Irrigation Company is $100,000 and the shares are valued at $100 each. Mr. A. S. Baker owns three-fourths of the stock, the remainder being owned by J. S. Courtney, F. E. Baker, E. E. Baker, W. C. Lothrop, the Glassey Brothers of Fort Collins, G. W. Warner, and Henry N. Rouse. To build the ditch and raise the money necessary for its construction, it was bonded for $160,000. It is represented by 350 water rights, which are as good as United States bonds, and can be used as collaterals in any bank. It is expected that the sale of these water rights will more than pay for the ditch. Then the rapid increase of the value of the land will greatly add to the worth of the property. Land has already been sold under the ditch for $15 an acre; of course the title for it has been obtained from the Government and the purchaser receives his share of water from the canal. With the exception of some 3,000 acres of State land (which is now owned by A. S. Baker), all the land in the Fort Morgan tract was taken up by actsal [sic] settlers under the pre-emption act[690].

One claim made by many towns on the Colorado plains was the health benefits thought to come with the dry air and altitude. The health benefits of Fort Morgan were included in the above article, but Dr. F. J. Bancroft's description of Colorado and especially the plains reads much like a prescription for those in ill health:

> Persons afflicted with asthma, bronchitis, liver complaints, almost any disorders induced by derangement of the digestive organs, or by over-taxation of the physical and mental forces, in whom the heart is sound, are improved by even a short residence in this invigorating air. Those suffering from emaciation and debility, almost invariably gain flesh and strength here; the appetite is increased, respiration is accelerated, and owing to the fact that the lessened atmospheric pressure at this high altitude induces much freer capillary circulation, nutrition goes on with renewed activity. On the contrary, obesity is a condition almost unknown, and very stout persons usually decline sensibly in size after coming here; the general tendency being to a normal state of weight and health. The prairies, within forty miles of the mountains, at an elevation of not more than 5,000 or 6,000 feet above sea-level, possess peculiar sanitary advantages for the relief, or cure of pulmonary troubles. They are protected from the cool, dry north winds by the "divides," which run out at right angles from the main range; the air is tempered in winter

from the extremes of cold, by a warm, bright and genial sun, and, in the summer, from the extremes of heat, by cool breezes which constantly flow down through the cañons from the snowy range to the plains below; these breezes possess a little moisture, gained by absorption from the melting snow, and, mingling with the dry atmosphere of the prairies, relieve it of any harshness which it may possess. There are but few cloudy days in the year, and fogs are scarcely ever seen; sudden changes in the temperature are common at all seasons, but as the dryness of the atmosphere lessens its powers of conducting heat, the variations effect the system less than they would in damper localities....

The usual effects of the atmosphere upon asthmatics before emphysema, or dilation of the right side of the heart has taken place, is to produce a complete cure, and those who suffer from the above complications often experience much relief here.

Chronic laryngitis and bronchitis, unconnected with a rheumatic or syphilitic diathesis, readily yield to the light, unirritating character of the air. In the incipient stage of pulmonary consumption the effect of the climate is very marked in its tendency to relieve local and chronic inflammation; to arrest the deposit of tubercles, and to prevent the ulceration of matter already deposited. It also often permanently arrests the progress of the disease, after small cavities have been formed in the lungs, in cases where there is no hereditary tendency to it. Even when this tendency strongly exists, Colorado may prove a haven of safety if sought as soon as the presence of the disease is detected; and to the young, especially, it will prove so, if resorted to before the occurrence of any of the premonitory symptoms; and thus, many a life that would otherwise be lost before reaching the meridian of manhood, could here be prolonged to a healthy and useful old age.

I believe that any person, with a fair constitution, who settles in this region, stands a better chance of enjoying a healthful life and of finally attaining the full period allotted to man – "three score years and ten" – than in any other portion of the land[691].

The vision for the town was in place from the beginning and the town sprang up quickly starting along Main Street. Obtaining the railroad was key to the town's success. A station had been established on the north bank of the river feeding the growing town of Deuel, but it was essential for Fort Morgan to have a railroad as well. The Burlington railroad initially established a station two miles west of Fort Morgan at Ensign. To encourage the railroad to move the station, Abner S. Baker deeded half of the town plots to the Lincoln Land Company, a subsidiary of the Chicago, Burlington & Quincy railroad. The railroad literally now owned the town, at least half of it[692,693] and the station at Ensign was moved. The budding town of Ensign disappeared as quickly as its railroad station.

The vision for the town was Abner Baker's, but building the town was a family affair with the Baker brothers, Edwin E., Lyman C., and Baker's brother-in-law, William H. Clatworthy building the first structures in the new town including a general store[694]. Soon followed Farnsworth's Hotel, a brickyard, a livery barn, a blacksmiths and a carpenter shop[695].

The town was laid out in a grid bounded north and south by Railroad and Platte Avenues and east and west by Lake and Deuel Streets with Main street in the middle. The grid was six by five blocks square. The lots were divided into 50'x140' segments with the lots boarding Main Street half the width[696]. It is interesting to note the names of the streets. The east-west streets were named after important rivers in the area, Platte, Bijou, Beaver, Kiowa. Deuel was named after the neighboring town to the north, Meeker Street named for the

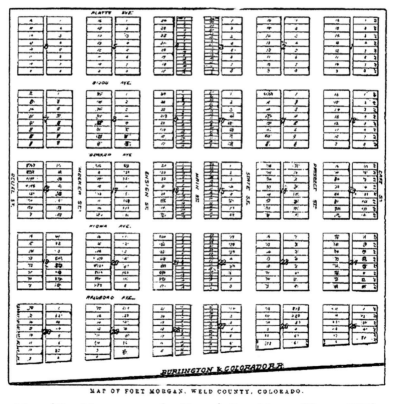

MAP OF FORT MORGAN. WELD COUNTY. COLORADO.

Map of Fort Morgan town plat. From the Fort Morgan Times, *1886.*

founder of Greeley's Union Colony, and Ensign for the railroad station on the Burlington that was moved to Fort Morgan.

Fort Ruins

The ruins of the old fort were located on the land of Lyman C. Baker north of the town. Indians had burned the fort and all that remained were the adobe walls, but the early settlers, none of whom had ever visited the active fort, adopted the ruins as a heritage site:

> L. C. Baker is breaking ground around the old fort, on his tree claim preparatory to planting five acres of trees. When a young forest has grown up around there, what fun it will be for the young fry to dangle their legs from the old walls, while the cotton from the trees sifts down the back....[697]

In 1885, an attempt was made to identify thirteen graves in an enclosure near the fort. A letter was sent to the War Department[698], but no records for the burials could be found. A small cemetery near the fort had been mentioned in a military inspection conducted in 1866, but there was no indication of whether the graves were civilian or military[699]. Whispering Ed Forrester (known for his booming voice), an old pioneer and guide, told to Bess Burtram, daughter of Frank Baker a story that could explain the anonymous graves near the old fort:

> First time I [Forrester] was in Ft. Morgan was in September 1872. There was just a sod fort there then. Built up on a hill on the south side of the river – kind of a bend there seems like. I was a scout in those days – long hair,

buckskin clothes with lots of fringe – big hat – not very old but plenty sure of myself. I was guidin' a wagontrain from Omaha along the old Ply Express Trail [sic]. It was Saturday, I remember, and we was aimin' to make the fort by sundown. There wasn't any soldiers there then, but there was a big sod stockade that made a safe campin' ground and plenty of water. Just before we got to the fort we ran onto a smoldering fire of ashes that had been a wagon – or several wagons. The ground was covered with fresh tracks – Indians, white men, women and children and there were naked, tomahawked and scalped corpses scattered over the ground. Eight men and women. They were all old people and one woman must have weighed three hundred pounds. The children and live stock were gone. There was just those dead people and that pile of ashes and the blood all over the ground to tell of the massacre that must have taken place less than 24 hours before we got there. We laid over Sunday to bury them. We took canvas from our wagon covers to wrap them in and dug graves in two rows on the hill where they were killed. Maybe you think that wasn't hard digging. It took all day. I took a board from a wagon and printed on it "Killed by Indians September – 1872" and set it up over the graves. There was nothing more we could do so the next day we were on our way – but do you know we never heard a word about any Indian outbreak or any massacre anywhere. I suppose it was just a roving band, and nobody was left alive to spread the news so nobody but our party ever knew anything about it – and we didn't know much. Yes indeed, I recollect Ft. Morgan real well[700].

The new settlers dug into the land around the fort and found history. Shells, rifle balls, bits of cavalry harness belt buckles and soldier buttons were found near the fort's ruins as well as an old carbine:

Captain E. D. Farley, of Fort Morgan, on the South Platte river, some time ago found near the banks of the river a mile below the Fort, an old, rusty and storm-beaten Spencer carbine. It is one of the old pattern which was patented two years before the war and with which many of the cavalry and mounted infantry regiments were armed.... They were surprise to the Indians who had never known any kind of gun except the muzzle loader, and they became...afraid of 'the guns that could be wound up and fired all day'.... When, how and by whom this gun was lost will perhaps, never be known. In the times when it must have been lost fights and skirmishes with the Indians were so common that no record could now be made of them, or the place of their occurrence. The region around Fort Morgan was prolific of them, but memory fail to tell of only one of which occurred in the exact region where this gun was found.... This rusty old weapon, a silent remembrance of the pioneer days, may be seen in the counting room of the *Tribune Republican* office. It will be kept on exhibition in the office for several days[701].

In pursuit of more history, the *Fort Morgan Times* placed a call in Colorado newspapers for information from soldiers stationed at the fort[702] and Captain M. H. Slater responded:

I have a distinct recollection of one incident, in 1864, when twenty men of my command had chased a party of Indians more than a hundred miles, and recovered from them about one hundred and thirty head of stock, a large portion of which belonged to the Overland stage company, and brought the bunch in to the point where Fort Morgan was afterwards built....

Apropos of the rusty reminiscence republished by you from the *Tribune-Republican*, let me add, that I could stand on the site of the old Fort and point out a spot where I once saw a white man surrounded by half a dozen Cheyennes. Twenty of us were saddling our horses one mile distant. In five minutes we were on the ground, but the Indians had taken to the adjacent bluffs. The poor wretch we went to succor laid as they had left him, literally pinned to the ground with arrows[703].

Despite local interest in the fort, by 1911[704], the remains had disappeared. The Daughters of the American Revolution placed a marker at the site of the old fort on October 26, 1912[705] at the corner of Grant and Riverview Avenue[706]. The monument is now located near the intersection of Main Street and Riverside.

First settlers

The town was Abner Baker's vision and he with friends and family members were among the first to settle in the new town. A short biography and celebration of Abner Baker was published in the Fort Morgan Times under the headline "The One Man who saw the Future of Fort Morgan":

Abner S. Baker was born in Norwalk, Ohio, in August 1844, the son of Geo. R. and Hannah A. Baker. At an early age he removed with his parents to Indiana and a little later settled in Baraboo, Wis. where he received an academic education. In 1861 he responded to the call of his country and enlisted in the First Wisconsin Cavalry and served throughout the war. At the close of the war he returned to his home in Wisconsin and was employed for some time as a salesman in one of the leading mercantile establishments, until the year 1866, he moved with other families to East Tennessee where he remained until the time of his joining the Greeley colony in 1870, being one of the original colonists.

Mr Baker was married in 1876 to Sarah F. Graham, who, after many years of feeble health died in Fort Morgan in June, 1895.

He followed farming in the Greeley Colony with varied success, and learned lessons in irrigation and the building of ditches which he was able to use for the bene-

A. S. BAKER,

Sketch of Abner S. Baker published in the Fort Morgan Times, *1889.*

fit of others in later years. In 1880 and 1881 he turned his attention to contract work, and was successfully engaged in the construction of several ditches in Weld county, also contract work on the U.P. railroad and Denver & New Orleans (now Colorado Southern).

In November, 1881 he moved his forces east of Greeley and commenced construction of the Ogilvy ditch, he being the projector of the enterprise, and the owner of much of the land under it. This ditch was completed in the early summer of 1882, and the ditch and lands sold to Lord Ogilvy, who later developed them and sold to the Studebakers. During the process of this work he was looking for other lands upon which to build ditches. Shortly after this the Earl of Airlie, who with his son, Lord Ogilvie, was interesting himself in these enterprises, died and the plans of Mr. Baker for the building of the Platte and Beaver canals and the acquirement of the lands under them had to be abandoned Mr. Baker then interested a company to take over the location and pursue the work, and this company became the builders of the canals known as the Platte & Beaver systems. This company included Mr. Baker, Lord Ogilvy, Governor Brush, Governor Eaton, Governor Cooper, Willard Teller, Bruce Johnson, H. N. Hayes, Judge Scott and others. Mr. Baker received a contract for a large part of the work, and moved his forces down the Platte in June 1882. Nearly all of the upper canal was built during that year, and much of the lower canal completed. While engaged in one enterprise he was always looking ahead, ever ready to take advantage of other enterprises that might be developed so while Mr. Baker had a large interest in the Platte and Beaver ditches and lands, then all owned by the company, it did not suit him to be tied down by the interests of others, and not be able to push the development of the enterprises in his own energetic way; he was ambitious to take up something in which he would be the central figure or have full control.

As early as May, 1882, Mr. Baker talked to the writer [G. W. Warner] about the feasibility of building a ditch to water the Fort Morgan flats above the line of the Platte & Beaver canal, and the writer spent some time along the banks of the Bijou to see how an available crossing could be had. We were told by everyone that it was impossible to flue the Bijou – it was too long a span and the piling would not stand. Nevertheless, a flume 2,100 feet long was constructed, and that stood for eleven years until rebuilt by the farmers.

It was as early as May, 1882, that a plan was formed to build a town at or near our present location…and its name to be Fort Morgan in honor of the old fort and post, which was well known at that time…. The Fort Morgan townsite having been surveyed, on May 1, 1884, the plat was filed, and active operations in building, which had already begun, were continued. In 1884 the store was then being conducted by Mr. Baker, Mr. Farnsworth was building a hotel, a brickyard was opened by Killebrew & Burk, and livery barn, blacksmith and carpenter shops were going up, as well as many dwellings, most of the material and money being furnished by Mr. Baker.

We who were on the ground were hopeful and enthusiastic for the new town, and believed then as now, that the location was ideal and the surrounding land unsurpassed for farming purposes in Colorado – the best state in the union….

In 1884 Mr. Baker encouraged everyone to farm and

water all the land that it was possible to cultivate, and water was furnished to everyone without consideration, only in notes, which were canceled. His theory was that the building of a ditch did not necessarily create a priority of right, the building must be followed by the application of water to the land, and an earlier constructed ditch might lose its prior rights by not actually applying the water to beneficial uses...

Mr. Baker's forsight [sic] into the possibilities of this locality was far in advance of his time. He could see Fort Morgan a city of 2,000 people in the near future, which, we are sorry to say, he did not live to see. His immediate friends advised him against this enterprise, that it was too far away from Greeley to amount to much, and so far down the Platte that we would get no water after running through the sand, that it was a fool hardy enterprise to try to build a flume across the Bijou; but he persisted in his undertaking with all the more determination....

The great part of his character was his indomitable will and nerve, coupled with assurance that he could accomplish his purpose, enabling him to attempt large undertakings. His vision gave him view of the future possibilities in the development of this country, but unfortunately the great results were delayed much longer than was then thought. No one who has ever lived in Fort Morgan was entitled to so much consideration for what he did.... No one has been so pooly rewarded[707].

Frank Hall's *History of the State of Colorado* published in 1889 described the founders of Fort Morgan including William H. Clatworthy, John H. Farnsworth (the first hotel keeper), J. E. Fisk, S. M. Prince (the first school teacher), W. S. Morton, C. N. Fisk, John L. Haff, the Flynts, and Lyman C. Baker. The first mayor was Manley E. Lowe with L. W. Bartlett serving as treasurer, H. M. Putnam as clerk and M. B. Howard, J. T. Devin, L. C. Baker, J. E. Brown, W. H. Clatworthy, and J. D. Johnson as trustees[708].

In 1889, the *Fort Morgan Times* also introduced important members of the Fort Morgan community including Amos A. Smith, Morgan County Sheriff[709]. The newspaper also introduced prominent businessmen – and women. These were among the first builders of Fort Morgan: A. C. Clarke, J. D. Johnson, W. H. Clatworthy, Thomas Brown, J. S. Courtney, F. E. Baker, E. C. Luce, J. M. Lytle, G. A. Garard, Michael Johnson, J. C. Coburn, E. W. Lowe, A. K. Hill, Walter T. Brown, G. W. Warner, Mrs. C. A. C. Flynt, F. S. Schoonover, M. I. Tuttle, Henry Stamm, F. H. McLain, L. H. Nelson, Captain W. B. Howard, Dr. E. R. Tibbals, S. A. Sherman Work, L. M. Piper, M. N. Wagner, H. M. Putnam, Dr. H. Work, J. J. Losh, Charles Gossman, Hovey G. Altman, I. C. Lefevre, J. P. Looney, Dr. J. J. Lutze, I. B. Price, and George Gordan.

Wilbur Fiske Stone's *History of Colorado* published in four volumes in 1918-1919 also included substantial biographies of influential Coloradans including people who had connections with Fort Morgan or Morgan County. Included are biographies of: John C. Andersen, pharmacist; Edwin E. Baker, irrigation engineer; Ernest E. Calkins, businessman; Harry T. Carroll, businessman; Robert A. Chace, rancher; Walter Scott Coen, attorney; James A. M. Crouch, businessman; Dennis Dailey, farmer; Ralph R. Drennen, businessman; Alfred W. Dulweber, attorney; Charles H. Gilbertson, mayor of Fort Morgan; A. C. Gillett, businessman; Tyler D. Heiskell, businessman; George E. Hosmer, newspaperman & editor; Marshall M. House, attorney; James E. Jewel, attorney; Arthur M. Johnson, banker; Lewis G. Johnson, attorney; James W. McCreery, a trial lawyer based in Greeley; Robert L. Patterson, businessman; Frank H. Potter, businessman; Willard Reid, Morgan County treasurer; Fred F. Reinert, postmaster; Judge Clayton C. Rickel; Corbin E. Robison, attorney; E. B. Roe, surgeon; Julian H. Roediger, businessman; Robert B. Spencer, newspaperman and editor; Arlington Taylor, attorney; George C. Twombly, district attorney; Hurd Warren Twombly, district attorney; David J. Van Bradt, attorney; Frank W. Vanderhoof, businessman; U. J. Warren, businessman; Roscoe C. Welsh, businessman; Jacob H. Welty, rancher; Hirah W. Woodward, banker; Robert M. Work, district attorney; and Joseph Austin Yenne, businessman[710].

Fort Morgan's first doctor was Hubert Work, coming to town in 1887 as a young man. Later, Dr. Work was politically active and would become Postmaster General and then Secretary of the Interior of the United States under Presidents Harding and Coolidge[711]. Work's advice was "men will simply do as best they can, the job before them, and finish it, - whether they like it or not, - the future will take care of itself[712]." This motto seems to apply to the founders of Fort Morgan.

Main Street & Businesses

When Fort Morgan began, "Main street was a few wagon tracks showing again the buffalo grass and cactus that covered the entire flat[713]," but he town would grow quickly. Almost uniform red brick characterizes Main Street, a result of one of the first established businesses in town - the Killebrew and Burk brickyard. The brickyard was soon joined by Hallack & Howard lumber on the 100 block of Main Street near the railroad depot. By 1886, Main Street included a restaurant, a bank, a hotel, a drug store, a confectionary store, a livery, a barber shop, and a number of hardware and dry goods stores[714].

The town developed northward, starting along Main Street at the railroad depot. The 100, 200, and to a lesser extent the 300 blocks of Main Street formed the first center of the town of Fort Morgan[715]. Most buildings started on one or two 25' lots constructing one- or two-story brick buildings. By the turn of the century, most of the spaces between buildings had been filled in resulting in a continuous brick montage of businesses. The buildings were constructed quickly, but there seemed a great deal of movement of businesses between buildings. Business owners often built new premises across the street or moved, seeming at random, a few doors down.

Depot

The railroad depot, relocated from Ensign in May of 1884, was placed on Railroad Avenue on the east side of Main Street. The present structure, west of Main Street was built in 1928[716]. The first agent was W. F. Callender who lived with his wife at the station house. He was also active on the school board and building associations and as an amateur musician[717]. The railroad report for the year 1885 shows a thriving business with $1147.20 in ticket sales, $6814.01 in freight received, $116.56 in telegraph business and 21 carloads of stock and produce shipped and 41 carloads of lumber and 18 carloads of coal received[718]. By the end of 1886, freight had risen to $12,842.26, ticket sales to $2,156.81, telegraph receipts to $227.83. During the year 51 carloads of stock and produce were shipped[719].

Newspaper

The *Fort Morgan Times* was among the first businesses established in Fort Morgan with the first issue printed September 4, 1884, just months after the town plat was filed. The town of Brush also had a newspaper, the *Lariat* which stated publishing in May of 1884, but the *Lariat* was short-lived and stopped publishing just a year later. Towards the turn of the century, the *Morgan County Herald* became the chief rival for the Times, but it too folded in July of 1918.

The first editor of the paper was Lyman C. Baker, brother of Abner, who had worked at the *Greeley Tribune* before coming to Fort Morgan. One of the early settlers in Fort Morgan, Lute H. Johnson, printer and sometime editor of the *Times* spoke of the paper and its first editor:

Lyman C. Baker, brother of Abner, had been a printer back in Wisconsin and had worked on the *Greeley Tribune*. It had been planned that a newspaper should be started to "put the town on the map." In the fall, while the first crop – almost entirely of oats – was being har-

THE FORT MORGAN TIMES.

VOL I   FORT MORGAN, WELD COUNTY, COLO., THURSDAY, SEPTEMBER 4, 1884.   NO 1

vested on the new farms, Lyme got hold of an army press
and a bootful of second hand type and, discovering that I
had been a printer, I was called in to help get out the *Fort
Morgan Times*. The first few issues were printed in Lyme's
coal house, which stood on his preemption adjoining the
east half of the townsite on the north. After a few issues
there, the claim shanty by which Grandpa Baker had
proved up the west half was papered inside and the mea-
gre [sic] plant moved into it. It stood in the extreme
northeast corner of the claim, almost in the middle of the
Main Street. I worked on as a printer for a time, walking
almost a mile to my meals. It was a poor community, but
the several settlers took pride in their paper and it managed to get by thru the winter. Lyme had a certain strain
of wit. We filled the few columns with the every day
doings of the settlers until any one felt injured if he failed
to see his name in the weekly paper at least twice. If he
went across the river to the Tracy ranch for hay, that was
news![720]

Baker and George Warner published their manifesto in the
first issue:

We take pleasure in presenting a new journal to the
citizens of Fort Morgan and the surrounding country this
week. Our increasing prosperity will amply support the
Times, and we trust that its first issue will meet a friendly
reception. Making no promises, except to stand by the
best interests of the community, we send the Times forth
to paralyze the enemies of our great State. The Times will
not be the organ of any party or clique, but will support
all that is calculated to build upon the country and ligh-

ten the burdens of the people. Outside of this, the Times will be run for our own amusement, and the general enlargement of the firm's pocket-book[721].

The newspaper would continue under the editorship of Lyman Baker and George Warner alternately and has published continuously since 1884.

As noted by Warner, the *Times* was first located in a shed on Baker's land and then in 1885 moved to 219 Main Street[722] before moving to its current location on the 300 block of Main Street. Crouch's dry goods store took over the *Times* building on Main Street[723].

Post Office

In 1884, a post office was opened in the new town in William H. Clatworthy's hardware store at the corner of Kiowa and Main Streets with Clatworthy as the first postmaster[724]. Soon, Clatworthy's store was expanded to house the Bank of Fort Morgan and G. W. Warner's office. Clatworthy announced in the *Times*: "I sell good goods, and endeavor to do business on the live and let live principle[725]"

Hotels

One of the first businesses on Main Street was Farnsworth's hotel opened in September 1884 by John H. Farnsworth[726]. The hotel was located on the southwest corner of Main and Railroad[727] and was large enough for 20 rooms[728]. During the building phase of Fort Morgan, the hotel was packed. Much of the social life of Fort Morgan revolved around the Farnsworth House with concerts and dances held at the hotel or in the nearby school building. J. H. Farnsworth was politically active in the Republican party and was appointed Justice of the Peace. Farnsworth was also instrumental in starting Fort Morgan's first school[729].

Other establishments soon sprang up including A. B. Daughtry's Fort Morgan Hotel in 1886[730] and in 1889, the Curry Hotel in the 300 block was built.

School

Fort Morgan's first schoolhouse was located on the 200 block of Main Street in a white frame structure built by J. H. Farnsworth in November 1884. The first classes were held in January of 1885[731] with Mr. Prince, nephew of Mrs. H. H. Baker, the first teacher[732]:

> The school opened on Tuesday [January 13, 1885], but it was found that no books of the desired kind were on hand and the school was adjourned until a supply was received, which will not be later than the last of the week. There were about 20 scholars enrolled. The seats are of the folding kind, and the school is furnished with maps, charts, globe, etc., and every appliance for a good school. Mr. Prince comes to us well recommended, and will no doubt do his duty to the school.[733]

The school house was used for meetings and social events functioning as a town hall and it wasn't long before the town began discussions of a larger, more permanent school. By the time Morgan County was established in 1889, there were 350 students and nine school buildings across the county[734].

Bank

Fort Morgan's first bank was the Bank of Fort Morgan located in Clatworthy's store on the 300 block of Main Street, but was soon to move to 201 Main Street. The bank was opened in 1887 with M. E. Lowe as president, C. S. Howard, vice president, and L. H. Bartlett as cashier[735]. The Bank of Fort Morgan became the Morgan County Bank in 1889[736]. The Morgan County offices occupied the second floor of the bank until the Court House was opened in 1906. When the Morgan County Bank moved, Creitz Drug Store occupied the first floor.

In 1890, the bank suspended trading when the cashier, L. H. Bartlett, was arrested for embezzling $20,000. He was later apprehended in Seattle, Washington[737].

General Stores

Abner S. Baker built a general store in 1884 on the corner of Main and Railroad[738], which he sold to W. B. Sinton in 1885[739]. Next door, to Baker's store was J. D. Johnson built a Cash store[740] opening in 1886 advertising that he desired to do business on the following conditions:

> ...Fair and honest treatment to all; Goods at as low prices as I can sell for and live; Equal treatment of all, whether Stockman, Farmer, Cow-boy or Laborer; One price to all and on the same terms. My stock is new, large and carefully bought. A life time spent in merchandizing will I treat, enable me to buy for the people in eastern markets at prices which they will find advantageous. As has been stated, I shall conduct a strictly CASH business, knowing it to be the most economical and satisfactory for both purchaser and dealer. In requiring cash on delivery of goods, I shall make no distinctions between millionaire or beggar, but shall treat both alike, sell them goods at the same prices and endeavor to please both. The cash system

Looking north to 200 block of Main Street c. 1890. Morgan County Bank is on the left, Barton block, white schoolhouse, and Restaurant No. 1 on the right. Courtesy of the Fort Morgan Museum.

grinds no man's nose; Trading by it you pay no laterest, no interest, no book-keeper's salary, no loss of bad accounts and a dozen little things for which the credit system must be paid in prices. The cash system keeps its own account. All goods marked in plain figures.... I am here to stay, and hope by these methods to win not only a share of the patronage, but the good will and esteem of the people I have chosen for neighbors.... Positively no goods sold on Sunday[741].

Completing the southern half of the 200 block was the two-story Barton Block housing J. W. Roberts Grocery store, Tibbals Furniture and dentist and later Shoonover law office.

A. K. Clarke's Emporium built in 1885 was located on the corner of Main Street and Kiowa, on lots that would later become the second home of the Morgan County Bank. Located on the second floor of Clarke's Emporium were offices of Morgan County, the Armory and the Masonic Hall[742].

Civic Organizations

The business infrastructure of Fort Morgan was in place, but bricks and businesses do not make a community. Within the first five years, the town had a baseball team, a Masonic lodge, an orchestra and a singing school, and two military organizations. The early settlers of Fort Morgan worked hard, but they also seem to play hard.

One of the first things the new town did was organize a baseball team.

Spring has revived the drooping spirits of the base ball fiend, and he is now very actively engaged in our midst. Scarcely had the snow left the ground when our players of

Looking south along Main Street from 300 block. Wagner-Simpson store on right side of photo is located at 309 Main Street. Courtesy of the Fort Morgan Museum.

the national game began the organization of a nine that would take the penant [sic] over any club in Colorado, and win the shekels of the game's devotees....

First and Second nines have been picked and lively competition will follow for the championship of our town, as well as among such clubs of neighboring towns as will meet the Fort Morgans in battle array. The grounds in thh [sic] town site have been smoothed down in fine shape, and the death dealing cacti removed. A full supply of accoutrements has been ordered, including a suit of mail and a small arsenal for the umpire. The club is ready to receive challenges – just knock a chip off of Joe Fisk's shoulder, if you dare[743].

Playing on the 1885 Fort Morgan baseball team was Gilbertson, Fisk, Courtney, Anderson, Warner, Bartlett, Hotchkiss, More, and Prince[744] with J. S. Courtney serving as captain[745].

Another organization begun in the first year of the town was the Singing School conducted by Prof. E. R. Crandall, the local music teacher and piano and organ salesman[746].

The Singing School opened Tuesday evening with a good attendance which bids fair to be increased as the term advances. Soon we will have a talented lot of warblers in our midst and the peaceful citizens will be forced to go into training in self defence [sic]. Although the school is just started, John Haff warble "Little Buttercup" with the greatest of ease, and Lou Bartlett goes about his work singing "Climbing up the Tenement Stairs" real beautifully. A concert will be given at the close of the term at which our people will see the shining musical lights in all their glory[747].

An orchestra added to the musical entertainment of the new town, giving its first dinner dance on August 1, 1885 at the Farnsworth House[748].

The young town was not without its secret organizations. The first home of the Masonic Lodge (Oasis Lodge No. 67), as well as the volunteer military, was Clarke's Emporium at Main and Kiowa Streets. George Robinson was the Worshipful Master and H. M. Putnam served as Secretary. Members included Walter T. Brown, W. B. Sinton, W. H. Clatworthy[749], Manley E. Lowe, Moses N. Wagner, Eugene W. Lowe, George S. Redfield, Tyler D. Helskel, Ibur F. Callender, Stafford R. McBratney, Louis H. Bartlett, J. Edwin Brown, George W. Warner, Heron G. Pyatt, and James T. Devin[750]. Another civic organization was the G. A. R. or the Grand Army of the Republic, a fraternal organization made up of Union soldiers who had served during the Civil War[751]. Fort Morgan also formed a company of men for the Colorado National Guard[752].

Within five years, the town had come from dust to a vibrant center of commerce and community. The next big step would government.

Morgan County

On February 19, 1889, Morgan County was established with Fort Morgan as the county seat. There had been fierce competition with Brush for the county seat; Fort Morgan was the larger town with a population of 488 to Brush's 112, but Brush had a longer history and was the center of the ranching trade[753]. But Fort Morgan had two railroad lines and was located, not by accident, in the exact center of the 36-mile square county. The town of Fort Morgan, the dream of one man who saw the promise of a flat tract of land near a ruined military fort, went from dust to county seat in five years.

∞

Epilogue

The town of Fort Morgan was born in 1884, but the land already had a rich history, one connected with westward expansion, with the rush for gold, and with the taming of the land for agriculture. Fort Morgan as a town survived and thrived while so many other towns faded. The success of this one town set amidst hundreds of acres of flat grassland lies both with its location, a point on an ancient Native American trail transformed into a junction with the rise of the golden town of Denver and the expansion of the railroads, and tenacity and foresight of the early settlers. The life-blood of the town was water. Without the canals flowing from not one source, but three, Fort Morgan would never have survived. In an age when most towns relied on railroads for commerce and connection, Fort Morgan achieved stations on two transcontinental railroad lines.

Fort Morgan was not a naturally beautiful place, but Fort Morgan has always been a land of promise. Nearly a dozen of Native American tribes found bountiful hunting on the land, early explorers looked up from the monotony of the plains and saw the wondrous sight of the Rocky Mountains soon to glisten with gold, and pioneers like John Iliff and Abner S. Baker saw promise in the land itself. Today, cattle still roam the pastures and farmers till the earth using water from the canals dug by shovel years before. The railroad thunders through the town daily and the businesses built on Main Street over a century and half ago still open their doors each morning, picking up a copy of the *Fort Morgan Times* as they do.

The town is named for a military fort, already in ruins before the town began. The fort, in turn was named for a much-loved military officer who died in a senseless accident 800 miles away. Fort Morgan seems an odd place for a loving memorial to a lost friend, but there was something special about the place that caused some to stop in their travels and take notice of the subtle beauty. The beauty of the plains, the beauty of the far-off mountains:

It was not long till we could discern a seemingly dark cloud, far-reaching, near the horizon, capped with white, which later I found to be the dear old Rocky Mountains, with their everlasting cap of snow. We were almost there and our past troubles we had left behind[754].

It was a harsh land and success came only with hard work but it was from these roots, Fort Morgan grew.

∞

Suggested Reading

Gray, John S., *Cavalry & Coaches: The Story of Camp and Fort Collins* (Fort Collins, CO: Old Army Press, 1978).

Hoig, Stan, *The Sand Creek Massacre* (Norman, OK: University of Oklahoma Press, 1961).

Jones, Robert Huhn, *Guarding the Overland Trails: The Eleventh Ohio Cavalry in the Civil War* (Spokane, WA: Arthur H. Clark Co, 2005).

Mehls, Steven F., *The New Empire of the Rockies: A History of Northeast Colorado* (Denver, CO: Bureau of Land Management, 1984).

Monahan, Doris, *Destination Denver: The South Platte Trail* (Athens OH: Swallow Press, 1985).

Propst, Nell Brown, *Forgotten People: A History of the South Platte Trail* (Boulder, CO: Pruett Publishing, 1979).

Root, Frank Albert & William Elsey Connelley. *The Overland stage to California* (Topeka, KS: F. A. Root, 1901).

Sabin, Edwin Legrand [fiction], *On the Overland Stage* (New York: Crowell, 1918).

End Notes

[1] Henry Dodge, "Dragoon Expedition – Indian Talks," *The Military and Naval Magazine of the United States* 6 (1836): 325.

[2] Delzell, James E., *Twenty-Third Biennial Report of the State Superintendent of Public Instruction* (Lincoln, NE: Woodruff Press, 1914), 600.

[3] Wilbur Fiske Stone, *History of Colorado, Vol. 1* (Chicago: S. J. Clarke Publishing, 1918), 199.

[4] Alvin Theodore Steinel & Daniel Webster Working, *History of Agriculture in Colorado*, (Fort Collins, CO: State Agricultural College, 1926), 13.

[5] Lilian L. Fitzpatrick, *Nebraska Place-Names* (Lincoln, NE: University of Nebraska Press, 1960), 180.

[6] William Bright, *Colorado Place Names* (Boulder, CO: Johnson Books, 2004), 140.

[7] Fitzpatrick, *Nebraska Place-Names*, 181.

[8] Floyd Benjamin Streeter, *Prairie Trails & Cow Towns: The Opening of the Old West* (New York: Devin Adair, 1963), 5-6.

[9] Howard Ensign Evans, *The Natural History of the Long Expedition to the Rocky Mountains* (New York: Oxford University Press, 1997), 115.

[10] Herbert M Hart, *Old Forts of the Northwest* (Seattle: Superior, 1963), 182.

[11] Colton, Ray Charles, *The Civil War in the Western Territories: Arizona, Colorado, New Mexico, and Utah* (Norman, OK: University of Oklahoma Press, 1959), 153.

[12] *Report of the National Society of the Daughters of the American Revolution for the Year Beginning October 11, 1913, and Ending October 11, 1914* (Washington: Government Printing Office, 1915), 58-59.

[13] Steven F. Mehls, *The New Empire of the Rockies: A History of Northeast Colorado*

(Denver: Bureau of Land Management, 1984),
www.nps.gov/history/history/online_books/blm/co/16/chap2.htm

14 Federal Writers' Project and Alan Boye, *Nebraska: A Guide to the Cornhusker State* (Lincoln, NE: University of Nebraska Press, 2005), 46.

15 The Long expedition reported covering the distance between Fort Morgan and the forks in 5 or 6 days and Fremont covered the distance in 4 days.

16 John Francis Bannon, *The Spanish Borderlands Frontier, 1513-1821* (New York: Holt, Rinehart, & Winston, 1970), 129-130.

17 Addison Erwin Sheldon, *History and Stories of Nebraska* (Chicago: University Pub., 1913), 15.

18 *Extract of the Journal of the Expedition of the Mallet Brothers to Santé Fe, 1739-1740*, www.americanjourneys.org/pdf/AJ-092.pdf

19 James W. Savage, "The Christening of the Platte," *Transactions and Reports of the Nebraska State Historical Society* 3, 67-73.

20 Donald Emmet Worcester, *Pioneer Trails West* (Caldwell, ID: Caxton Printers, 1985), 268.

21 *Extract of the Journal of the Expedition of the Mallet Brothers to Santé Fe, 1739-1740.*

22 Hiram Martin Chittenden, *The American Fur Trade of the Far West* (New York: F. P. Harper, 1902), 489.

23 Caroline Bancroft, *Colorful Colorado: Its Dramatic History* (Boulder, CO: Johnson, 1966), 19.

24 Zebulon Montgomery Pike, & Elliott Coues, *The Expeditions of Zebulon Montgomery Pike*, Vol. 2 (New York: F. P. Harper, 1895), 758.

25 David Sievert Lavender & Duane A. Smith, *The Rockies* (Lincoln, NE: University of Nebraska Press, 2003), 49

26 Pike & Coues, *The Expeditions of Zebulon Montgomery Pike*, 602-604.

27 Junius P.Rodriguez, *The Louisiana Purchase: A Historical and Geographical Encyclopedia* (Santa Barbara, CA: ABC-CLIO, 2002), 198.

28 Edwin James, Stephen Harriman Long, & Thomas Say, *James's Account of S. H. Long's Expedition, 1819-1820* (Cleveland: A. H. Clark, 1905), 11.

29 Ibid., 9.

30 Evans, *The Natural History of the Long Expedition to the Rocky Mountains*, 7.

31 LeRoy R.Hafen, "Joseph Bissonet dit Bijou," *The Mountain Men and the Fur Trade of the Far West, vol. 9* (Glendale, CA: A. H. Clark Co., 1965), 27-32.

32 "Messages and Documents," *Old Santa Fe: A Magazine of History, Archaeology, Genealogy and Biography 1* (1914): 375-376.

33 John R. Bell, *The Journal of Captain John R. Bell: Official Journalist for the Stephen H. Long Expedition to the Rocky Mountains, 1820* (Glendale, CA: A. H.

Clark, 1973), 141-143.

[34] Evans, *The Natural History of the Long Expedition to the Rocky Mountains*, 114.

[35] James, Long, & Say, *James's Account of S. H. Long's Expedition*, 20.

[36] LeRoy R. Hafen, "Fort St. Vrain," *Colorado Magazine* 29 (1952): 241-255.

[37] Ibid.

[38] Henry Inman, *The Great Salt Trail* (New York: Macmillan, 1898), 51.

[39] Glenn R. Scott, *Historical Trail Maps of the Sterling 1°X2° Quadrangle, Northeastern Colorado. Department of the Interior U. S. Geological Survey.*

[40] David J.Weber, *The Taos Trappers: The Fur Trade in the Far Southwest, 1540-1846* (Norman, OK: University of Oklahoma Press, 1971), 41.

[41] John C. Luttig, & Stella Madeleine Drumm, *Journal of a Fur-Trading Expedition on the Upper Missouri: 1812-1813* (St. Louis: Missouri Historical Society, 1920), 18.

[42] LeRoy R. Hafen & Harvey Lewis Carter, *Trappers of the Far West: Sixteen Biographical Sketches* (Lincoln, NE: University of Nebraska Press, 1983), 153.

[43] LeRoy R. Hafen, *Broken Hand: The Life of Thomas Fitzpatrick, Mountain Man, Guide and Indian Agent* (Lincoln, NE: University of Nebraska Press, 1981), 44.

[44] Harrison Clifford Dale & William Henry Ashley, *The Ashley-Smith Explorations and the Discovery of a Central Route to the Pacific: 1822-1829* (Cleveland: Arthur H. Clark, 1918), 125-127.

[45] Robert Newell, *Memorandum of Robert Newell's Travels in the Teritory of Missourie* (1959), www.xmission.com/~drudy/mtman/html/newell.html, 33.

[46] *Robert Newell Notebooks* www.manuellisaparty.com/articles/docs/newell's%20notebook.doc, 12.

[47] LeRoy Reuben Hafen & Ann Woodbury Hafen, "The E. Willard Smith Journal 1839-1840," *To the Rockies and Oregon 1839-1842* (Glendale, CA: A. H. Clark, 1955), 146-148.

[48] Luttig, & Drumm, *Journal of a Fur-Trading Expedition on the Upper Missouri*, 140.

[49] David Lavender, *Bent's Fort* (Garden City, NY: Doubleday, 1954), 208-209.

[50] John Charles Frémont, *Narrative of the Exploring Expedition to the Rocky Mountains in the Year 1842, and to Oregon and North California, in the Years 1843-44* (New York: D. Appleton, 1849), 5.

[51] Ibid., 23.

[52] Ibid., 26.

[53] Ibid., 27.

[54] Ibid.

[55] Ibid., 28-29.

[56] Ibid., 30-31.

[57] Rufus B. Sage, *Wild scenes in Kansas and Nebraska, the Rocky Mountains, Oregon, California, New Mexico, Texas, and the Grand Prairies* (Philadelphia: G. D. Miller, 1855), 13-14.

[58] Ibid., 158-160.

[59] Ibid.

[60] Theodore Talbot, *The Journals of Theodore Talbot* (Portland, OR: Metropolitan Press, 1931), 17.

[61] Frémont, *Narrative of the Exploring Expedition to the Rocky Mountains*, 99.

[62] Talbot, *The Journals of Theodore Talbot*, 18-21.

[63] Loretta Fowler, *Arapahoe Politics, 1851-1978: Symbols in Crises of Authority* (Lincoln, NE: University of Nebraska Press, 1982), 42.

[64] *Annual report of the Secretary of War, Volume 2*, United States War Department. Ex. Doc. No. 11. (Washington: William A. Harris, 1858), 455.

[65] Ibid., 469.

[66] Louis Pelzer, *Marches of the Dragoons in the Mississippi Valley* (NY: Arno Press, 1975), 35.

[67] *American State Papers, Military Affairs, VI*, http://memory.loc.gov/cgi-bin/ampage, 130-46.

[68] Fred S. Perrine, "Hugh Evans' Journal of Colonel Henry Dodge's Expedition to the Rocky Mountains in 1835," *The Mississippi Valley Historical Review* 14 (1927): 192-214.

[69] Hafen & Carter, *Trappers of the Far West*, 213.

[70] Robert Marshall Utley, *Frontiersmen in Blue: the United States Army and the Indian, 1848-1865* (Lincoln, NE: University of Nebraska Press, 1981), 121-122.

[71] William Y. Chalfant, *Cheyennes and Horse Soldiers: The 1857 Expedition and the Battle of Solomon's Fork* (Norman, OK: University of Oklahoma Press, 1989), 131.

[72] Chalfant, *Cheyennes and Horse Soldiers*, 141.

[73] Frederick E. Hoxie, *Encyclopedia of North American Indians* (Boston: Houghton Mifflin Co., 1996), 453.

[74] Francis Paul Prucha, *Documents of United States Indian Policy* (Lincoln, NE: University of Nebraska Press, 1975), 84.

[75] Joseph Kappler (Ed.), "Treaty of Fort Laramie with the Sioux, etc., 1851," *Indian affairs: Laws and treaties, Volume 2* (Washington: Government Printing Office, 1904), 594-596.

[76] Doris Monahan, *Destination, Denver City: The South Platte Trail* (Athens, OH: Swallow Press, 1985), 14.

[77] Thom Hatch, *Black Kettle: The Cheyenne Chief who Sought Peace but Found*

War, (Hoboken, NJ: John Wiley & Sons, 2004), 72-73.

[78] *Annual Report of the Commissioner of Indian Affairs for the Year 1865*, (Washington: Government Printing Office, 1865), 524.

[79] William C. Sturtevant, *Handbook of North American Indians: Vol. 13 Plains, Part 2*, (Washington, D.C.: Smithsonian, 2001), 939.

[80] George B. Grinnell, "Who Were The Padouca?" *American Anthropologist* 22 (1920): 248-260.

[81] David Bailie Warden, *A Statistical, Political, and Historical Account of the United States of North America* (Edinburgh: A. Constable & Co., 1819), 562.

[82] Ibid.

[83] Ibid.

[84] Samuel G. Goodrich, *History of the Indians of North and South America* (Boston: Bradbury, Soden, & Co., 1844). 259.

[85] Grinnell, "Who Were The Padouca?," 248-260.

[86] George E. Hyde, *Indians of the High Plains: From the Prehistoric Period to the Coming of Europeans* (Norman, OK: University of Oklahoma Press, 1959), 100.

[87] Chittenden, *The American Fur Trade of the Far West*, 877.

[88] William C. Meadows, *Kiowa, Apache, and Comanche Military Societies: Enduring Veterans, 1800 to the Present*, (Austin, TX: University of Texas Press, 1999), 180

[89] Hoxie, *Encyclopedia of North American Indians*, 25.

[90] Loretta Fowler, *The Columbia Guide to American Indians of the Great Plains* (NY: Columbia University Press, 2003), 19.

[91] Frank Raymond Secoy & John Canfield Ewers, *Changing Military Patterns of the Great Plains Indians* (Lincoln, NE: University of Nebraska Press, 1992), 81-83.

[92] Fowler, *The Columbia Guide to American Indians of the Great Plains*, 28.

[93] Sally Crum, *People of the Red Earth: American Indians of Colorado* (Santa Fe, NM: Ancient City Press, 1996), 183-185.

[94] Hyde, *Indians of the High Plains*, 199.

[95] Thomas W. Kavanagh, *The Comanches: A History, 1706-1875* (Lincoln, NE: University of Nebraska Press, 1999), 87.

[96] Goodrich, *History of the Indians of North and South America*, 270-271.

[97] George I. Cropley, "Impressions of the Indians Gained by Early American Explorers of Eastern Colorado," *Southwestern Lore 16* (1951): 49-55.

[98] George E Hyde, *The Pawnee Indians* (Norman, OK: University of Oklahoma Press, 1988), 145.

[99] Edwin James & Stephen Harriman Long. *Account of an Expedition from Pittsburgh to the Rocky Mountains, Performed in the Years 1819, 1820, Volume 2* (London: A. & R. Spottiswoode, 1823), 164-165.

[100] Ruby Esther Wilson, *Frank J. North, Pawnee Scout Commander and Pioneer*

(Athens, OH: Swallow Press, 1984), 116.

[101] Earl Alonzo Brininstool, *Fighting Indian Warriors: True Tales of the Wild Frontiers* (Harrisburg, PA: Stackpole, 1953), 217.

[102] Robert Bruce, *The Fighting Norths and* Pawnee *Scouts* (Lincoln, NE: University of Nebraska Press, 1932).

[103] Peter C. Mancall & James Hart Merrell, *American Encounters: Natives and Newcomers from European Contact to Indian Removal, 1500-1850* (NY: Routledge, 2000), 553-554.

[104] Jedidiah Morse, *A Report to the Secretary of War of the United States, on Indian Affairs,* (Washington, D. C.: Davis & Force, 1822), 239.

[105] Fowler, *The Columbia Guide to American Indians of the Great Plains*, 28.

[106] Morse, *A Report to the Secretary of War of the United States, on Indian Affairs*, 253.

[107] Sturtevant, *Handbook of North American Indians*, 970.

[108] Meriwether Lewis, William Clark, & Elliott Coues, *The History of the Lewis and Clark Expedition, Vol. 1*, (NY: Dover, 1979), p. 58.

[109] Warden, *A Statistical, Political, and Historical Account*, 562.

[110] George Bird Grinnell, *Trails of the Pathfinders*, (NY: C. Scribner's Sons, 1911), 143.

[111] Fowler, *Arapahoe Politics*, 310.

[112] Lewis, Clark, & Coues, *The History of the Lewis and Clark Expedition*, 58.

[113] Sturtevant, *Handbook of North American Indians*, 970.

[114] James Mooney & Rodolphe Charles Petter, *The Cheyenne Indians* (Lancaster, PA: American Anthropological Assoc., 1907), 376.

[115] George Bird Grinnell, *The Fighting Cheyennes* (NY: Charles Scribner's Sons, 1915), 33.

[116] Ibid., 40.

[117] George E. Hyde, *Life of George Bent: Written from His Letters* (Norman, OK: University of Oklahoma Press, 1968), 55-56.

[118] Fowler, *The Columbia Guide to American Indians of the Great Plains*, 62.

[119] Crum, *People of the Red Earth*, 201

[120] *Annual Report of the Commissioner of Indian Affairs 1847-1848* (Washington: Wendell and Van Benthuysen, 1848), 127.

[121] *Report of the Commissioner of Indian Affairs. 1860* (Washington: George W. Bowman, 1860), 93.

[122] George E. Hyde, *Red Cloud's Folk: A History of the Oglala Sioux Indians* (Norman, OK: University of Oklahoma Press, 1937), 58.

[123] Meriwether Lewis & William Clark, *The Travels of Capts. Lewis & Clarke, from St. Louis, by way of the Missouri and Columbia Rivers, to the Pacific Ocean* (Lon-

don: Longman, 1809), 171-172.

[124] Goodrich, *History of the Indians of North and South America*, 244-245.

[125] Stan Hoig & Frank W. Porter, *The Cheyenne*, (NY: Chelsea House, 1989), 20-21.

[126] Chalfant, *Cheyennes and Horse Soldiers,* 18.

[127] Cropley, "Impressions of the Indians," 49-55.

[128] Margaret Coel, *Chief Left Hand: Southern Arapaho* (Norman, OK: University of Oklahoma Press, 1981), 9.

[129] Goodrich, *History of the Indians of North and South America*, 272.

[130] Morse, *A Report to the Secretary of War of the United States, on Indian Affairs*, 253.

[131] Chittenden, *The American Fur Trade of the Far West*, 878-879.

[132] Cropley, "Impressions of the Indians," 49-55.

[133] Fowler, *The Columbia Guide to American Indians of the Great Plains*, 62.

[134] Hoig &Porter, *The Cheyenne*, 20-21.

[135] William Philo Clark, *The Indian Sign Language: With Brief Explanatory Notes of the Gestures* (Philadelphia: L. R. Hamerly, 1885), 102.

[136] Grinnell, *The Fighting Cheyennes*, 40.

[137] Goodrich, *History of the Indians of North and South America*, 274.

[138] Hyde, *The Pawnee Indians*, 182.

[139] Hatch, *Black Kettle*, 35.

[140] Ibid.

[141] Stan Hoig, *The Peace Chiefs of the Cheyennes* (Norman, OK: University of Oklahoma Press, 1980), 144.

[142] Hatch, *Black Kettle*, 35.

[143] George Bird Grinnell & Joseph A. Fitzgerald, *The Cheyenne Indians: Their History and Lifeways*, (Bloomington, IN: World Wisdom, 2008), 68.

[144] Lewis & Clark, *The Travels of Capts. Lewis & Clarke*, 173-174.

[145] Hoxie, *Encyclopedia of North American Indians*, 113-114.

[146] Lavender, *Bent's Fort*, 341.

[147] Hatch, *Black Kettle*, 72-73.

[148] *Report of the Commissioner of Indian Affairs. 1860* (Washington: George W. Bowman, 1860), 138-139.

[149] Stephen Grace, *It Happened in Denver* (Guilford, CN: TwoDot, 2007), 2.

[150] William H. Goode, *Outposts of Zion: With Limnings of Mission Life* (Cincinnati, OH: Poe & Hitchcock, 1864), 402.

[151] Worcester, *Pioneer Trails West,* 268.

[152] *Rocky Mountain News*, May 30, 1860, p. 2.

[153] Frank Albert Root & William Elsey Connelley, *The Overland Stage to Califor-*

nia (Topeka, KS: Crane & Co., 1901), 301.

[154] "The Great Routes Over the Plains," *New York Times*, July 19, 1866.

[155] Charles M. Clark, *A Trip to Pike's Peak and Notes by the Way* (Chicago, IL: S. P. rounds' steam book, 1861), 63-67.

[156] Ralph Moody, *Stagecoach West* (Lincoln, NE: University of Nebraska Press, 1998), 156.

[157] Chicago, Burlington & Quincy Railroad Company, *Traveler's Guide to the New Gold Mines in Kansas and Nebraska* (New York: Polhemus & de Vries, 1859).

[158] Obridge Allen, *Allen's Guide Book and Map to the Gold Fields of Kansas & Nebraska and Great Salt Lake City* (Washington: R. A. Waters, 1859.)

[159] Luke D. Tierney, Stephen William Smith, & D. C. Oaks [sic], *History of the Gold Discoveries on the South Platte River with A Guide to the Gold Mines on the South Platte* (Pacific City, IA: Herarld Office A. Thomson, 1859), 21.

[160] Robert L. Brown, *The Great Pikes Peak Gold Rush* (Caldwell, ID: Caxton Printers, 1985), 45-46.

[161] Louise Barry (ed.), "Albert D. Richardson's Letters on the Pike's Peak Gold Region Written to the Editor of the Lawrence Republican, May 22-August 25, 1860" *Kansas Historical Quarterly* 12 (1943): 14-57. Retrieved from www.kancoll.org/khq/1943/43_1_barry.htm

[162] Coel, *Chief Left Hand*, 85.

[163] Goode, *Outposts of Zion*, 402-403.

[164] Bancroft, *Colorful Colorado*, 42-44.

[165] Isaac Smith Homans & William Buck Dana, "Commerce of the Prairies," *The Merchants' Magazine and Commercial Review* 44 (1861): 37-38.

[166] Le Roy Reuben Hafen, *To the Pike's Peak Gold Fields, 1859* (Lincoln, NE: University of Nebraska Press, 2004), 154-155.

[167] Helen E. Clark, "The Diary of Helen E. Clark," In *Two Diaries with Calvin Perry Clark* (Denver, CO: Denver Public Library, 1962), 30-36.

[168] Emma Shepard Hill, *A Dangerous Crossing and What Happened on the Other Side* (Denver, CO: Press of the Smith-Brooks Co., 1914), 35-39.

[169] Francis Crissey Young, *Across the Plains in '65: A Youngster's Journal from "Gotham" to "Pike's Peak"* (Denver, CO: Lanning Bros,1905), 196-207.

[170] Sarah Raymond Herndon, *Days on the Road* (NY: Burr Printing House, 1902), 119-124.

[171] Agnes Miner "The Story of a Colorado Pioneer," In Sharon Niederman (ed.) *A Quilt of Words: Women's Diaries, Letters, and Original Accounts of Life in the Southwest, 1860-1960* (Boulder, CO: Johnson Books, 1988), 13.

[172] LeRoy R. Hafen, "Early Mail Service to Colorado," *Colorado Magazine* 2 (1925): 23-32.

[173] *Rocky Mountain News*, August 20, 1859, p. 2.

[174] John M. Townley, *The Overland Stage: A History and Guidebook* (Reno, NV: Jamison Station Press, 1994), 6-7.

[175] "Tips to Stagecoach Travelers," www.uni.edu/iowahist/Frontier_Life/Stagecoach/Stagecoach.htm

[176] Leroy R. Hafen, & David Dary, *Overland Mail, 1849-1869* (Norman, OK: University of Oklahoma Press, 2004), 232.

[177] Townley, *The Overland Stage*, 36.

[178] Taft, "Crossing the Plains in 1862," *Fort Collins Express*, May 20, 1923, p. 9.

[179] Stone, *History of Colorado* 574.

[180] Monahan, *Destination, Denver City*, 241.

[181] Townley, *The Overland Stage*, 50.

[182] Root & Connelley, *The Overland Stage to California*, 64-65.

[183] Grinnell, *The Fighting Cheyennes*, 191.

[184] E. Douglas Branch, *Hunting of the Buffalo* (Lincoln, NE: University of Nebraska Press, 1962), 124-5.

[185] William A. Kelley to Governor John Evans, June 14, 1864, in *The War of the Rebellion: A Compilation of the Official Records of the Union and Confederate Armies, Series I, Volume 34, Part 4* (Washington: Government Printing Office, 1891), 513-514.

[186] Perry Eberhart, *Ghosts of the Colorado Plains* (Athens, OH: Swallow Press, 1986), 12-13.

[187] Inman, *The Great Salt Trail*, 113.

[188] Monahan, *Destination, Denver City*, 229.

[189] Root & Connelley, *The Overland Stage to California*, 379-380.

[190] Carol Rein Shwayder, *Chronology of Weld County, Colorado, 1836-1983* (Greeley, CO: Unicorn Ventures, 1983), A28

[191] Charles Collins, *Rocky Mountain Gold Regions and Emigrants' Guide* (Denver City, CO: Rocky Mountain News Printing Company, 1861), 64.

[192] U.S. Department of the Interior, Census Office, 1870 Census, Weld County, district 5, Colorado Territory, "Holon Godfrey," *Ancestory.com*.

[193] Stanley Buchholz Kimball, *Historic Sites and Markers along the Mormon and Other Great Western Trails* (Urbana, IL: University of Illinois Press, 1988), 199.

[194] Hubert Howe Bancroft, *West American History* (NY: The Bancroft Company, 1902), 353.

[195] "A Tour Through the Rocky Mountains. No. III," *New York Tribune*, May 25, 1867, p. 2.

[196] "How a Frontiersman Fights Indians," *The [Huntingdon, PA] Globe*, August 21, 1867, p. 1.

[197] Charles Dawson, *Pioneer Tales of the Oregon Trail and of Jefferson County* (Topeka, KS: Crane & Co., 1912), 59.

[198] Root & Connelley, *The Overland Stage to California*, 223-224.

[199] Young, *Across the Plains in '65*, 202+.

[200] Benjamin Ross Cauthorn, *Trip to Montana by Wagon Train, 1865 April 14-November 9*, 34-39.

[201] Monahan, *Destination, Denver City*, 120.

[202] Emma Burke Conklin, *A Brief History of Logan County, Colorado: With Reminiscences by Pioneers* (Denver, CO: Welch-Haffner, 1928), 141.

[203] Nell Brown Propst, *Forgotten People: A History of the South Platte Trail* (Boulder, CO: Pruett Publishing, 1979), 38-39.

[204] Collins, *Rocky Mountain Gold Regions and Emigrants' Guide*, 64.

[205] Fitz Hugh Ludlow, *The Heart of the Continent* (NY: Hurd & Coughton, 1870), 134-136.

[206] Edwin Legrand Sabin, *On the Overland Stage* (NY: Crowell, 1918), 107-109.

[207] Frank Hall, *History of the State of Colorado* (Chicago, Blakely Printing, 1889), 239.

[208] Conklin, *A Brief History of Logan County, Colorado*, 141.

[209] Grinnell, *The Fighting Cheyennes*, 148.

[210] Ibid., 191.

[211] Eberhart, *Ghosts of the Colorado Plains*, 111-112.

[212] Worcester, *Pioneer Trails West*, 236.

[213] Eugene Parsons, *A Guidebook to Colorado* (Boston: Little, Brown, & Co., 1911), 238.

[214] Eberhart, *Ghosts of the Colorado Plains*, 13.

[215] Hall, *History of the State of Colorado*, 239.

[216] Ibid.

[217] Document Number 105253. Accession/Serial Number COCOAA 042309. Retrieved from www.glorecords.blm.gov/PatentSearch/Detail.asp?PatentDocClassCode=SER&Accession=COCOAA+042309&Index=12&QryID=46550.13&DetailTab=1

[218] *Report of the National Society of the Daughters of the American Revolution*, 58.

[219] *Rocky Mountain News*, September 29, 1865, p. 4.

[220] *Rocky Mountain News*, July 30, 1866, p. 4.

[221] Collins, *Rocky Mountain Gold Regions and Emigrants' Guide*, 64.

[222] U.S. Department of the Interior, Census Office, 1860 Census, Weld County, district 5, Colorado Territory, "Frederick Samb [Lamb]," *Ancestory.com*.

[223] Monahan, *Destination, Denver City*, 75-76.

[224] Scott, *Historic Trail Maps of the Sterling 1°X2° Quadrangle, Northeastern Colo-*

rado.

[225] Silas Wright Burt & Edward L. Berthoud, *The Rocky Mountain Gold Regions* (Old West Pub. Co., 1861).

[226] Collins, *Rocky Mountain Gold Regions and Emigrants' Guide*, 64.

[227] Hall, *History of the State of Colorado*, 239-240.

[228] *Journal of the Telegraph*, 1(15), June 15, 1868, p. 6.

[229] Edward J Lewis, "Diary of a Pike's Peak Gold Seeker in 1860," *Colorado Magazine* 14 (1937): 201-219.

[230] William N. Byers & John H. Kellom, *A Hand Book to the Gold Fields of Nebraska and Kansas* (Chicago: D. B. Cooke, 1859), 73-75.

[231] Hafen, *To the Pike's Peak Gold Fields, 1859*, 154-155.

[232] Ludlow, *The Heart of the Continent*, 134-136.

[233] Eberhart, *Ghosts of the Colorado Plains*, 24.

[234] Ibid.

[235] Hafen, *To the Pike's Peak Gold Fields, 1859*, 154-155.

[236] Benjamin Ross Cauthorn, *Trip to Montana by Wagon Train, 1865 April 14-November 9*, 34-39. Retrieved from
http://contentdm.lib.byu.edu/Diaries/image/4253.pdf

[237] Grinnell, *The Fighting Cheyennes* 191.

[238] Dawson, *Pioneer Tales of the Oregon Trail and of Jefferson*, 59.

[239] Monahan, *Destination, Denver City*, 50.

[240] George A. Crofutt, *Crofutt's Overland Tours* (Chicago: Rand McNally, 1890), 35.

[241] *Rocky Mountain News*, May 30, 1860, p. 5.

[242] *Western Mountaineer*, April 25, 1860, p. 2

[243] Burt & Berthoud, *The Rocky Mountain Gold Regions.*

[244] http://en.wikipedia.org/wiki/United_States_dollar

[245] *General Laws, Joint Resolutions, Memorials, and Private Acts Passed at the Sixth Session of the Legislative Assembly of the Territory of Colorado* (Central City, CO: David C. Collier, 1867), 211-212.

[246] Monahan, *Destination, Denver City*, 58-59.

[247] *General Laws, Joint Resolutions, Memorials, and Private Acts Passed at the Sixth Session of the Legislative Assembly of the Territory of Colorado* (Central City, CO: David C. Collier, 1867), 97.

[248] Shwayder, *Chronology of Weld County, Colorado, 1836-1983*, 94.

[249] Root & Connelley, *The Overland Stage to California*, 383-387.

[250] "Tyson, T. K. Rev. Walter McD Potter – A memorial Tribute," *The Baptist Home Mission Monthly* 15-16: 315.

[251] Clark, *A Trip to Pike's Peak and Notes by the Way*, 63-67.

252 *Rocky Mountain News*, February 29, 1860, p. 2.

253 John D. Young & Dwight La Vern Smith, *John D. Young and the Colorado Gold Rush* (Chicago, R. R. Donnelly & Sons, 1969), 31-35.

254 Ellis Paxson Oberholtzer, *A History of the United States Since the Civil War*, Volume 1(NY: Macmillan, 1936), 316.

255 Robert Luther Thompson, *Wiring a Continent* (Princeton, NJ: Princeton University Press, 1947), 360.

256 Ibid.

257 Samuel S. Wallihan & T. O. Bigney, *The Rocky Mountain Directory and Colorado Gazetteer, for 1871* (Denver, CO: S. S. Wallihan, 1870), 128.

258 Stone, *History of Colorado*, 384.

259 Root & Connelley, *The Overland Stage to California*, 136.

260 "Telegraph Comes to Colorado" *Essays in Colorado History* 7 (1987): 1-26.

261 Thomas Powers, *The Killing of Crazy Horse* (New York: Alfred A. Knopf, 2010), 266.

262 "Telegraph Comes to Colorado," 1-26.

263 Root & Connelley, *The Overland Stage to California*, 135.

264 "Colorado – Brief Land History," *Yearbook of the State of Colorado* (Denver, CO: Eames Brothers, 1922), 43-45.

265 "Laws of the Provisional Government of the Territory of Jefferson," *Rocky Mountain News,* January 25, 1860, p. 1.

266 William Gilpin, "Report of the Secretary of the Interior. No. 35," in *Message of the President of the United States to the Two Houses of Congress at the Commencement of the Second Session of the Thirty-Seventh Congress, Volume 1* (Washington: Government Printing Office, 1861), 710.

267 Monahan, *Destination, Denver City,* 129.

268 John Evans, "Papers Accompanying the Annual Report…: No. 50," *Message of the President of the United States and Accompanying Documents to the Two Houses of Congress at the Commencement of the First Session of the Thirty-Eighth Congress* (Washington: Government Printing Office, 1863) 240-1.

269 Ibid.

270 Elbridge Gerry, "Papers Accompanying the Annual Report…: No. 52," *Message of the President of the United States and Accompanying Documents to the Two Houses of Congress at the Commencement of the First Session of the Thirty-Eighth Congress* (Washington: Government Printing Office, 1863) 247-248.

271 John Evans to E. M. Stanton, December 14, 1863, in *Report of the Commissioner of Indian Affairs, for the Year 1864* (Washington: Government Printing Office, 1865), 225-6.

272 Stone, *History of Colorado,* 704.

[273] Ibid.

[274] Ancestry.com. 1860 United States Federal Census [database on-line]. Provo, UT, USA: Ancestry.com Operations, Inc., 2009. Original data: 1860 U.S. census, population schedule. NARA microfilm publication M653, 1,438 rolls. Washington, D.C.: National Archives and Records Administration, n.d.

[275] Clark Dunn, "Report of Lieut. Clark Dunn, First Colorado Cavalry," *The War of the Rebellion: A Compilation of the Official Records of the Union and Confederate Armies, Series 1, Volume 34, Part I*, (Washington: Government Printing Office, 1891), 884-5.

[276] Clark Dunn interviewed by J. M. Chivington (April 27, 1865), of the Secretary of War…Ordered to inquire into the Sand Creek Massacre, November, 1864 (Washington: Government Printing Office, 1867), pp. 180-1.

[277] Monahan, *Destination, Denver City*, 138.

[278] David Fridtjof Halaas & Andrew Edward Masich, *Halfbreed: The Remarkable True Story of George Bent* (Cambridge, MS: Da Capo Press, 2004), 113 & 115.

[279] Ralph K. Andrist, *The Long Death: The Last Days of the Plains Indian* (New York: Macmillan, 1965), 75-76.

[280] George L. Sanborn to John M. Chivington, April 13, 1864, in *The War of the Rebellion: A Compilation of the Official Records of the Union and Confederate Armies, Series 1, Volume 34, Part I*, (Washington: Government Printing Office, 1891), 884.

[281] Clark Dunn, "Report of Lieut. Clark Dunn, First Colorado Cavalry, April 18, 1864," *The War of the Rebellion: A Compilation of the Official Records of the Union and Confederate Armies, Series 1, Volume 34, Part I*, (Washington: Government Printing Office, 1891), 887.

[282] Monahan, *Destination, Denver City*, 138.

[283] Dunn, "Report of Lieut. Clark Dunn, First Colorado Cavalry, April 18, 1864," 887.

[284] Ibid.

[285] Ibid.

[286] George H. Stilwell to Jacob Downing, April 16, 1864, in *The War of the Rebellion: A Compilation of the Official Records of the Union and Confederate Armies, Series I, Volume 34, Part 3* (Washington: Government Printing Office, 1891), 189.

[287] J. Downing to J. M. Chivington, April 18, 1864, in *The War of the Rebellion: A Compilation of the Official Records of the Union and Confederate Armies, Series I, Volume 34, Part 3* (Washington: Government Printing Office, 1891), 218.

[288] "Valley Station, 19th," in *Daily Mining Journal*, April 19, 1864, p. 2.

[289] Hubert Howe Bancroft & Frances Fuller Victor, *History of Nevada, Colorado,*

and Wyoming, 1540-1888 (San Francisco: History Co., 1890), 460-61.

[290] George L. Sanborn to J. M. Chivington, April 20, 1864, in *The War of the Rebellion: A Compilation of the Official Records of the Union and Confederate Armies, Series I, Volume 34, Part 3* (Washington: Government Printing Office, 1891), 243.

[291] J. Downing to J. M. Chivington, April 21, 1864, in *The War of the Rebellion: A Compilation of the Official Records of the Union and Confederate Armies, Series I, Volume 34, Part 3* (Washington: Government Printing Office, 1891), 250-52.

[292] J. Downing to J. M. Chivington, April 27, 1864, in *The War of the Rebellion: A Compilation of the Official Records of the Union and Confederate Armies, Series I, Volume 34, Part 3* (Washington: Government Printing Office, 1891), 314.

[293] J. Downing to J. M. Chivington, April 21, 1864, in *The War of the Rebellion: A Compilation of the Official Records of the Union and Confederate Armies, Series I, Volume 34, Part 3* (Washington: Government Printing Office, 1891), 250-52.

[294] Ibid.

[295] Shwayder, *Chronology of Weld County, Colorado, 1836-1983*, 65.

[296] J. Downing to J. M. Chivington, "Reports of Maj. Jacob downing, First Colorado Cavalry," May 3, 1864, in *The War of the Rebellion: A Compilation of the Official Records of the Union and Confederate Armies, Series I, Volume 34, Part 1* (Washington: Government Printing Office, 1891), 907.

[297] Ibid., 907-908.

[298] Marshall Sprague, *Colorado: A Bicentennial History* (New York, Norton, 1976), 39.

[299] Colton, *The Civil War in the Western Territories,* 153.

[300] J. P. Dunn, *Massacres of the Mountains: A History of the Indian Wars, Volume 2* (New York: Harper & Brothers, 1886), 412.

[301] Andrew Gulliford, *Preserving Western History* (Albuquerque: University of New Mexico Press, 2005), 177.

[302] J. S. Brown, D. C. Corbin, & Thomas J. Darrah to Captain Maynard, June 13, 1864, in *The War of the Rebellion: A Compilation of the Official Records of the Union and Confederate Armies, Series I, Volume 34, Part 4* (Washington: Government Printing Office, 1891), 354-5.

[303] "A Horrible Sight!," *Weekly Commonwealth,* June 15,1864, p. 3.

[304] LeRoy Henry Fischer, *The Western Territories in the Civil War* (Manhattan, KS: Sunflower University Press, 1977), 66.

[305] J. S. Maynard to Joseph C. Davidson, June 11, 1864, in *The War of the Rebellion: A Compilation of the Official Records of the Union and Confederate Armies, Series I, Volume 34, Part 4* (Washington: Government Printing Office, 1891), 320-321.

[306] J. C. Davidson to J. S. Maynard, June 12, 1864, in *The War of the Rebellion: A Compilation of the Official Records of the Union and Confederate Armies, Series I, Volume 34, Part 4* (Washington: Government Printing Office, 1891), 330-331.

[307] "Troops in the Department of Kansas, Maj. Gen. Samuel R. Curtis, U. S. Army, commanding, June 30, 1864," in *The War of the Rebellion: A Compilation of the Official Records of the Union and Confederate Armies, Series I, Volume 34, Part 4* (Washington: Government Printing Office, 1891), 620.

[308] J. S. Maynard to John Evans, June 12, 1864, in *The War of the Rebellion: A Compilation of the Official Records of the Union and Confederate Armies, Series I, Volume 34, Part 4* (Washington: Government Printing Office, 1891), 329-330.

[309] John Evans to E. M. Stanton, June 14, 1864, in *The War of the Rebellion: A Compilation of the Official Records of the Union and Confederate Armies, Series I, Volume 34, Part 4* (Washington: Government Printing Office, 1891), 381.

[310] Evans, John, "Statement," June 21, 1864, in *Report of the Commissioner of Indian Affairs for the Year 1864* (Washington: Government Printing Office, 1865), 227-228.

[311] William James Ghent, *The Road to Oregon: A Chronicle of the Great Emigrant Trail* (London: Longmans & Co., 1929), 274.

[312] Fischer, *The Western Territories in the Civil War.*

[313] Root & Connelley, *The Overland Stage to California,*

[314] John Evans to Brigadier General Mitchell, June 21, 1864, in *Executive Documents printed by the order of the House of Representatives during the Second Session of the Thirty-Eighth Congress, 1864-'65* (Washington: Government Printing Office, 1865), 371-372.

[315] "Another Indian Raid," Rocky Mountain News Week, July 20, 1864 p. 2.

[316] "Indian Murders," *Rocky Mountain News Weekly*, July 27, 1864, p. 2.

[317] Leroy, "Statement of Mr. Leroy," August 20, 1864, in *Report of the Commissioner of Indian Affairs for the Year 1864* (Washington: Government Printing Office, 1865), 232.

[318] John Evans, in *Report of the Commissioner of Indian Affairs for the Year 1864* (Washington: Government Printing Office, 1865), 219.

[319] Worcester, *Pioneer Trails West*, 278.

[320] Ghent, *The Road to Oregon: A Chronicle of the Great Emigrant Trail,* 274.

[321] Monahan, *Destination, Denver City,* 162.

[322] Curtis P.Nettels, *A History of the Overland Mail* (M. A. thesis, University of Wisconsin, Madison, 1922), 134.

[323] Lonnie J. White & Jerry Keenan, *Hostiles and Horse Soldiers: Indian Battles and Campaigns in the West* (Boulder, CO: Pruett Publishing, 1972), 6.

[324] J. Downing to J. M. Chivington, April 20, 1864, in *The War of the Rebellion: A*

Compilation of the Official Records of the Union and Confederate Armies, Series I, Volume 34, Part 3 (Washington: Government Printing Office, 1891), 242.

[325] J. Downing to J. M. Chivington, May 11, 1864, "Report of Maj. Jacob Downing, First Colorado Cavalry," in *The War of the Rebellion: A Compilation of the Official Records of the Union and Confederate Armies, Series I, Volume 34, Part 1* (Washington: Government Printing Office, 1891), 916.

[326] Grinnell, *The Fighting Cheyennes*, 191.

[327] Stan Hoig, *The Sand Creek Massacre* (Norman, OK: University of Oklahoma Press, 1961), 44.

[328] Root & Connelley, *The Overland Stage to California*, 310.

[329] J. M. Chivington to S. M. Logan, October 14, 1864, in *The War of the Rebellion: A Compilation of the Official Records of the Union and Confederate Armies, Series I, Volume 41, Part 2* (Washington: Government Printing Office, 1893), 876.

[330] Robert Huhn Jones, *Guarding the Overland Trails: The Eleventh Ohio Cavalry in the Civil War* (Spokane, WA: Arthur H. Clark, 2005), 15.

[331] "Troops in the District of Nebraska, Brigadier General Robert B. Mitchell, commanding," in *The War of the Rebellion: A Compilation of the Official Records of the Union and Confederate Armies, Series I, Volume 41, Part 4* (Washington: Government Printing Office, 1893), 989.

[332] Mehls, *The New Empire of the Rockies*, 43.

[333] J. M. Chivington to Benjamin Holladay, December 2, 1864, *Reports of Committees of the Senate of the United States for the First and Second Sessions of the Forty-Sixth Congress, 1879-'80* (Washington: Government Printing Office, 1880), 363.

[334] John S. Gray, *Cavalry & Coaches: The Story of Camp and Fort Collins* (Fort Collins, CO: Old Army Press, 1978), 75.

[335] Ibid., 79.

[336] Worcester, *Pioneer Trails West*, 278.

[337] James F. Willard, "The Tyler Rangers: The Black Hawk Company and the Indian Uprising of 1864," *Colorado Magazine 7* (1930): 147-51.

[338] "Address of Governor Evans," *Rocky Mountain News,* September 30, 1864, p. 1.

[339] National Parks Service, *Civil War Soldiers & Sailors System,* www.itd.nps.gov/cwss/index.html

[340] John Evans to E. M. Stanton, June 14, 1864, in *The War of the Rebellion: A Compilation of the Official Records of the Union and Confederate Armies, Series III, Volume 4* (Washington: Government Printing Office, 1891), 432.

[341] E. M. Stanton to Governor Evans, August 19, 1864, in *The War of the Rebel-*

lion: A Compilation of the Official Records of the Union and Confederate Armies, Series III, Volume 4 (Washington: Government Printing Office, 1891), 627.

[342] J. B. Fry to Governor of Colorado Territory, August 11, 1864, in The War of the Rebellion: A Compilation of the Official Records of the Union and Confederate Armies, Series III, Volume 4 (Washington: Government Printing Office, 1900), 608.

[343] "Proclamation," Rocky Mountain News, August 11, 1864, p. 2.

[344] Robert V. Hine & John Mack Faragher, The American West: A New Interpretive History (New Haven, CT: Yale University Press, 2000), 229.

[345] J. M. Chivington to S. R. Curtis, August 30, 1864, in The War of the Rebellion: A Compilation of the Official Records of the Union and Confederate Armies, Series I, Volume 41, Part 2 (Washington: Government Printing Office, 1893), 946.

[346] Raymond G. Carey, "The 'Bloodless Third' Regiment, Colorado Volunteer Cavalry," Colorado Magazine 38 (1961): 275-300.

[347] "Troops in the Department of Kansas, Maj. Gen. Samuel R. Curtis, commanding," in The War of the Rebellion: A Compilation of the Official Records of the Union and Confederate Armies, Series I, Volume 41, Part 4 (Washington: Government Printing Office, 1893), 375.

[348] Forbes Parkhill, The Wildest of the West (New York: Holt, 1951) 66.

[349] Thomas J. Noel, The City and the Saloon: Denver, 1858-1916 (Niwot, CO: University Press of Colorado, 1996), 37.

[350] Raymond G. Carey, "The 'Bloodless Third' Regiment, Colorado Volunteer Cavalry," Colorado Magazine 38 (1961): 275-300.

[351] "Troops in the Department of Kansas, Maj. Gen. Samuel R. Curtis, commanding," in The War of the Rebellion: A Compilation of the Official Records of the Union and Confederate Armies, Series I, Volume 41, Part 4 (Washington: Government Printing Office, 1893), p. 989.

[352] Monahan, Destination, Denver City, 182.

[353] Stone, History of Colorado, 702.

[354] Carey, "The 'Bloodless Third' Regiment," 275-300.

[355] Hubert Howe Bancroft, History of the Pacific States of North America (San Francisco: A. L. Bancroft, 1882), 463.

[356] R. W. Clarke & David H. Louderback, January 27, 1865, in The War of the Rebellion: A Compilation of the Official Records of the Union and Confederate Armies, Series I, Volume 31, Part 1 (Washington: Government Printing Office, 1893), 972.

[357] Captain L Wilson. "Testimony," Report of the Joint Special Committee, Appointed under Joint Resolution of March 3, 1865 (Washington: Government Printing Office, 1867), 67.

[358] John S. Smith interviewed by Mr. Doolittle, March 8, 1865, *Report of the Joint Special Committee, appointed under Joint Resolution of March 3, 1865* (Washington: Government Printing Office, 1867), 41.

[359] Wilson, "Testimony," 67.

[360] *Official Army Register of the Volunteer Force of the United States Army for the Years 1861, '62, '63, '64, '65, Volume 8: Territories of Washington, New Mexico, Nebraska, Colorado, Dakota...* (Washington: Adjutant General's Office, 1865), 26.

[361] J. M. Chivington to S. R. Curtis, December 16, 1864, in *The War of the Rebellion: A Compilation of the Official Records of the Union and Confederate Armies, Series I, Volume 31, Part 1* (Washington: Government Printing Office, 1893), 948-950.

[362] Gary L. Roberts & David Fridtjof Halaas, "Written in Blood: The Soule-Cramer Sand Creek Massacre Letters," in Ben Fogelberg' *Western Voices: 125 Years of Colorado Writing* (Golden, CO: Fulcrum, 2004), 319-337.

[363] "Big Indian Fight!," *Rocky Mountain News,* December 7, 1864, p. 2.

[364] "Coming Back," *Rocky Mountain News*, December 13, 1864, p. 2.

[365] "Arrival of the Third Regiment – Grand March Through Town," *Rocky Mountain News*, December 22, 1864, p. 2.

[366] J. M. Chivington, "To the President and Members of the Military Commission Convened as per Special Orders No. 23, Headquarters District of Colorado," in *Index to the Senate Executive Documents for the Second Session of the Thirty-Ninth Congress of the United States of America 1866-'67* (Washington: Government Printing Office, 1867), 189.

[367] John S. Smith interviewed by Mr. Doolittle, 42.

[368] "Cheyenne Indian Massacre," July 25, 1865 *Chicago Tribune,* p. 3.

[369] "Governor Evans' Resignation," *Rocky Mountain News*, September 4, 1865, p. 1.

[370] Hyde, *Red Cloud's Folk,* 109.

[371] Halaas & Masich, *Halfbreed,* 171-2.

[372] R. R. Livingston to C. S. Charlot, January 2, 1865, in *The War of the Rebellion: A Compilation of the Official Records of the Union and Confederate Armies, Series I, Volume 48, Part 1* (Washington: Government Printing Office, 1896), 400.

[373] Chivington, J. M., "General Orders, No. 1," January 4, 1865, in *The War of the Rebellion: A Compilation of the Official Records of the Union and Confederate Armies, Series I, Volume 48, Part 1* (Washington: Government Printing Office, 1896), 416.

[374] Moonlight reports to Elbert as acting-governor almost immediately upon taking his command. Moonlight, T. January 7, 1865, in *Report of the Joint*

Committee on the Conduct of the War, at the Second Session Thirty-Eighth Congress (Washington: Government Printing Office, 1865), 97.

[375] S. R. Curtis to H. W. Halleck, "Report of Maj. Gen. Samuel R. Curtis, U. S. Army, Commanding Department of Kansas," January 9, 1865, in *The War of the Rebellion: A Compilation of the Official Records of the Union and Confederate Armies, Series I, Volume 48, Part 1* (Washington: Government Printing Office, 1896), 23.

[376] T. Moonlight to Major-General Curtis, "Report of Col. Thomas Moonlight, Eleventh Kansas Cavalry, Commanding District of Colorado," January 7, 1865, in *The War of the Rebellion: A Compilation of the Official Records of the Union and Confederate Armies, Series I, Volume 48, Part 1* (Washington: Government Printing Office, 1896), 23-24.

[377] Charles Griffin Coutant, *The History of Wyoming from the Earliest Known Discoveries, Volume 1* (Laramie, WY: Chaplin, Spafford & Mathison, 1899), 464.

[378] T. Moonlight to Major-General Curtis, "Report of Col. Thomas Moonlight, Eleventh Kansas Cavalry, Commanding District of Colorado," January 7, 1865, in *The War of the Rebellion: A Compilation of the Official Records of the Union and Confederate Armies, Series I, Volume 48, Part 1* (Washington: Government Printing Office, 1896), 23-24.

[379] Ira I. Taber to J. J. Kennedy, January 7, 1865, in *The War of the Rebellion: A Compilation of the Official Records of the Union and Confederate Armies, Series I, Volume 48, Part 1* (Washington: Government Printing Office, 1896), 454.

[380] T. Moonlight to James Olney, January 7, 1865, in *The War of the Rebellion: A Compilation of the Official Records of the Union and Confederate Armies, Series I, Volume 48, Part 1* (Washington: Government Printing Office, 1896), 454.

[381] Taber, Ira I., "General Orders, No. 7," January 23, 1865, in *The War of the Rebellion: A Compilation of the Official Records of the Union and Confederate Armies, Series I, Volume 48, Part 1* (Washington: Government Printing Office, 1896), 624.

[382] W. S. Cobern, "Raid up the Platte," in Luella Shaw (ed.) *True History of Some of the Pioneers of Colorado* (Hotchkiss, CO: W. S. Coburn, J. Patterson, & A. K. Shaw, 1909), 23-32.

[383] Gregory Michno, *Encyclopedia of Indian Wars: Western Battles and Skirmishes, 1850-1890* (Missoula, MT: Mountain Press, 2003), 164.

[384] "From the Big Train," *Rocky Mountain News*, January 20, 1865, p. 2.

[385] "Body Found," *Rocky Mountain News*, April 14, 1865, p. 3.

[386] "History of Mrs. Sarah Morris...," *Frontier Scout 1*, 2 (1865): 3.

[387] "Wants the Government to Repay it," *Chicago Daily Tribune*, April 9, 1894: 7

[388] Ghent, *The Road to Oregon*, 225-6.

[389] Paul Iselin Wellman, *Death on the Prairie: The Thirty Years' Struggle for the Western Plains* (New York: Macmillan, 1934), 68.

[390] T. Moonlight to Speaker of the House of Representatives," January 31, 1865, in *The War of the Rebellion: A Compilation of the Official Records of the Union and Confederate Armies, Series I, Volume 48, Part 1* (Washington: Government Printing Office, 1896), 843.

[391] R. R. Livingston to G. M. Dodge, February 9, 1865, in *The War of the Rebellion: A Compilation of the Official Records of the Union and Confederate Armies, Series I, Volume 48, Part 1* (Washington: Government Printing Office, 1896), 793-4.

[392] Thomas Moonlight to C. S. Charlot, February 2, 1865, in *The War of the Rebellion: A Compilation of the Official Records of the Union and Confederate Armies, Series I, Volume 48, Part 1* (Washington: Government Printing Office, 1896), 726-77.

[393] Richard G. Hardoff, *Washita Memories: Eyewitness Views of Custer's Attack on Black Kettle's Village* (Norman, OK: University of Oklahoma Press, 2006), 353.

[394] Hyde, *Life of George Bent:* 179-81.

[395] Nettels, *A History of the Overland Mail,* 136.

[396] G. M. Dodge to Colonel Livingston & Moonlight, February 11, 1865, in *The War of the Rebellion: A Compilation of the Official Records of the Union and Confederate Armies, Series I, Volume 48, Part 1* (Washington: Government Printing Office, 1896), 821.

[397] "Good News," *Rocky Mountain News*, February 13, 1865, p. 2.

[398] "How it Looks to Us," *Rocky Mountain News*, February 13, 1865, p. 2.

[399] "Telegraph Dispatches," *Daily Mining Journal,* July 29, 1865, p. 2.

[400] "'Friendlies' Near Fremont's Orchard," *Rocky Mountain News,* September 28, 1865, p. 1.

[401] Sanborn, John B., & J. H. Leavenworth, August 15, 1865, in *Report of the Commissioner of Indian Affairs for the Year 1865* (Washington: Government Printing Office, 1865), 394-395.

[402] "Gen. Sanborn's Treaty," *Rocky Mountain News*, November 8, 1865, p. 1.

[403] Note: The fort which would later be called Fort Morgan established at the Junction is not the same Fort Junction discussed by Augusta Bloc in her article "Lower Boulder and St. Vrain Valley Home Guards and Fort Junction." In *Colorado Magazine*, 1939. It is clear that the military reports sent from the Junction, refer to the site of Fort Morgan on the South Platte River.

[404] James F. Rusling to M. C. Meigs, September 4, 1866, in *Executive Documents Printed by Order of the House of Representatives, during the Second Session of the Thirty-Ninth Congress, 1866-'67* (Washington: Government Printing Office,

1867), 36-40.

[405] Root & Connelley, *The Overland Stage to California*, 380.

[406] Hall, *History of the State of Colorado*, 239-240.

[407] *Report of the National Society of the Daughters of the American Revolution*, 58.

[408] James Florant Meline, *Two Thousand Miles on Horseback* (NY: Hurd and Houghton, 1867), 48-52.

[409] T. Moonlight to D. H. Nichols, January 25, 1865, in *Report of the Joint Committee on the Conduct of the War, at the Second Session Thirty-Eighth Congress* (Washington: Government Printing Office, 1865), 99.

[410] "Organization of Troops in the Military Division of the Missouri...," *The War of the Rebellion: A Compilation of the Official Records of the Union and Confederate Armies, Series I, Volume 48, Part 1* (Washington: Government Printing Office, 1896), 1041-2.

[411] "From the Big Train," *Rocky Mountain News*, January 20, 1865, p. 2.

[412] Albert Walter to T. Moonlight, "Report of Lieut. Albert Walter, Second Colorado Cavalry," February 1, 1865, *The War of the Rebellion: A Compilation of the Official Records of the Union and Confederate Armies, Series I, Volume 48, Part 1* (Washington: Government Printing Office, 1896), 43-44.

[413] "Organization of Troops in the Military Division of the Missouri...," April 30, 1865, *The War of the Rebellion: A Compilation of the Official Records of the Union and Confederate Armies, Series I, Volume 48, Part 2* (Washington: Government Printing Office, 1896), 276.

[414] Livingston to Colonel Moonlight, February 13, 1865, *The War of the Rebellion: A Compilation of the Official Records of the Union and Confederate Armies, Series I, Volume 48, Part 1* (Washington: Government Printing Office, 1896), 845.

[415] T. Moonlight to Colonel Livingston, February 13, 1865, *The War of the Rebellion: A Compilation of the Official Records of the Union and Confederate Armies, Series I, Volume 48, Part 1* (Washington: Government Printing Office, 1896), 845.

[416] T. Moonlight to Major-General Dodge, February 13, 1865, *The War of the Rebellion: A Compilation of the Official Records of the Union and Confederate Armies, Series I, Volume 48, Part 1* (Washington: Government Printing Office, 1896), 838.

[417] T. Moonlight to Speaker of the House of Representatives, January 31, 1865, *Report of the Joint Committee on the Conduct of the War, at the Second Session Thirty-Eighth Congress* (Washington: Government Printing Office, 1865), 99-100.

[418] "Martial Law," *Rocky Mountain News*, February 8, 1865, p. 2.

[419] T. Moonlight to S. E. Browne, March 2, 1865, *The War of the Rebellion: A*

Compilation of the Official Records of the Union and Confederate Armies, Series I, Volume 48, Part 1 (Washington: Government Printing Office, 1896), 1061-2.

[420] e.g., E. W. Hayes, March 10, 1865, in *Foothills Inquirer 9* (1989): 32 retrieved from www.rootsweb.ancestry.com/~cofgs/inquirer/pdfs/Volume_9_Issue_2.pdf

[421] E. W. Hayes, "Special Order No. 8," March 29, 1865, in *Foothills Inquirer 9* (1989): 33 retrieved from www.rootsweb.ancestry.com/~cofgs/inquirer/pdfs/Volume_9_Issue_2.pdf

[422] S. E. Brown to E. W. Hayes, March 30, 1865, in *Foothills Inquirer 9* (1989): 38 retrieved from www.rootsweb.ancestry.com/~cofgs/inquirer/pdfs/Volume_9_Issue_2.pdf

[423] S. E. Brown, "Regimental Order No 12," March 10, 1865, in *Foothills Inquirer 9* (1989): 5-6 retrieved from www.rootsweb.ancestry.com/~cofgs/inquirer/pdfs/Volume_9_Issue_2.pdf

[424] P. Edward Connor to G. M. Dodge, April 14, 1865, *The War of the Rebellion: A Compilation of the Official Records of the Union and Confederate Armies, Series I, Volume 48, Part 2* (Washington: Government Printing Office, 1896), 100-101.

[425] "Local and Miscellaneous," *Daily Mining Journal*, April 27, 1865, p. 3.

[426] Thomas Kenny, June 4, 1865, Bloedorn Research Center, Fort Morgan Museum (Fort Morgan, Colorado).

[427] P. Edward Connor to G. M. Dodge, April 14, 1865, *The War of the Rebellion: A Compilation of the Official Records of the Union and Confederate Armies, Series I, Volume 48, Part 2* (Washington: Government Printing Office, 1896), 100-101.

[428] G. M. Dodge to Joseph McC. Bell, March 5, 1865, *The War of the Rebellion: A Compilation of the Official Records of the Union and Confederate Armies, Series II, Volume 8* (Washington: Government Printing Office, 1899), 358-9.

[429] Samuel Bowles, *Across the Continent* (New York: Hurd & Houghton, 1865), 11.

[430] Dee Alexander Brown, *The Galvanized Yankees* (Urbana, IL: University of Illinois Press, 1963), 1

[431] "The Galvanized Yankees," *The Museum Gazette* (National Park Service, U. S. Department of the Interior, Jefferson National Expansion Memorial), retrieved from www.nps.gov/jeff/historyculture/upload/galvanized_yankees.pdf

[432] James F. Rusling to M. C. Meigs, September 4, 1866, *Executive Documents Printed by Order of the House of Representatives, during the Second Session of the Thirty-Ninth Congress, 1866-'67* (Washington: Government Printing Office, 1867), 36-40.

[433] Gatlin, Jeffry, "James D. Rowland – Galvanized Yankee," retrieved from

www.rootsweb.ancestry.com/~mscivilw/rowland/jdrowland.htm

[434] William Best Hesseltine, *Civil War Prisons* (Kent, OH: Kent State University Press, 1972), 50.

[435] Ibid., 58.

[436] P. Edward Connor to G. M. Dodge, April 14, 1865, *The War of the Rebellion: A Compilation of the Official Records of the Union and Confederate Armies, Series I, Volume 48, Part 2* (Washington: Government Printing Office, 1896), 100-101.

[437] Thomas Kenny, May 2, 1865, Bloedorn Research Center, Fort Morgan Museum (Fort Morgan, Colorado).

[438] Morse H. Coffin, "Early Days in Boulder County," *The Trail 3* (1911): 14-19.

[439] Brown, *The Galvanized Yankees*, 144.

[440] W. Willard Smith to Graham, June 29, 1865, Bloedorn Research Center, Fort Morgan Museum (Fort Morgan, Colorado).

[441] W. Willard Smith to Graham, July 19, 1865, Bloedorn Research Center, Fort Morgan Museum (Fort Morgan, Colorado).

[442] W. Willard Smith to Graham, June 29, 1865.

[443] Scott Reynolds Nelson, *Steel Drivin' Man: John Henry, the Untold Story of an American Legend* (New York: Oxford University Press, 2006), 65.

[444] Gatlin, "James D. Rowland – Galvanized Yankee".

[445] Frederick H. Dyer, "5th Regiment Infantry," *A Compendium of the War of the Rebellion, Volume 3, Regimental Histories* (New York: T. Yoseloff, 1959), 1717.

[446] George F. Price to C. H. McNally, May 30, 1865, *The War of the Rebellion: A Compilation of the Official Records of the Union and Confederate Armies, Series I, Volume 48, Part 2* (Washington: Government Printing Office, 1896), 690.

[447] Brown, *The Galvanized Yankees*, 43.

[448] Steinel & Working, *History of Agriculture in Colorado*, 62.

[449] H. G. Litchfield, "Consolidated Report of Trains passing Fort Sedgwick, Colorado Territory, from February 1, 1867, to September 28, 1867," *Message of the President of the United States and Accompanying Documents to the Two Houses of Congress at the Commencement of the Second Session of the Fortieth Congress* (Washington: Government Printing Office, 1867), 62-64.

[450] John Pope to E. Upton, August 22, 1865, *The War of the Rebellion: A Compilation of the Official Records of the Union and Confederate Armies, Series I, Volume 48, Part 2* (Washington: Government Printing Office, 1896), 1204-1205.

[451] "From the Plains: Exaggerated Report of Indian Troubles," *Chicago Tribune*, July 10, 1867, p. 2.

[452] January 27, 1866, *The Missouri Republican*, p. 3.

[453] "Road Agents on the Platte: Robbing and Murder!," *Rocky Mountain News*

Weekly, January 10, 1866, p. 3.

[454] "Prisoners Brought In," *Rocky Mountain News*, January 30, 1866, p. 4.

[455] "Prisoners Sentenced," *Rocky Mountain News*, April 28, 1866, p. 4.

[456] "Confessions of Stone and Foster," *Rocky Mountain News*, May 17, 1866, p. 1.

[457] Ibid.

[458] "Execution of Franklin Foster and Henry Stone for the Murder of Isaac H. Augustus and --- Sluman," *Rocky Mountain News*, May 24, 1866, p. 1.

[459] Ibid.

[460] Nathanial Pitt Langford, *Vigilante Days and Ways: The Pioneers of the Rockies* (New York: AMS Press, 1973), 426-427.

[461] John C. Bonnell, *Sabres in the Shenandoah: The 21st New York Cavalry, 1863-1866* (Shippensburg, PA: Burd Street Press, 1996), 195.

[462] "21st Cavalry Regiment: Civil War: Griswold Light Cavalry," *New York State Military Museum and Veterans Research Center. Retrieved from* www.dmna.state.ny.us/historic/reghist/civil/cavalry/21stCav/21stCavMain.htm

[463] "From Fort Wardwell," *Rocky Mountain News*, May 15, 1866, p. 2.

[464] Charles G. Otis to L. Thomas, April 8, 1866, Bloedorn Research Center, Fort Morgan Museum (Fort Morgan, Colorado).

[465] Bonnell, *Sabres in the Shenandoah,* 195.

[466] "From Fort Wardwell," *Rocky Mountain News*, May 15, 1866, p. 2.

[467] "Nathaniel P. Hill Makes Second Visit to Colorado, 1865," *Colorado Magazine 34* (1957): 130-131.

[468] "In Memoriam," *Rocky Mountain News*, June 30, 1866, p. 3.

[469] Letter announcing arrival of unit notes 18th U. S. Infantry (Otis, Charles G., "General Order No. 12," June 13, 1866, Bloedorn Research Center, Fort Morgan Museum (Fort Morgan, Colorado). Letter announcing the unit has left the fort notes 36th U. S. Infantry (Sheridan, M. V., January 11, 1867, Bloedorn Research Center, Fort Morgan Museum (Fort Morgan, Colorado).

[470] Dennis S. Lavery & Mark H. Jordan, *Iron Brigade General: John Gibbon, a Rebel in Blue* (Westport, CN: Greenwood Press, 1993), 136.

[471] Charles G. Otis, "General Order No. 12," June 13, 1866, Bloedorn Research Center, Fort Morgan Museum (Fort Morgan, Colorado).

[472] Merrill J. Mattes, *Indians, Infants, and Infantry* (Denver, CO: Old West Pub.), 46.

[473] Freeman Cleaves, *Rock of Chickamauga: The Life of General George H. Thomas* (Westport, CN: Greenwood University Press, 1974), 50.

[474] Mark Wells Johnson, *That Body of Brave Men: The U. S. Regular infantry and the Civil War in the West* (Cambridge, MA: Da Capo Press, 2003), 20.

[475] E. D Townsend, "General Orders, No. 106," August 14, 1862, *Reports of*

Committees of the Senate of the United States for the First Session of the Forty-Eighth Congress, 1883-'84 (Washington: Government Printing Office, 1884).

[476] E. D Townsend, "General Orders, No. 205," June 1, 1864, *Reports of Committees of the Senate of the United States for the First Session of the Forty-Eighth Congress, 1883-'84* (Washington: Government Printing Office, 1884).

[477] "Lyman M. Kellogg," *Biographical Register of the Officers and Graduates of the U. S. Military Academy, from 1802 to 1867, Volume 2* (New York: James Miller, 1879), 328-329.

[478] Charles Otis, May 22, 1866, Bloedorn Research Center, Fort Morgan Museum (Fort Morgan, Colorado).

[479] Lyman M. Kellogg to Ulysses S. Grant, November 23, 1866, *The Papers of Ulysses S. Grant: January 1-September 30, 1867* (Carbondale, IL: Southern Illinois University Press, 1967), 364.

[480] Grant endorsed the letter from Lyman M. Kellogg "Recommendation for this transfer reconsidered and disapproved" in *The Papers of Ulysses S. Grant: January 1-September 30, 1867* (Carbondale, IL: Southern Illinois University Press, 1967), 364.

[481] Albert Barnitz, Jennie Barnitz & Robert Marshall Utley, *Life in Custer's Cavalry: Diaries and Letters of Albert and Jennie Barnitz* (New Haven, CN: Yale University Press, 1877), 29-30.

[482] "Resources of Colorado: Weld County," *Colorado Transcript*, January 23, 1867, p. 1.

[483] "Affairs in the West, Colorado," *New York Times*, July 19, 1866, p. 2.

[484] Lavery & Jordan, *Iron Brigade General*, 136.

[485] Francis Paul Prucha, *Guide to the Military Posts of the United States 1789-1895* (Madison, WI: State Historical Society of Wisconsin, 1964), 93.

[486] "Name Changed," *Rocky Mountain News*, June 26, 1866, p. 4.

[487] Robert Walter Frazer, *Forts of the West* (Norman, OK: University of Oklahoma Press, 1965), 40.

[488] "Interments: 15795," Spring Grove Cemetery, Cincinnati, Ohio, www.springgrove.org/sg/genealogy/stats/15795.tif.pdf

[489] National Parks Service, *Civil War Soldiers & Sailors System*, www.itd.nps.gov/cwss/index.html

[490] John Pope, "General Orders, No. 8," February 24, 1862, *Index to the Miscellaneous Documents of the House of Representatives for the Second Session of the Forty-Seventh Congress 1882-'83* (Washington: Government Printing Office, 1883), 566.

[491] John Pope, "The Capture of New-Madrid, Mo. General Pope's Official Report," *The Rebellion Record: A Diary of American Events, Volume 4* (New York:

G. P. Putnam, 1862), 297-299.

[492] John Pope, *Directory...City of St. Louis for 1866* (St. Louis: Edwards, Greenough, & Deved, 1866), 667.

[493] "Terrible and Unexpected Death of a Prominent Staff Officer – The Ceremonies To-Day," *Missouri Republican*, January 21, 1866, p. 3

[494] "Interments: 15795," Spring Grove Cemetery, Cincinnati, Ohio.

[495] Meline, *Two Thousand Miles on Horseback*, 49-50.

[496] Thomas Worthington Whittredge, *The Autobiography of Worthington Whittredge, 1820-1910* (New York: Arno Press, 1969), 45.

[497] T. Moonlight to Colonel Brown, March 23, 1865, *Foothills Inquirer 9* (1989): 36 retrieved from
www.rootsweb.ancestry.com/~cofgs/inquirer/pdfs/Volume_9_Issue_2.pdf

[498] James F. Rusling to M. C. Meigs, September 4, 1866, *Executive Documents Printed by Order of the House of Representatives, during the Second Session of the Thirty-Ninth Congress, 1866-'67* (Washington: Government Printing Office, 1867), 36-40.

[499] *Report of the National Society of the Daughters of the American Revolution,* 58.

[500] Peter Cozzens, *General John Pope: A Life For The Nation* (Urbana, IL: University of Illinois Press, 2000), 272.

[501] R. O. Woodward, "With the Troops in Colorado, 1865," *Colorado Magazine 3* (1926): 53-54.

[502] John E. Mayo to Samuel P. Simpson, December 10, 1865, *Annual Report of the Adjutant General of Missouri, for the year ending December 31, 1865* (Jefferson City: Emory S. Foster, 1866), 385-387.

[503] James Fowler Rusling, *Men and Things I saw in Civil War Days* (New York: Eaton & Mains, 1899), 394.

[504] James Fowler Rusling, *The Great West and Pacific Coast* (New York: Sheldon, 1877), 45, 50-1, & 75.

[505] James F. Rusling to M. C. Meigs, September 4, 1866, *Executive Documents Printed by Order of the House of Representatives, during the Second Session of the Thirty-Ninth Congress, 1866-'67* (Washington: Government Printing Office, 1867), 36-40.

[506] Thom Hatch, *The Custer Companion: A Comprehensive Guide to the Life of George Armstrong Custer and the Plains Indian Wars* (Mechanicsburg, PA: Stackpole Books, 2002), 35.

[507] Ibid., 52-3.

[508] M. V. Sheridan to Chauncy McKeever, January 17, 1867, Bloedorn Research Center, Fort Morgan Museum (Fort Morgan, Colorado).

[509] Ibid.

[510] "Colorado," *New York Times*, January 15, 1867, p. 5.

[511] "Untitled," *Rocky Mountain News*, January 15, 1867, p. 4.

[512] Ibid.

[513] "The Deserters," *Rocky Mountain News*, January 23, 1867, p. 1.

[514] Melbourne C. Chandler, *Of GarryOwen in Glory: The History of the Seventh United States Cavalry Regiment* (Annandale, VA, 1860), 7.

[515] Peter Cozzens, *Eyewitnesses to the Indian Wars, 1865-1890: Conquering the Southern Plains* (Mechanicsburg, PA: Stackple Books, 2003), 240.

[516] "Eye Witnesses of a Massacre. Regular Soldiers Saw Indians Murder Whites. An Intervening River Prevented Succor – Disappearance of a Party of Thirty Deserters," *New York Times*, August 3, 1895, p. 5.

[517] "Untitled," *Rocky Mountain News*, January 15, 1867, p. 4.

[518] "A Complaint," *Rocky Mountain News*, April 18, 1867, p. 2 .

[519] Cozzens, *Eyewitnesses to the Indian Wars, 1865-1890*, 240.

[520] Hatch, *The Custer Companion*, 39-40.

[521] Brininstool, *Fighting Indian Warriors*, 217.

[522] Luther H. North, *Man of the Plains: Recollections of Luther North, 1856-1882* (Lincoln, NE: University of Nebraska Press, 1961), 54-55.

[523] Dan L. Thrapp, *Encyclopedia of Frontier Biography: A-F* (Glendale, CA: A. H. Clark, 1988), 364.

[524] Hatch, *The Custer Companion*, 39-40.

[525] Chandler, *Of GarryOwen in Glory*, 5

[526] "From the Plains. The Trial and Sentence of Gen. Custer," *New York Times*, December 7, 1867, p. 2.

[527] Custer, George A. "Custer on the Defensive: General's Letter to the Sandusky Register Gives his Version of Events for which he was Court-Martialed," *The Westerners Brand Book 25*, 41-43 & 47-48.

[528] Minnie Dubbs Millbrook, "Mrs. General Custer at Fort Riley, 1866," *The Kansas Historical Quarterly* 40 (1974): 63-71.

[529] Morris F. Taylor, "Fort Stevens, Fort Reynolds, and the Defense of Southern Colorado" *Colorado Magazine* 49 (1972): 134-162.

[530] Ibid., 134-162.

[531] "Protection for the Plains," *The Colorado Transcript*, April 17, 1867, p. 2.

[532] David M. Jordan, *Winfield Scott Hancock: A Soldier's Life* (Bloomington, IN: Indiana University Press, 1988), 194.

[533] W. T. Sherman to George K. Leet, "Report of Lieutenant General Sherman," October 1, 1867, *Message of the President of the United States and Accompanying Documents to the Two Houses of Congress at the Commencement of the Second Session of the Fortieth Congress* (Washington, Government Printing Office, 1867),

31-38.

[534] "The Indian War," *New York Tribune,* June 26, 1867, p. 1.

[535] " The Indian Troubles," *New York Times,* June 9, 1867, p. 5.

[536] Bancroft & Victor, *History of Nevada, Colorado, and Wyoming, 1540-1888,* 724

[537] Lewis Randolph Hamersly, "Captains," *Records of Living Officers of the United States Army* (Philadelphia: L. R. Hamersly & Co., 1884), 248.

[538] William H.Powell, *A History of the Organization and Movements of the Fourth Regiment of Infantry...* (Washington: M'Gill & Witherow, 1871), 65-66.

[539] "Eye Witnesses of a Massacre. Regular Soldiers Saw Indians Murder Whites. An Intervening River Prevented Succor – Disappearance of a Party of Thirty Deserters," *New York Times,* August 3, 1895, p. 5.

[540] *Treaty with the Cheyenne and Arapaho, 1867,* retrieved from http://digital.library.okstate.edu/kappler/Vol2/treaties/che0984.htm#mn5

[541] Mehls, *The New Empire of the Rockies: A History of Northeast,* 46.

[542] Monahan, *Destination, Denver City,* 235-6.

[543] Powell, … *Fourth Regiment of Infantry…,* 66-7.

[544] J. D. Ward, "A Chicago Company at Pike's Peak," *Chicago Press and Tribune,* May 10, 1860, p. 2.

[545] "Resources of Colorado," *Colorado Transcript,* February 13, 1867, p. 1.

[546] Frémont, *Narrative of the Exploring Expedition to the Rocky Mountains,* 25-26.

[547] A. R. Ross, "Hunting Buffalo in the Seventies," *Colorado Magazine 23* (1946), pp. 84-87.

[548] Elliott West, *Contested Plains: Indians, Goldseekers, & the Rush to Colorado* (Lawrence, KS: University Press of Kansas, 1998), 241.

[549] Hall, *History of the State of Colorado,* 239-240.

[550] "George A. Hodgson's Reminiscences of Early Weld county. As assembled and prepared by H N Haynes," *Colorado Magazine 12* (1935): 70-78.

[551] "Successful Stock-Men. Ilife's Herds on Crow Creek," *New York Times,* May 11, 1872, p. 11.

[552] Eugene Williams. "The Cattle Roundup." *The Colorado Magazine* 5 (1928): 179-181.

[553] Ernest Ingersoll, "Cattle Ranching in the United States," *The Chautauquan, 6* (1886): 555-558.

[554] "Meeting of the County Commissioners," *Rocky Mountain News,* April 7, 1875, p. 4.

[555] "A Great 'Round-up,'" *Chicago Daily Tribune,* July 4, 1884, p. 9.

[556] Charles Wayland Towne & Edward N. Wentworth, *Cattle & Men* (Norman, OK: University of Oklahoma Press, 1955), 165.

[557] "Potter and Blocker Trail," *The Handbook of Texas, Volume 2* (Austin, TX:

Texas State Historical Association, 1952), 401-2.

[558] Jack Potter, "Potter-Bacon Cut-off Trail," *Cattle Trails of the Old West* (Clayton, NM: Laura R. Krehbiel, 1939), 7.

[559] "About the Late J. W. Iliff," *Cheyenne Daily Sun*, February 12, 1878, p. 4.

[560] Linda Wommack, *From the Grave: A Roadside Guide to Colorado's Pioneer Cemeteries* (Caldwell, ID: Caxton Press, 1998), 10.

[561] William Thomas Hagan, *Charles Goodnight: Father of the Texas Panhandle* (Norman, OK: University of Oklahoma Press, 2007), 16.

[562] J. Evetts Haley, *Charles Goodnight, Cowman and Plainsman* (Norman, OK: University of Oklahoma Press, 1949), 206.

[563] Ibid., 140.

[564] Ibid., 206.

[565] Hall, *History of the State of Colorado*, 240.

[566] William Burton Hartley, *Agricultural Settlement in the South Platte Valley, 1860-1890* (M. S. Thesis, University of Wisconsin, Madison, 1962), 86.

[567] "The Cattle King of the West," *New York Times*, November 26, 1875, p. 3.

[568] Sue Flanagan, "Charles Goodnight in Colorado," *Colorado Magazine 43* (1966):1-21.

[569] West, *Contested Plains*, 247-248.

[570] Lewis Eldon Atherton, *The Cattle Kings* (Bloomington, IN: Indiana University Press, 1961), 222.

[571] Donald LaGrande Oglesby, *J.W. Iliff: Cattle King of Colorado* (M. A. Thesis, Western State College of Colorado, 1953), 23-24.

[572] "Report of the Surveyor General of Wyoming Territory: Stock Growing," September 4, 1875, *Report of the Secretary of the Interior, Volume 1* (Washington: Government Printing Office, 1875), 364-5.

[573] Shwayder, *Chronology of Weld County, Colorado, 1836-1983* , 399.

[574] George Washington Saunders, "Experiences of a Texas Pioneer," in John M. Sharpe's *The Trail Drivers of Texas: Interesting Sketches of Early Cowboys* (Austin, TX: University of Texas Press, 1985), 721-29.

[575] James Albert Young & B. Abbott Sparks, *Cattle in the Cold Desert* (Reno, NV: University of Nevada Press, 2002), 77.

[576] Kathleen A. Brosnan, *Uniting Mountain & Plain: Cities, Law, and Environmental Change Along the Front Range* (Albuquerque: NM: University of New Mexico Press, 2002), 67.

[577] Shwayder, *Chronology of Weld County, Colorado, 1836-1983*, 45.

[578] "Indians. Murders and Depredations at Latham…," *Rocky Mountain News*, August 29, 1868: 1.

[579] "Untitled," *Rocky Mountain News*, 2 January, 1869, p. 4.

[580] "Indians," *Rocky Mountain News*, 15 January, 1869, p. 4.

[581] "Reported Killing of 15 Men by Sioux," *Cheyenne Daily Leader*, 17 June, 1876, p. 3.

[582] Eberhart, *Ghosts of the Colorado Plains,* 11-12.

[583] "Fort Morgan. A History," *Fort Morgan Times,* 30 August 1889 p. 1.

[584] "Untitled," *Chicago Daily Tribune*, 2 October, 1881, p. 4.

[585] "Fort Morgan," *Fort Morgan Times,* 4 September, 1884, p. 2.

[586] "Irrigating Canals," *Fort Morgan* Times, 30 August, 1889, p. 6.

[587] Lyman C. Baker, *Morgan County Colorado: What Ten Years of Irrigation has Done for a Part of the Colorado Desert* (Denver, CO: W. F. Robinson & Co., 1895), 5.

[588] "Meeting of the Arapahoe County Claim Club," *Rocky Mountain News Weekly*, 15 February, 1860, p. 2.

[589] Steinel & Working, *History of Agriculture in Colorado,* 45.

[590] "An Act to Secure Homesteads to Actual Settlers on the Public Domain," May 20, 1862, retrieved from www.und.edu/dept/indian/Treaties/Homestead%20Act%201862.pdf

[591] Land Patent Details www.glorecords.blm.gov/PatentSearch/

[592] James A. Ramage, *Gray Ghost: The Life of Col. John Singleton Mosby* (Lexington, KY: University Press of Kentucky, 1999), 319.

[593] Mehls, *The New Empire of the Rockies: A History of Northeast,* www.nps.gov/history/history/online_books/blm/co/16/chap4.htm

[594] Ramage, *Gray Ghost,* 319.

[595] Mehls, *The New Empire of the Rockies: A History of Northeast,* www.nps.gov/history/history/online_books/blm/co/16/chap4.htm

[596] Ramage, *Gray Ghost,* 319

[597] Walter Ebeling, *The Fruited Plain: The Story of American Agriculture* (Berkeley, CA: University of California Press, 1979), 228.

[598] Mehls, *The New Empire of the Rockies: A History of Northeast,* www.nps.gov/history/history/online_books/blm/co/16/chap4.htm

[599] "Stock Raising," *Fort Morgan Times,* 30 August, 1889, p. 5.

[600] D. E. Cameron, "City of Fort Morgan, Colorado," *National Magazine 28* (1908): 240-244.

[601] "Population of the 100 Largest Urban Places: 1880," retrieved from www.census.gov/population/www/documentation/twps0027/tab11.txt

[602] Henry Kirke White, *History of the Union Pacific Railway* (Chicago: University of Chicago Press, 1895), 13.

[603] "The Plate and Kansas Valley Railroads," *Chicago Tribune*, 18 October, 1866, p. 2.

[604] W. F.Bailey, *The Story of the First Trans-Continental Railroad* (Pittsburgh, PA: Pittsburgh Printing Co., 1906), 37.

[605] J. L. Williams, "Report of the Government Director, November 23, 1866," November 23, 1866, *Reports of the Government Directors of the Union Pacific Railroad Company made to the Secretary of the Interior from 1864 to 1865* (Washington: Government Printing Office, 1886), 18-24.

[606] Anthony J. Bianculli, *Trains and Technology: Track and Structures* (Newark: University of Delaware Press, 2003), 63.

[607] George Woodman Hilton, *American Narrow Gauge Railroads* (Stanford, CA: Stanford University Press, 1990), 340-41.

[608] "Colorado; Progress of Railways in the Territory. Interesting Litigation Threatened Between Corporations…," *Chicago Daily Tribune*, 3 January, 1874, p. 2.

[609] "Denver and Julesburg Railroad," *Denver Daily Times*, 14 September, 1872, p. 1.

[610] Elmer Orville Davis, *The First Five Years of the Railroad Era in Colorado* (Golden, CO: Sage Books, 1948), 187.

[611] "Golden and Julesburg," *Colorado Transcript*, 3 April, 1872, p. 2.

[612] Robert Manley Ormes, *Railroads and the Rockies* (Denver, CO: Sage Books, 1963), 171.

[613] "City and Vicinity," *Golden Weekly Globe*, 17 May, 1873, p. 3.

[614] "The Julesburg Road," *Golden Weekly Globe*, 5 April, 1873, p. 2.

[615] "Untitled," *Daily Register Call*, 10 July, 1873, p. 2.

[616] "Railroad Progress," *Denver Daily Times*, 27 May, 1873, p. 2.

[617] "Untitled," Golden Weekly Globe, 21 June, 1873, p. 3.

[618] "Denver's Latest," *Colorado Transcript*, 18 June, 1873, p. 3.

[619] "Jefferson County Bonds," *Denver Daily Times*, 18 March, 1874, p. 4.

[620] M. John Lubetkin, *Jay Cooke's Gamble: The Northern Pacific Railroad, the Sioux, and the Panic of 1873* (Norman, OK: University of Oklahoma Press, 2006), xv.

[621] "The Case of the Colorado Central," *Fort Collins Standard*, 24 June, 1874, p. 1.

[622] Hilton, *American Narrow Gauge Railroads*, 340-41.

[623] Robert G. Athearn, *Union Pacific Country* (Chicago: Rand McNally, 1971),220.

[624] Bailey, *The Story of the First Trans-Continental Railroad*, 128-9.

[625] "Untitled," *Fairplay Flume*, 10 November, 1881, p. 2.

[626] "Denver Junction," *Crofutt's New Overland Tourist and Pacific Coast Guide* (Omaha, NE & Denver, CO: Overland Publishing Company, 1884), 40.

[627] "Julesburg Cut-Off Abandoned," *Chicago Daily Tribune*, 1 February, 1894, p.

2.

[628] "Colorado Central Railroad," *UtahRails.net* retrieved from http://utahrails.net/up/colorado-central.php

[629] "The Railroads," *Chicago Daily Tribune*, 24 August, 1881, p. 2.

[630] "Untitled," *Colorado Transcript*, 15 October, 1879, p. 2.

[631] "State Exchange Notes," *Fairplay Flume*, 22 September, 1881, p. 2.

[632] "Burlington Route," *Rand-McNally Official Railway Guide and Hand Book* (Chicago: Rand, McNally, & Co, 1886), 245-6.

[633] Shwayder, *Chronology of Weld County, Colorado, 1836-1983*, A60.

[634] Stone, *History of Colorado,* 370.

[635] "Construction – Burlington & Missouri River," *The Railway Age 30* (1900): 234.

[636] "The 'Union Colony' of Colorado," *New York Times*, 19 December, 1870, p. 4.

[637] Shwayder, *Chronology of Weld County, Colorado, 1836-1983*, 401.

[638] Eberhart, *Ghosts of the Colorado Plains*, 65-67.

[639] Shwayder, *Chronology of Weld County, Colorado, 1836-1983* , 401.

[640] "Untitled," *Daily Colorado Miner*, 20 December, 1873, p. 3.

[641] Shwayder, *Chronology of Weld County, Colorado, 1836-1983*, 49.

[642] LeRoy Ruben Hafen, *Colorado and its People: A Narrative and Topical History of the Centennial State, Volume 1* (New York: Lewis Historical Pub. Co., 1948), 430.

[643] Federal Writers' Project. *Colorado A Guide to the Highest State*, 1946, 201.

[644] "Statistics of Population," *Thirteenth Census of the United States Taken in the Year 1910: Statistics for Colorado* (Washington: Government Printing Office, 1913), 580.

[645] *Colorado: 2000 Population and Housing Unit Counts,* retrieved from www.census.gov/prod/cen2000/phc-3-7.pdf

[646] Shwayder, *Chronology of Weld County, Colorado, 1836-1983*, 45.

[647] Ibid., 399.

[648] LeRoy Reuben Hafen & Ann W. Hafen, *Our State, Colorado: A History of Progress* (Denver, CO: Old West Pub. Co, 1966), 203.

[649] Ray Shaffer, *A Guide to Places on the Colorado Prairie, 1540-1975* (Boulder, CO: Pruett Publishing, 1978), 252.

[650] Bright, *Colorado Place Names*, 25.

[651] Hall, *History of the State of Colorado*, 241.

[652] Hafen, *Colorado and its People,* 432

[653] "Statistics of Population," *Thirteenth Census of the United States Taken in the Year 1910: Statistics for Colorado* (Washington: Government Printing Office,

1913), 585.

654 *Colorado: 2000 Population and Housing Unit Counts*, retrieved from
www.census.gov/prod/cen2000/phc-3-7.pdf

655 Scott, *Historic Trail Maps of the Sterling 1°X2° Quadrangle, Northeastern Colorado*, 4.

656 David Boyd, *A History: Greeley and the Union Colony of Colorado* (Greeley, CO:
Greeley Tribune Press, 1890), 434-437.

657 Ibid., 194-5.

658 Lute H. Johnson, *Reminiscences of Fort Morgan*, Bloedorn Research Center,
Fort Morgan Museum (Fort Morgan, Colorado).

659 "In and around Town," *Fort Morgan Times*, 18 September, 1884, p. 3.

660 *Crofutt's Grip-Sack Guide of Colorado: A Complete Encyclopedia of the State 1885
Vol. 2* (Omaha, ME: Overland Publishing Co.), 93.

661 Shwayder, *Chronology of Weld County, Colorado, 1836-1983*, 147.

662 Ibid., 300-301.

663 Ibid., A62.

664 Hall, *History of the State of Colorado*, 241.

665 George A. Crofutt, *Crofutt's Overland Tours* (Chicago-Philadelphia: H. J.
Smith & Co, 1889), 33-35.

666 "Deuel, William A.," *The Biographical Directory of the Railway Officials of
America* (New York: Simmons-Boardman Publishing Company, 1913), 145.

667 Shwayder, *Chronology of Weld County, Colorado, 1836-1983*, 104.

668 Thomas J. Noel, *Guide to Colorado Historic Places* (Englewood, CO: Westcliffe
Publishers, 2006), 204.

669 "Untitled," *Fort Morgan Times*, 26 March, 1886, p. 8.

670 Boyd, *A History: Greeley and the Union Colony of Colorado*, 196.

671 "Deuel Cash Store," *Fort Morgan Times*, 25 December, 1885, p. 1.

672 "In and Around Town," *Fort Morgan Times*, 18 January, 1889, p. 5.

673 George F. Cram, "Colorado Chicago: The Fort Dearborn Publishing Company, 1901" *The National Standard Family and Business Atlas of the World* 1901

674 Shaffer, *A Guide to Places on the Colorado Prairie*, 253.

675 "Denver Public Library – Place Names," retrieved from
http://history.denverlibrary.org/research/place_names/place_names_weld.pdf

676 Shwayder, *Chronology of Weld County, Colorado, 1836-1983*, A59.

677 Writers' Program of the Work Projects Administration…, *Place Names in Colorado* (Denver, CO: State Historical Society of Colorado, 1943), 110-114.

678 Shaffer, *A Guide to Places on the Colorado Prairie*, 251-2.

679 "The Southwestern Colony," *Rocky Mountain News*, 14 March, 1871, p. 4.

680 James F. Willard, *The Union Colony at Greeley, Colorado, 1869-1871* (Boulder,

CO: 1918), xviii.

[681] Shwayder, *Chronology of Weld County, Colorado, 1836-1983*, 186.

[682] "Homes for All; The Southwestern Colony of Colorado. The Paradise of the Workingman Discovered. Mr. Abernethy's Account of What He Found There. Mr. Green's Explanation of the Whole Affair…," *Chicago Daily Tribune*, 15 March, 1874, p. 12.

[683] "The Southwestern Colony of Colorado," *Chicago Daily Tribune*, 11 April, 1874, p. 2.

[684] "An Act: Changing the Name of the Town of Green City, in Weld County, to the name of Corona," in *General Laws, Private Acts, Joint Resolutions, and Memorials passed at the Tenth Session of the Legislative Assembly of the Territory of Colorado* (Central City, CO: Register Printing House, 1874), 296.

[685] Shwayder, *Chronology of Weld County, Colorado, 1836-1983*, 89.

[686] "The Towns and Cities of Colorado," *Rocky Mountain News*, 7 June, 1874, p. 2.

[687] Shwayder, *Chronology of Weld County, Colorado, 1836-1983*, 88.

[688] Shaffer, *A Guide to Places on the Colorado Prairie*, 251.

[689] LeRoy R. Hafen & Harvey Lewis Carter, *Mountain Men and Fur Traders of the Far West: Eighteen Biographical Sketches* (Lincoln, NE: University of Nebraska Press, 1982), 176.

[690] "Fort Morgan," *Fort Morgan Times*, 4 September, 1884, p. 2.

[691] F. J. Bancroft, "Untitled," *Official Information. Colorado* (Denver, CO: Rocky Mountain News Steam Printing House, 1872), 14-15.

[692] Hafen, *Colorado and its People*, 431.

[693] Johnson, *Reminiscences of Fort Morgan*.

[694] Stone, *History of Colorado*, 721.

[695] Hafen, *Colorado and its People*, 431.

[696] *Historical/ Architectural Survey of Fort Morgan*, Bloedorn Research Center, Fort Morgan Museum (Fort Morgan, Colorado), p. 4.

[697] "Untitled," *Fort Morgan Times*, 19 March, 1885, p. 3.

[698] "Old Fort Morgan's Dead," *Fort Morgan Times*, 26 February, 1885, p. 3.

[699] James F. Rusling to M. C. Meigs, September 4, 1866, *Executive Documents Printed by Order of the House of Representatives, during the Second Session of the Thirty-Ninth Congress, 1866-'67* (Washington: Government Printing Office, 1867), 36-40.

[700] Bess L. Bertram, "Whispering Ed Forrester Recollects Fort Morgan," Bloedorn Research Center, Fort Morgan Museum (Fort Morgan, Colorado).

[701] "Old Fort Morgan Again," *Fort Morgan Times*, 5 March, 1885, p. 3.

[702] E.g., "Fort Morgan," *Fort Collins Courier*, 29 October, 1885, p. 8 & "Un-

titled," *Fort Collins Courier*, 5 March, 1885, p. 1.

703 "Untitled," *Fort Morgan Times*, 12 March, 1885, p. 3.

704 Parsons, *A Guidebook to Colorado*, 342.

705 *Report of the National Society of the Daughters of the American Revolution*, 58-59.

706 *Standard Atlas of Morgan County, Colorado*, (Chicago, IL: George A. Ogle, 1913), 11.

707 "The One Man who saw the Future of Fort Morgan," *Fort Morgan Times*, 19 December, 1907.

708 Hall, *History of the State of Colorado*, 240-1.

709 "County Officers," *Fort Morgan Times*, 30 August, 1889, p. 3.

710 Stone, *History of Colorado*.

711 Hafen, *Colorado and its People*, 430-432.

712 "Herbert Work: Postmaster-General," *The Administration of a New Era* (Boston, MA: George H. Ellis Co., 1922), 41-43.

713 Johnson, *Reminiscences of Fort Morgan*.

714 "Fort Morgan Businessmen," *Fort Morgan Times*, 24 December, 1886, p. 1.

715 *Historical/ Architectural Survey of Fort Morgan*, 5.

716 *Historical/ Architectural Survey of Fort Morgan*, 5MR465

717 "The Citizens Building Association," *Fort Morgan Times*, 18 September, 1884, p. 2 & "The Ball, *Fort Morgan Times*, 18 September, 1884, p. 3.

718 "Untitled," *Fort Morgan Times*, 15 January, 1886, p. 4.

719 "Railroad Business," *Fort Morgan Times*, 28 January, 1887, p. 1.

720 Lute H. Johnson "Reminiscences of Fort Morgan," in "Morgan and Sedgwick Counties," C. W. A. manuscripts in State Historical Society library, 61.

721 "To the Public," *Fort Morgan Times*, 4 September, 1884, p. 2.

722 "In and Around Town," *Fort Morgan Times*, 20 November, 1885, p. 4.

723 *Historical/ Architectural Survey of Fort Morgan*, 5MR431

724 "Post-Offices and Postmasters – Colorado," *Official Register of the United States, Volume 2* (Washington: Government Printing Office, 1885), 411.

725 e.g., "Advertisement," *Fort Morgan Times*, 6 August, 1885, p. 3.

726 *Historical/ Architectural Survey of Fort Morgan*, 5MR407

727 "John H. Farnsworth," *One Hundred Eleven Trees* (Fort Morgan Heritage Foundation: 1976), 80-81.

728 "Improvements of 1884," *Fort Morgan Times*, 8 January, 1885, p. 2.

729 "In and Around Town," *Fort Morgan Times*, 20 November, 1884, p. 3.

730 *Fort Morgan Times* 11 June, 1886 Page: 1

731 *Historical/ Architectural Survey of Fort Morgan*, 5MR453

732 "In and Around Town," *Fort Morgan Times*, 11 December, 1884, p. 3.

733 "In and Around Town," *Fort Morgan Times*, 15 January, 1885, p. 3.

734 Stone, *History of Colorado*, 596.

735 "Advertisement," *Fort Morgan Times*, 5 October, 1888, p. 4.

736 *Historical/ Architectural Survey of Fort Morgan*, 5MR423

737 "State News," Castle Rock Journal, 16 July, 1890, p. 2.

738 *Historical/ Architectural Survey of Fort Morgan*, 3.

739 "Improvements of 1884," *Fort Morgan Times*, 8 January, 1885, p. 2.

740 *Historical/ Architectural Survey of Fort Morgan*, 5MR455

741 "Now Open. J. D. Johnson's Cash Store," *Fort Morgan Times*, 3 December, 1886, p. 4.

742 "Fort Morgan Businessmen," *Fort Morgan Times*, 24 December, 1886, p. 1.

743 "Untitled," *Fort Morgan Times*, 9 April, 1885, p. 2.

744 "Victory at Last, Boys. The Fort Morgans Bring Home the Bat Won from them by the Sterlings," *Fort Morgan Times*, 28 May, 1885, p. 3.

745 "In and Around Town," *Fort Morgan Times*, 23 April, 1886, p. 4.

746 "In and Around Town," *Fort Morgan Times*, 23 October, 1885, p. 4.

747 "In and Around Town," *Fort Morgan Times*, 13 November, 1885, p. 4.

748 "In and Around Town," *Fort Morgan Times*, 6 August, 1885, p. 3.

749 "Fraternally," *Fort Morgan Times*, 23 August, 1889, p. 11.

750 *Proceedings of the Grand Lodge of A. F. and A. M. of Colorado. Twenty-Seventh Annual Communication. 1887,* 9 & 147

751 Stuart McConnell, *Glorious Contentment: The Grand Army of the Republic, 1865-1900* (Chapel Hill, NC: University of North Carolina Press, 1992), xiii.

752 "I am a Soldier," *Fort Morgan Times*, 26 March, 1886, p. 1.

753 "Statistics of Population," *Thirteenth Census of the United States Taken in the Year 1910: Statistics for Colorado* (Washington: Government Printing Office, 1913), 585-586.

754 Mrs. George Brubaker, "Across the Plains in the Early '60s by Mrs. George Brubaker," *The Trail 12* (1919), 17-20.